ADOPTION,
SEARCH &
REUNION

ADOPTION, SEARCH & REUNION

THE LONG TERM EXPERIENCE
OF ADOPTED ADULTS

David Howe
University of East Anglia, Norwich

Julia Feast
The Children's Society

with ### Denise Coster
The Children's Society

First published in 2000

The Children's Society
Edward Rudolf House
Margery Street
London WC1X 0JL

A catalogue record of this book is available from
the British Library.

ISBN 1 899783 30 X

Contents

Foreword

When I carried out my study, *In Search of Origins*, in 1973, I said at that time that the research was based solely on adopted people who felt the need to search for genealogical information and in many cases reunions with members of their birth family. In other words, we didn't know anything about those who did not set out on a quest and how similar or otherwise they were to those searching. Subsequent studies known to me continued to suffer from the same drawback. This did not make any less real the experiences of those who searched. On the contrary, many new insights were gained into the adoption experience, the importance of genealogical continuity and wider identity issues, including self-esteem. Life-story work was a practical application of those early insights.

We had to wait for over twenty-five years before the nearest to a comparative study of searchers and non-searchers could be made available. In my view, the wait for the present study has been most worthwhile. The comparative element that the researchers successfully introduced into the study has proved highly successful in helping to advance much further our understanding of the process of searching and of reunions. It is difficult for me not to feel very excited about this study because it has provided answers to many questions that both myself and others have been asking over the years about possible similarities and differences between searchers and non-searchers in such matters as:

> biographical characteristics, timing of adoption revelation, the sharing of background genealogical information, the adoption experience, sense of belonging, motivation to search, the aftermath of contact and reunions and feelings towards adoptive and birth parents.

Similarities and differences found between searchers and non-searchers are carefully analysed, discussed and possible explanations offered. Whilst some of the findings confirm those of previous studies, others provide surprises to established thinking. It is not my job to provide a review of the book, as no doubt others will do this, but if you have no time to read the whole study, I urge you to read Chapter 11 on 'Difference and belonging', Chapter 16 on 'Identity and relationships', Chapter 17 on 'Roots, reasons and relationships: a model of the searching process' and the concluding chapter which discusses practice implications. I doubt whether I will be the only one to find this a real gem of a study. Of equal satisfaction to me is that this study continues to keep UK research on adoption, origins, search and reunions at the forefront of international research on the subject.

John Triseliotis
Emeritus Professor, University of Edinburgh
Visiting Professor and Senior Research Fellow,
University of Strathclyde

Preface

In 1997, The Nuffield Foundation awarded The Children's Society a grant to undertake a study into adopted people's experience of searching and reunion. The Children's Society's decision to carry out research in this field grew out of a wish to learn more about the searching and reunion process. In particular, there was a desire to understand more about the long-term impact of a reunion with a birth relative on adopted people and the effect, if any, it has on relationships within the adoptive family. There was also a wish to know more about why some adopted people seek information about their origins and attempt to find birth relatives, while others do not. All of these matters have been under-explored in the UK.

Historically, The Children's Society was one of the largest adoption agencies in the UK and placed over 16,000 babies for adoption. Since the 1975 Children's Act was introduced, giving adopted people the right to access information from their birth certificate, The Children's Society has received thousands of enquiries from people who have been adopted.

During the past decade The Children's Society has also received an increasing number of enquiries from birth relatives (mainly birth mothers) who want basic information about the child (now adult) they placed for adoption. Since 1991, a number of birth relatives have used The Children's Society's Intermediary Service to try to obtain information about whether or not their child is alive and well and to let the adopted adult know of their interest in having contact.

The development of The Children's Society's counselling, advice, information and intermediary services has been directly influenced by the adopted people, adoptive parents and birth relatives who have used the services. It soon became apparent that there are no hard and fast rules, and that each case raises unique issues and dilemmas. However, there is still a need to identify general principles and practice skills to help social workers and counsellors assist and steer people through a major life event. Searching and achieving a reunion with a birth relative is, for many, a time of strong emotion and much turmoil.

The study claims three particular strengths. First, the investigation involved surveying the experiences, views and reunion outcomes of a relatively large number of adopted people who had either searched or been searched for. Second, the study was able to compare and contrast the experiences of adopted people who had initiated a search for information and birth relatives with those who had not. Third, an assessment was made of the long-term outcome of the searching and reunion experience and the impact this had had on people's relationships with their adoptive family.

One of the underlying purposes of the research has been to increase adoption practitioners' knowledge and understanding of the search and reunion process. We hope that the present report will be of value to researchers, practitioners, academics, policy-makers and managers in developing practices that are increasingly sensitive and helpful. We also hope that our findings will be of support and interest to all those more personally and directly involved – adopted people, adoptive parents and birth family members themselves.

Acknowledgements

In every sense the project that has lead to this book has been a team effort. From an initial idea to research the experiences of adopted people who had had a reunion with a birth relative to the collection, analysis and interpretation of the findings, many people have given generously of their time and expertise. One group in particular require special mention. The Children's Society Post Adoption and Care Team, based in Peckham, were pivotally involved at every stage of the project. In fact, they became the research team. They guided the design of the questionnaires from tentative beginnings to final product, they travelled far and wide to carry out in-depth interviews with a large sub-sample of adopted people, they made sharp suggestions about the kind of questions we should ask. Throughout, their commitment and support was unwavering. With great thanks then to

Erica Peltier	Rose Wallace
Jenny Setterington	Liz Webb
Janet Smith	Penny Whittingham.

No project succeeds or keeps on track without the back-up of a strong administrative team. Danielle Sawyer of The Children's Society established monitoring systems that helped us keep on top of the increasingly complex paper flow, and undertook the difficult task of liaising between the Peckham office and the University of East Anglia. Julia Warner of the School of Social Work at the University of East Anglia patiently and skilfully helped design the lay-out of the questionnaires and created diagrams to illustrate our ideas in the book. Ann Stephens typed several chapters of the book, and Sue Hyam and Mandy Priest transcribed all the interviews. More generally, we should like to thank all of the staff at the Peckham office for their interest and encouragement, including Ruth Timlett, Philip West, Carole Crossley and Agnes Asare. The research certainly put extra stresses and strains on everyone there, but the collective willingness to absorb these pressures was much appreciated. As the book entered its final stages of preparation, The Children's Society provided us with the skills of its publishing department.

The project had the benefit of an Advisory panel: Rose Dagoo, Carol Edwards, Derek Kirton and Jill Walker. Their wisdom and experience in the field of adoption practice helped shape many aspects of the enquiry, particularly a number of difficult ethical issues. Derek Kirton also went out of his way to furnish us with material about transracial adoptions that we were pleased to incorporate into our review of the literature. Along the way we received many acts of kindness and, in particular, we should like to thank Kieron Mahoney, Michael Brennan, Terry Connor, Tony Jeeves, Adam and Ben Timlett, Anne Barton, and the staff of the National Health Service Central Register.

We must also record our thanks to the Nuffield Foundation whose generous grant made the study possible. Sharon Witherspoon, the Assistant Director (Social Research and Innovation) at the Nuffield Foundation, has been particularly helpful in the amount of support and guidance she has given. The Fishmongers' Company also made a grant enabling the research team to buy equipment that helped locate the whereabouts of adopted people who had moved from their last known address.

And finally, our deepest thanks go to the hundreds of adopted people who willingly completed long questionnaires, volunteered to be interviewed, commented on draft survey schedules, and helped us to understand the search and reunion experience. We hope they feel that the threads of their own unique tales have helped weave a story that speaks to everyone.

The Children's Society would like to thank the members of the Publications Advisory Group for their valued advice: Kathy Aubeelack; Nicola Baboneau; Ron Chopping (Chair); Annabelle Dixon; Sara Fielden; Judy Foster; Christopher Walsh.

SETTING THE SCENE

Adoption research, once concentrated on placement outcomes, now takes a lifespan perspective. Increasing interest has been taken in adopted people's search for identity. For many, this involves a search for background information and a possible reunion with one or more birth relatives. Others are content not to embark on such a journey. This study compares the experiences of adopted people who initiated a search for a birth relative with adopted people who were sought out by a birth relative. The research looked in detail at the differences and similarities between these two groups in terms of their adoption and reunion experiences. In total, 472 adopted people took part in the research project.

Part I introduces the policy and practice background to birth records counselling and the search process, reviews the existing research literature on the subject of adopted people's search for identity and reunion, and describes the methodology employed by the study.

CHAPTER 1

Social, Historical and Legislative Perspectives on Adoption

Introduction

The themes of birth, separation and reunion raised by adoption hold universal interest. Adoption, particularly over the last decade, has attracted considerable media coverage. People enjoy hearing stories with 'happy endings'. They are intrigued by accounts of how alike children and their parents, brothers and sisters can be, even when they have been separated all their lives. There is great fascination with the coincidences that appear in so many of the reunion stories told by adopted people – birth mothers who lived two streets away, adopted sons pursuing the same careers as their birth fathers, two separately adopted birth siblings searching for their birth mother at the same time. All adoption stories are about the interplay of nature and nurture.

Professionals working in the field of adoption have increasingly become aware that transplanting a child from one family to another rarely represents a 'clean break'. For many adopted children, their origins continue to be both relevant and important. More generally, adoption is now seen as a life-long process which each individual manages and deals with in his or her own way. As part of this process, many adult adopted people decide to search for and seek contact with one or more of their birth relatives.

Adoption and the search for birth relatives is complex. Professionals providing counselling advice and intermediary services realise the importance of basing their practice on the findings of good quality research rather than relying on simple anecdote. Prior to beginning a search or having a reunion, adopted people, adoptive parents and birth relatives ask many questions: 'Why do some adopted people search for birth relatives while others do not?' 'What happens when people do search?' 'If adopted people do find and have contact with their birth relatives, how short lived or long lasting is the relationship?' Although providing neat answers to such questions is never going to be easy, studies which examine the experiences of those who have searched and had a reunion promise to increase the confidence with which counsellors are likely to deal with them.

Since adoption was first legalised in the UK in 1926 there have been many developments and changes that have influenced attitudes and practices. In particular, section 26 of the Children Act 1975 (later to form part of the Adoption Act 1976 (section 51)) was a particularly significant piece of legislation. It gave adopted people aged 18 years and over the right to access information that enabled them to obtain a copy of their birth certificate showing their original name, place of birth, and their birth parent(s) name(s) and address(es) at the time of birth. It also gave adopted people the right to apply to the court to find out the name of the agency or the local authority involved in the adoption. The information shown on the birth certificate helped adopted people to begin a search for their birth mother, if they wished to do so. Haimes and Timms (1985, p. 11) described this as 'a law which at least some social workers considered "made history" in its retrospective undoing of previous "promises" turns around the complex ways in which history-making is crucial for individuals.'

The Act stipulates that people adopted before 12 November 1975 should receive counselling before being allowed to apply for their birth certificate. (This would not apply to people who do know their original name.) This statutory counselling interview gave practitioners, academics and policy makers the first real opportunity to gain a much broader understanding of adopted people's need to reconnect with their past and origins. The knowledge gained from working with adopted adults has had a significant impact on informing adoption practice today: adoption work is now guided by the principle of openness. At the stages of recruitment and preparation, prospective adoptive parents are actively encouraged to acknowledge the children's adoption status. They are helped to understand that children need to have knowledge about their past so that important questions about identity and inheritance are not avoided or ignored.

Long gone are the days when adoptive parents were advised that 'provided that he has not grown up with the idea that his adoptive parents do not love him, or that there is some mystery about his origins, he will not dwell unduly on these matters or want to get in touch with his natural parents' (Standing Committee, 1949). 'In the past,' observes a recent Government White Paper (Department of Health, 1993, pp. 4.19–20),

> adoption was often a secretive process. Adopted children were often not informed of their status and could be traumatised to discover it by accident. It was impossible or difficult for them to discover anything about their birth parent, or for birth parents to discover anything about their children after adoption … A good deal of progress has been made on these issues since the 1976 Act. It is sensible and humane to encourage an open approach, provided always that the prospects for a secure and successful adoption are not jeopardised.

Acknowledging and valuing a child's origins and history is now an intrinsic part of good adoption practice.

The history of adoption

In 1926 the first adoption law was introduced in England and Wales. Although it may not have been uncommon at that time for the adoptive parents and birth parent to know each other's identity, secrecy and stigma generally prevailed. Adoptive parents were encouraged to pass the child off as their own genetic son or daughter so that the stigma of the child's illegitimacy and their own infertility remained hidden.

The Adoption Act 1926 made no provision for access to birth records. An adopted person could only make an application to a Court for information if there were exceptional circumstances (Section 11, subs. (7)). However, in the Adoption Act of Scotland, implemented in 1930, there was a provision that allowed the adopted person, on reaching the age of 17 years, to apply for the original birth certificate direct from the Registrar General, without using an intermediary such as a court or social worker. In Scotland, unlike England and Wales, an adopted person did not lose his or her inheritance rights. The identifying information on the birth certificate helped adopted people who wished to search to locate their birth family.

The Adoption of Children Act (1949 England and Wales) brought in a major change in that it gave adopted children the same status as birth children by giving them the rights to inherit. It made provision for the treatment of adopted people as children of adopters for the purposes of intestacies, wills and settlement (Section 9). At the same time the Adoption of Children (County Court) Rules 1949, the Adoption of Children (summary jurisdiction) Rules 1949 and the Adoption of Children (High Court) Rules 1950 introduced a significant provision in that it enabled adoptive parents to conceal their identity from birth parents. Serial numbers rather than names appeared on the application form. Access to the identity of the parent could only be given if an application was made to the Registrar General by a court order.

The Adoption Act 1950 (England and Wales) consolidated previous legislation, confirming and emphasising the prevailing 'clean break – fresh start' view of adoption.

In 1954, the Hurst Committee recommended that adopted people aged 21 years and over should be able to apply to the Court for a full copy of their adoption order, which would include details of the birth parent(s)' names. The Hurst Report stated: 'it is not in the interests of adopted children to be permanently precluded from satisfying their natural curiosity' (para 201, p. 53). However, the 1958 Adoption Act did not include this recommendation of the Hurst Committee but maintained the status quo, making no substantial changes to previous legislation.

The Houghton Committee was appointed on 21 July 1969 to look at the adoption of children and address the issue of access to birth records. The Houghton Committee Report (1972) acknowledged the importance of being 'open' and telling children about their adoption. It stated:

> The importance of telling a child that he is adopted has long been
> recognised and there is growing recognition that the child should be told

early and helped to understand it more fully as he grows older. It is also increasingly recognised that at some stage the child will need to know about his origins – the positive factors about his parents, such as any special qualities, gifts or interests; their appearance; their reason for giving him up; and any medical background which may be relevant. This kind of information helps the proper development of a sense of identity and gives the child and his adoptive parents a fuller understanding of him as an individual with his own unique combination of characteristics, both inherited and acquired from his upbringing and environment. (para 28, p.8)

The Houghton Committee's final submission was influenced by the findings of Triseliotis' (1973) ground-breaking Scottish study, *In Search of Origins*. Triseliotis' findings confirmed the importance of adopted people having access to information and knowledge about their origins and background.

The adoptees' quest for their origins was not a vindictive venture but an attempt to understand themselves and their situation better ... The self perception of us all is partly based on what our parents and ancestors have been, going back many generations. Adoptees, too, wish to base themselves not only on their adoptive parents, but also on what their original parents and forebears have been, going back many generations ... no person should be cut off from his origins. (Triseliotis, 1973, p. 166)

The Houghton Committee concluded:

The weight of the evidence as a whole was in favour of freer access to background information, and this accords with our wish to encourage greater openness about adoption. We take the view that on reaching the age of majority an adopted person should not be denied access to his original birth records. We therefore recommend that all adopted adults in England and Wales, whenever adopted, should in the future be permitted to obtain a copy of their original birth entry, and that in Scotland the age at which access to original birth records is permitted should similarly be 18, instead of 17 as at present. (Houghton Report, 1972, para 303, p. 85)

The Houghton Report and its recommendations provided the blueprint for sections in the Children Act 1975 relating to services for adopted adults. Prior to the Act's implementation, there was much debate about the impact that such a radical change in legislation might have on the birth mother and also on the adoptive parents. It generated diverse and opposing views. Of particular concern was the proposal that the legislation would be retrospective, thus overturning the assurances that adoption would mean a complete severance from the birth family.

There was also concern for the birth mother who had been assured at the time of the adoption that her identity would be kept in the strictest confidence.

People feared that knowing that one's adopted child could now turn up unannounced on the doorstep might disturb birth mothers, wreck lives and upset marriages. There was also much worry that potential adopters would be deterred from coming forward because adoption no longer meant a 'clean break' and a 'fresh start'. To address these concerns, Section 26 of the Children Act 1975 included a facility for compulsory counselling before an adopted person would be given access to the information held on their original birth certificate. The provision of compulsory counselling was seen as a way of managing the disquiet generated by the introduction of retrospective legislation. The purpose of counselling interviews was to give the adopted adult an opportunity to reflect on the possible implications a subsequent search might have on his or her birth family. Advice and guidance was issued to counsellors about the areas of discussion that should be covered with an adopted person applying for access to information. The guidance notes issued to counsellors were suffused with cautionary advice, as the following extract shows:

> The counsellor has a responsibility to discuss the implications of such a search while conveying an understanding of the applicant's needs and feelings.
>
> The possible distress and disappointment at not being able to trace one's parents or of being rebuffed should be mentioned. The counsellor may advise against continuing the search because of the other people who could be hurt. The applicant must be helped to accept the responsibility for the pain he might cause to himself and to others if he pursues his quest. Some discussion about the variety of situations that may lead to a child being placed for adoption may be appropriate and may help the applicant to have a greater understanding of the feelings of all those involved in the original placement, both the natural and adoptive families.
>
> (*Access to Birth Records*, 1976, p. 6)

With such guilt-laden overtones, it is perhaps not surprising that some adopted people decided against searching for birth relatives.

The guidance currently issued by the Registrar General explains that the counsellor has an obligation to pass on information to enable the adopted person to obtain a certificate of their birth. However, where there is serious concern about the possible consequences of giving the information, the counsellor should seek advice from the Registrar General. In 1989, there was a court ruling upholding the Registrar General's decision not to fulfil her duty to give birth records information on the grounds that there were public policy considerations. This decision was upheld in the Court of Appeal in 1990 (*R. v. Registrar General ex parte Smith* (1989)).

Accurate figures about how many adopted people actually seek information about their origins are not available. For the period 1927–97 over 850,000 adoption orders were made. Between 1975 and 1997, the Registrar General's office received approximately 74,000 applications for birth record counselling. The figures produced by the Registrar General's office suggest that less than 9% of all adopted people make an application for access to birth records. However, if an adopted person knows their original name, they do not need to apply to the Registrar, thereby avoiding the compulsory counselling required by the Act. Many adopted people contact the adoption agency directly for the information they need and therefore do not appear in the figures given by the Registrar General's Office. In a study carried out by The Children's Society's in 1992, out of 132 people who had approached the organisation for counselling and access to information held on the agency's adoption record, only 26 were referred after receiving counselling from either the Registrar General (16) or the local authority (10) (Feast, 1992).

An important provision was introduced when the Children Act (England and Wales) 1989 amended the Adoption Act 1976 by adding Section 51A. This required the Registrar General to establish an Adoption Contact Register. The Register allowed adopted people and birth relatives to register their willingness for contact. In the same year, adopted people who lived abroad were no longer required to travel to the UK to receive counselling to obtain a copy of their birth certificate. Arrangements could be made for people to receive counselling in their country of residence.

In 1990, a review of adoption law began with the production of four discussion papers. The review included a look at the needs of birth mothers and their rights to have access to information about the child they had relinquished to adoption, and intermediary services. The review subsequently produced a White Paper, *Adoption – The Future* (Department of Health, 1993), published in November 1993, and a draft Adoption Bill that appeared in 1996. Part of the Bill has now become law and forms the Adoption (Intercountry Aspects) Act 1999. However, the majority of the Bill has still to begin its parliamentary journey and become statute. Amendments to the current adoption legislation to allow birth relatives to receive information held on the adoption records therefore remain on hold.

In spite of the lack of new legislation, the last decade has seen a growing lobby of birth relatives, particularly birth mothers, campaigning for a change in the law so that they have similar rights to those of adopted people to obtain information enabling them to search, in their case for their adopted son or daughter. Some local authorities and adoption agencies are sympathetic to the needs and position of these birth relatives and, where they hold the adoption record, they will provide an intermediary service allowing the adopted person to be located and informed of the birth relative's enquiry and interest. Intermediary services for birth relatives have been provided throughout the UK in an uneven and disparate way. However, the Department of Health plans to issue guidance to encourage more uniform practice, with all local authorities and adoption agencies providing intermediary services for birth relatives using existing legislation as the framework.

Nevertheless, although provisions and practices are becoming increasingly widespread and consistent, anomalies still occur. For example, unless new legislation is introduced, birth mothers who agreed to a private adoption will not have the same rights of access to such services, because unlike agency adoptions, the child's adoptive details – for example, their new surname – are often not known. Without such information, locating the adopted adult or the adoptive family is very difficult. Generally, the only option open to birth mothers where there has been a private adoption is to make an application to the courts for an order under Section 50 (5). Applications of this kind are typically very few in number, the courts making only one or two such orders a year. An application is more likely to succeed when an inheritance or a serious hereditary or medical condition is involved. Applications made on grounds of wanting to establish contact are unlikely to succeed unless the applicant can demonstrate to the court that there is an exceptional need.

Legislation and current practice

Opportunities for social workers to listen to the experiences of adopted adults during the 'compulsory counselling' session has enabled professionals to gain much greater insight into the world of the adopted adult. They have learned how important it is for adopted people to obtain information that helps them feel connected to their past. As a result, practice has often developed far beyond the requirements of the law. Many agencies exercise their discretionary powers and allow adopted people access to confidential information held on the adoption file. Agencies have to exercise a duty of care to all people mentioned in the adoption record. However, this duty has to be balanced against the adopted person's need for information. 'Whose information is it?' is a question with which policy makers and practitioners alike struggle. Are the adopted person's needs for information paramount? Will the information help the adopted person make informed decisions about his or her life? These, and other such questions, are asked and considered with great care. Agencies have to try to ensure that the dilemmas presented by providing people with access to information are addressed, considered and resolved.

The past few decades have thus witnessed a gradual shift towards a more open model of adoption. The best interests of the child is now the guiding principle, informing, for example, decisions about whether or not a child should retain links with his or her birth family, and how such contact should be managed. The need for openness and a general awareness by children of their birth parents and family runs through all adoption practice, from the recruitment and preparation of prospective adoptive parents to the provision of post-adoption services.

Section 1 of the Adoption Act 1976 places a duty on each local authority to provide a comprehensive adoption service to all those involved in adoption including (a) children who have been or may be adopted, (b) parents and guardians of such children, and (c) persons who have adopted or may adopt a child. The Act acknowledges that people who have a personal connection to adoption should have a right to a service if they have unresolved issues and counselling needs. While adoption legally severs children from their birth families, it does not necessarily cut the psychological and emotional ties. Understanding this helps adoptive parents see the importance for their children of knowing as much as possible, all else being equal, of their origins and background. During the 1980s, the development of organisations such as the National Organisation for Counselling Adoptees and Parents (NORCAP), the Natural Parents Network, and the Post Adoption Centre, did much to highlight the emotional and developmental needs of both adopted people and birth mothers.

The knowledge and experience of other countries, particularly New Zealand, has also influenced practice in the UK. For example, Ryburn and Rockel (1988), reported the benefits and the possibilities of opening up the channels of communication in what hitherto had been seen as closed models of adoption. Winkler and van Keppel's (1984) research in Australia, looking at the long-term adjustment patterns of mothers whose children had been adopted, found that parting with a child for adoption had life-long repercussions for many birth mothers. They found an above average susceptibility to physical illness and nervous disorders in their sample of birth mothers. More recent research in the UK by Bouchier *et al.* (1991), Howe *et al.* (1992), Wells (1993), and Hughes and Logan (1993) has confirmed that the loss of a child through adoption may profoundly affect the mental health and coping mechanisms of many birth mothers and that the effects may be life-long. It is now believed by many counsellors and support workers that the high incidence of emotional and physical disorders described by birth mothers is likely to be the result of repressed mourning and the consequences of living with the unresolved losses and traumas associated with their child's adoption.

Conclusion

From the time of the Adoption Act 1926, there has been a gradual trend for adoption to become increasingly open. Adopted people have been given more and more information about their backgrounds and origins. Adoptive parents have been given increased knowledge about their children's early years and they have been encouraged to be open in acknowledging and discussing adoption with their children. The psychological relevance to adopted children of birth parents is now recognised as playing a significant role in development and identity. The recognition that openness in adoption has a range of developmental benefits has led to an increasing number of placements being planned with provision for some form of contact between children and their birth families. The psychological tasks associated with adoption appear to continue into adulthood, showing that adoption is frequently a life-long process. The experiences of adopted people who search for birth relatives follows the story of openness into adulthood, a story which throws light on not only adopted people's search for identity but on the universal themes of who we are and where we belong.

CHAPTER 2

A Review of the Research Literature

Introduction

Researchers from a wide range of disciplines and theoretical viewpoints have looked at adopted people's experiences of searching and reunion. Sociologists, social and clinical psychologists, social workers, biologists, policy specialists and journalists have all taken an interest in adopted people's desire to search for and have contact with their birth relatives. There are also autobiographical accounts that provide more immediate, personal and emotionally charged descriptions of what it is like to look for and find a birth mother or father.

Earlier studies concentrated mainly on the pre-search period – what seemed to trigger the search, and the characteristics of those who searched. More recently, there has been growing interest in people's experiences of reunion. Looked at chronologically in terms of the search and reunion process, existing research is reviewed under the following headings:

- Who searches?
- How many adopted people search?
- What are adopted people searching for?
- What triggers adopted people's decision to search?
- Why do adopted people search?
- Who is sought?
- Why do some adopted people not search?
- What is the effect of the search on adoptive parents?
- Search as a process.
- Outcome of reunions with birth relatives.
- Post-reunion experiences.
- Long-term impact of a reunion.
- Transracial adoptions.

Who searches?

The question that dominates the literature is, why do adopted people search for their birth parents? Since not all adopted people undertake a search for their birth parents, it might seem reasonable to assume that there must be some differences between searchers and non-searchers that might provide clues about why some people decide to seek information and others do not. Much research has concentrated on trying to identify the characteristics of searchers. However, to date, there has been only limited agreement on what seems to characterise searchers as a group (March, 1995; Pacheco and Eme, 1993). Also, because of sampling problems, research so far has concentrated on trying to identify the characteristics, circumstances and experiences of searchers rather than non-searchers.

Gender has proved to be the factor that most frequently distinguishes searchers from non-searchers: roughly, twice as many women as men appear to search (Gonyo and Watson, 1988; Stevenson, 1976; Pacheco and Eme, 1993). The high proportion of women searchers is typically explained by suggesting that women are more interpersonally oriented than men (Pacheco and Eme, 1993). Sachdev (1992) suggests that women are more interested in their birth family because of pregnancy and identity issues.

A small number of studies have found that adopted people with low *self-esteem* and a poor self-image are more likely to search than those whose self-esteem is high and self-image positive (Aumend and Barrett, 1984; Sobol and Cardiff, 1983). However, as self-esteem is a difficult quality to measure and can change over time, confidence in these findings remains uncertain.

Another factor which may affect whether people search is the *degree of openness* in their adoption – how much the adopted person is told about their birth parents and how they are told it. It has been suggested that people with very little knowledge of their birth parents might be more likely to search because they feel there is more to discover. Triseliotis (1973) found that non-disclosure of background information was related to searching for birth parents (also see also Aumend and Barrett, 1984). However, in contrast, a study by Sobol and Cardiff (1983) found that the greater the information provided about the birth parent, the higher the probability that the adopted person would search. The study also found that adopted people who felt unable to discuss their adoption at home were more likely to search. Haimes and Timms (1985) saw the disclosure of adoption and its discussion as a two-way exchange between adopted people and adoptive parents. Just as sometimes an adoptive parent may be unforthcoming with information, an adopted person may refuse to take up the subject themselves, leading to a mutual silence.

The *quality of the adoption* has been found to affect whether or not adopted people search. Increased 'seeking' behaviour has been observed in adopted people who perceived the relationship with their adoptive parents in a negative light. Raynor (1980) found a link between the urge to meet biological relatives and an unsatisfactory experience of adoption (see also Sobol and Cardiff, 1983; Aumend and Barrett, 1984; Kowal and Schilling, 1985). However, a number of more recent studies failed to find a link between the quality of the adoption and the decision to search (Campbell *et al.*, 1991; Sachdev, 1992; Pacheco and Eme, 1993).

Age at placement has also been examined as a significant factor in whether people search or not. Sobol and Cardiff (1983) found that the older the adopted person was at the time of adoption, the greater probability that they would conduct a search.

Some analysts have wondered whether the division between searchers and non-searchers might be somewhat arbitrary. Haimes and Timms (1985) query whether in fact there are any adopted people who never question their adoption. They argue that searching behaviour occurs on a continuum and adopted people change their minds about searching over time. Adopted people who might have shown no interest in searching may suddenly decide to search.

Brodizinsky *et al.* (1992) suggest that every adopted person conducts an intrapsychic search. This involves fantasies and curiosity about why they were given up. Bertocci and Schecter (1991) agree that searching behaviour can take many forms – from unconscious associations and fantasies, to reunion with a biological parent. While it might be true that most adopted people wonder about their birth parents, it still allows researchers to ask what it is that makes some adopted people take that extra step and turn their thoughts into an active search.

How many adopted people search?

It is difficult to know what proportion of all adopted people search. A 1975 report to Parliament on the working of the Children Act reported that only between 1 and 2% of those eligible (i.e. adopted people affected by the new legislation) had chosen to apply for their birth certificates (Day and Leeding, 1980). Since 1975, more adopted people have embarked on a formal search. In 1976, 2600 people applied for counselling, and 309 people were actually counselled. In 1995, 4906 people applied for counselling and 3669 people were counselled. Although these figures show that the number of people searching appears to be rising, it remains difficult to calculate what proportion of all adopted people have searched or are currently searching. Although there are records for those who seek counselling, there may be many more who search independently, having obtained all the information they needed from their adoptive parents.

Organisations that provide counselling and advice to adopted people seeking reunion suggest that the number who search at some time is probably quite high. Brodizinsky *et al.* (1992) quote figures of 30 to 40% of adopted people searching at some time in their lives.

What are adopted people searching for?

Adopted people do not always search hoping for a reunion and a long-lasting relationship with their birth parents. Many search only for information. And yet others begin by searching for information but then go on to seek a reunion. Feast (1992) found that of 132 adopted adults who received information about their birth parents from The Children's Society, only six decided definitely not to go on and search for their birth relatives.

Although a number of studies report that many adopted people seek background medical information, proportions vary widely from 20% (Slaytor, 1986) to 75% (Kowal and Schilling, 1985). Sobol and Cardiff (1983) found that of those searching, nearly 51% wanted factual information, 21% said they were curious about their birth parents, and 29% said they were searching for reasons of fulfilment and identity. Haimes and Timms (1985) reported that the majority of subjects in their research wanted to trace a birth relative. They noted that people seemed to have trouble explaining the reason for their enquiry. 'Something so self evidently reasonable as, say, wanting to know who your parents are becomes immediately complex when needing an explanation' (Haimes and Timms, 1985, p. 53).

Although some adopted people are clearly searching for information, the desire behind the need for information appears to be more complicated. People might want information but want more than paper information; they might want to meet their birth parents but not wish to develop a relationship with them. A number of studies observe that adopted people often search to find somebody who looks like them. Kowal and Schilling (1985), Haimes and Timms (1985), and Hollingsworth (1998) note that parents' physical appearance seems very important to many adopted people. They might also want, as Haimes and Timms (1985) argue, an adequate account of their early life, provided by their birth parent. Campbell et al. (1991) suggest that some adopted people wish to create an extended family by searching. What people want from searching may also change at different times in their lives. A discussion paper produced by the Post Adoption Centre (1990, p. 10) suggests that 'as a generalisation the older the adopted adult and the more information they had, the more realistic and less idealised the expectations of reunion and the post reunion period.'

The many different reasons given for searching by adopted people possibly reflect different ways of expressing the same underlying desire to discover something about one's identity and origins. For many people, it seems this desire can only be fulfilled by having an actual meeting with their birth parents.

What triggers adopted people's decision to search?

A number of studies have sought to identify what triggers an adopted person's decision to search. It has been suggested that particular life experiences might trigger the search. For example, Kowal and Schilling (1985) found that 24% of respondents said their search was triggered by pregnancy, birth or adoption of a child. Having a child raises issues of biology. Becoming a parent makes people wonder even more why their own birth parents gave them up for adoption.

Although one particular event may appear to trigger the search, in practice people report a slow build-up in which they wonder about their birth relatives and think about a possible reunion. Anderson (1988) believes that trigger explanations, for example needing to find medical information, obscure deeper reasons to do with identity and feelings of loss. The actual reasons that people give in the course of their search may not be central, so looking for one event that triggers an adoptive person to search may be misleading. 'I think,' writes Anderson (1988, p. 19), 'that the search is most fundamentally an expression of the wish to undo the trauma of separation. Adopted people either hope to relive the life that was lost at the time of separation, or hope to heal the wound caused by the separation, and thereby provide a more authentic base for their lives.'

Why do adopted people search?

Explanations for the desire to search are broadly captured by two models – the normative and the pathological. The normative model sees searching as a natural outcome of adoption and not as a negative response to an adverse adoptive situation. This model stresses the fluidity of identity, and sees searching as an attempt to integrate one's roots and to develop a fuller understanding of who one is. The act of searching adds to, rather than replaces, one's existing identity. Adopted people's desire to know their roots is a universal phenomenon and is part of normal personality development (Sachdev, 1989, p. 14). For adopted people, finding out who one is and where one comes from just happens to be a more complex process (see also Rozenburg and Groze, 1997).

The pathological model suggests that the desire to search arises out of a dissatisfaction or difficulty with one's adoption. The adopted person is seeking a new, or reclaiming some lost, original identity. The model predicts that those with mental health or personality problems are more likely to search to fulfil a need (Humphrey and Humphrey, 1989). It is suggested that knowledge of one's origins is essential for mental health and identity formation. Triseliotis (1973) interviewed 70 people in Scotland who had sought further information about their parents. He found evidence of mental health problems and/or disturbed family relationships, concluding that the need to seek genealogical information and search for birth parents was activated by some deeply felt psychological need and rarely related to a matter-of-fact attitude (Triseliotis, 1973, p. 154).

The idea that adopted people have trouble with their identity is prevalent in the literature. Sorosky et al. (1974) believed that many adopted people cannot realise their full identity until they have information about their birth parents. 'For some, the existing block to the past may create the feeling that there is a block to the future as well' (Sorosky et al., 1974, p. 205). The authors describe feelings of 'genealogical bewilderment' caused by a lack of biological connection. The term genealogical bewilderment was first used by Sants (1964) to describe an adopted person not having access to information about their ancestry. Feeling a lack of connectedness is not necessarily caused by an unhappy adoption experience; it is simply a lack of knowledge about one's past that interferes with identity formation (see also Ryburn, 1995).

Supporters of the normative model argue that since adoption is essentially a social construct, and that adoption is constructed through interactions within a social environment, it is not useful to talk about adopted people being psychologically impaired. Being adopted marks people out *socially* as being either different and special; or different, disadvantaged, and in a sense not 'normal'. Searching, then, is seen as an attempt to account for this difference and establish a more complete social identity.

March (1995) formulated the idea that searching was associated with adopted people's feelings of stigma (see Goffman, 1963). In order to gain social acceptance, adopted people must neutralise their stigma. This they do by searching: normalising themselves by identifying a past that is theirs. In the study by March (1995, p. 658), adopted people's 'search and reunion activities were not symptomatic of adoption breakdown. They represented an attempt to neutralise the stigma trait by placing self within a biosocial context valued by their community.' In a similar vein, Haimes and Timms (1985) describe adopted people who search as trying to place themselves in a narrative framework. For adopted people, parts of their narrative are missing and by searching for birth relatives they seek to fill in the gaps (also see Bertocci and Schechter, 1991).

Searching, therefore, can either be seen as a normal part of development or as an adverse response to adoption. Adopted people who search can be viewed as either psychologically impaired or mentally healthy, fully exploring their pasts in a positive manner. Searching for identity involves either trying to connect with one's biological past or seeking to place oneself in a social context. Adopted people also search to neutralise feelings of loss, cancel out the past, or connect the past to the future. Summing up her research of people who had sought access to their Barnardo's childcare records, Pugh (1999) identified three motivations to search: the wish to understand the meaning and significance of one's roots, the need to know about one's history, and the need to make sense of one's past.

Who is sought?

To some extent, who is sought appears to affect the outcome of the search and reunion process. The emotional agenda with birth parents, particularly birth mothers, is complex and often highly charged. In terms of issues of loss and rejection, meeting birth siblings is likely to be more neutral. In practice, most adopted people set out initially to search for their birth mother. However, Humphrey and Humphrey (1989) suggest that it is easier to build a more comfortable relationship with siblings than with birth parents. McMillan and Irving (1994, p. 24) echo this, saying 'starting from a position of loss without the responsibility for the loss, siblings are freer for their relationship to develop in a more normal way, on the basis of relatedness and compatibility' (see also Sachdev, 1992).

Sachdev (1992) reports that few of his respondents expressed a desire to meet their biological father. Only 20% said they ever thought about their biological father.

It is not always the adoptive person who searches for the birth relative. Sometimes the birth relative decides to search for the adopted person. The Children's Society has been providing an intermediary service for birth relatives since 1991. They found that search and reunion for this group was, in many ways, more complicated. Feast and Smith (1993, 1995) reported that contacts initiated by birth relatives had a number of positive effects for both adopted adults and birth parents in terms of identity fulfilment and reassurance about lost relatives.

Why do some adopted people not search?

Gaining research access to adopted people who do not search for their birth parents has proved difficult and many studies of the search and reunion process have omitted this group from their investigations. However, a small number of studies have looked at why some adopted people delay or forestall their search. The speculation is that the reasons for some adopted people stopping their search might be similar to the reasons that non-searchers choose not to search at all.

Gonyo and Watson (1988) suggest that a decision to search is inhibited by three things: (i) a hesitancy to intrude on the life of the unknown party; (ii) fear of failure, discovering unforeseen problems, or upsetting the adoptive parents; and (iii) guilt or feeling disloyal to the adoptive family (see also Haimes and Timms, 1985; and Sachdev, 1992). Bertocci and Schecter (1991) and Sorosky *et al.* (1978) reported that a search was delayed, or not undertaken at all, because of fears about upsetting or losing adoptive parents. Sobol and Cardiff (1983) found that 29% of adopted people said they did not search for fear of hurting their adoptive parents, and that 20% of adopted people in their study said that there was no reason to search because they were satisfied with their adoptive families.

What is the effect of the search on the adoptive family?

Adopted people embarking on reunion often worry about the effect their search will have on their adoptive family. They might delay their search until their adoptive parents are dead (McMillan and Irving, 1994). They might simply not tell their parents: 34% of Sachdev's (1992) sample and about half of Pacheco and Eme's (1993) sample of adopted people did not tell their parents that they had started a search.

McMillan and Irving (1994) believe that their study shows that there is no need for adoptive parents to feel threatened when they learn about the search. A third of their participants reported an improvement in relations with their adoptive parents as a result of the search. Sachdev (1992) found that three-fifths of searchers told their parents about the search and two-thirds of those who had told their parents felt no change had occurred in the relationship because of their searching (also see Bertocci and Schecter, 1987; Depp, 1982; Slaytor, 1986; Sorosky *et al.*, 1978).

Lichtenstein (1996) argues that this improvement in relations with adoptive parents may be the result of resolving 'the romance fantasy'. The romance fantasy is a stage in child development first suggested by Freud (1973). At some stage in their development, children imagine themselves to be adopted in order to cope with the normal ambivalence of child–parent relations. However, this is obviously true for adopted children and therefore they might not integrate the good and bad parts of their parents but will direct different feelings to different parents – loving feelings towards the biological parents and hating feelings towards adoptive parents. When adopted adults search they test these fantasies. 'Postsearch adoptees can no longer construct an imaginary story about their origins or the reasons for their adoption, nor can they project on to biological parents feelings that they initially developed in relation to adoptive parents' (Lichtenstein, 1996, p. 63). This leads to improved relations with the adoptive parents.

Search as a process

Searching for birth parents is not a one-off event but an ongoing process of change and adjustment. Searching itself can be lengthy and after the reunion there may be a long-term relationship with the birth relative.

Betty Jean Lifton (1979), an adopted person, was probably the first to identify stages in the search process (see also Winkler *et al.*, 1988). Gonyo and Watson (1988) identify a process that starts with the decision to search, usually after a long period of internal struggle and ambivalence. The authors suggest that once the search is begun, it is pursued obsessively to the exclusion of other things in the searcher's life (see also Parish and Cotton, undated). Although there may be periods of respite, the search is typically resumed with the same obsessive energy. When the relative is located, the emotional impact can be great, but there is also a fear of loss of control. Adopted people describe reunions as emotionally draining experiences.

Outcome of reunions with birth relatives

The majority of studies report that most people who search and have a reunion with birth relatives describe their experiences as positive. Reunion has been found to enhance adopted people's feelings of completeness, improve their sense of identity and self-esteem, make them feel more whole and integrated, and improve interpersonal relations (Sorosky *et al.*, 1974; Depp, 1982; Boult, 1992; Pacheco and Eme, 1993).

Cowell *et al.* (1996) reported that the majority of searchers described the reunion relationship positively: 74% rated the reunion as satisfactory or very satisfactory, and 99% of adopted people had no regrets about carrying out a search. Campbell *et al.* (1991) found that when adopted people who search were asked if they would search again, 100% said they would. Bertocci and Schecter (1987), Slaytor (1986), and Sorosky *et al.* (1978) also report high levels of satisfaction.

March (1995) points out that high levels of satisfaction with reunion experiences seem to have little correlation with the actual outcome of the reunion, people's experience of adoption, or whether they maintain contact with the birth relative. She suggests that adopted people simply want to fill in the gaps in their lives, and find those who are biologically similar. Many adopted people say they feel more 'connected' after their search is completed. This is confirmed by Sachdev (1992) who found that 97% of adopted people in his study said they had no regrets about searching, although only 51% of adopted people had regular ongoing contact with their birth mothers.

Pacheco and Eme (1983) also identified why some people were dissatisfied with their reunion experience. Fourteen per cent said they disagreed or were uncertain that the reunion was a positive experience. Most disappointment centred around having unrealistic expectations, but some people said that they found their birth parents to be too needy or their extended family to be something of a shock. A small number of adopted people said they were simply rejected for unknown reasons. Slaytor (1986) identified a number of areas where difficulties were reported, including differences resulting from mis-matched expectations of the relationship, disapproval by or upsets to current families, and differences in values and family patterns. Sachdev (1992) also suggested that different expectations of the relationship after reunion can lead to conflict.

Post-reunion experiences

The reunion itself is seen as just the start of a process of readjustment and perhaps integration of the new found person into the adopted person's life. Post-reunion outcomes have been found to vary a great deal. For some, there is a long-lasting and fulfilling relationship with their birth family. For others, the differences between them and their birth families feel too great and the relationship ceases. Some adopted people feel that it is the actual relationship with the new family that is important while others value the acquisition of new information and the resolution of issues about their past.

Even at first contact, adopted people report very different experiences. Campbell *et al.* (1991) found that at the initial meeting 75% of birth parents were said to be warm and welcoming, 22% fearful, reserved or unsure, and 3% indifferent, hostile or rejecting (see also Sachdev, 1992; Pacheco and Eme, 1993).

Once the initial contact has been made, Gonyo and Watson (1988) suggest that the most common outcome of a successful search is an intense period of getting to know the person. This then tails off as people begin to accommodate the new person in their lives. In some cases, the adopted person and birth relative drift apart, finding they have little in common. Parish and Cotton (undated) observed that some adopted people found the social differences between themselves and their birth relatives to be too great and this appeared to interfere with and upset the relationship.

In Scotland, McMillan and Irving (1994) carried out a study to provide a longer-term view of the reunion process. Participants were mainly one to three years on from their initial reunion. They suggest that people need to go through stages of integration as the relationship progresses: 'the task over time is to integrate the contact with a related stranger into a network of existing relationships' (McMillan and Irving, 1994, p. 33). However, for the adopted person it is not just a case of getting to know a new person, but also of getting to know more about themselves. This helps resolve feelings of loss. Further developments can then take place in the formation of identity as new information is absorbed.

A number of studies have noted that once a reunion has taken place, continued contact does not necessarily follow. Sachdev (1988) followed 157 reunions. Of the 107 adopted people who met their birth mothers, only 19.8% said that the relationship was like a mother–child relationship. The remaining 73.2% described it as a friendship or said that they felt like acquaintances. Pacheco and Eme (1993) found that there was generally a pattern of decreasing contact which eventually settled down to contact on a monthly, bi-monthly or holidays only basis. Sachdev (1992) found that 17% terminated the relationship after the first meeting.

Haimes and Timms (1985) identified the different ways that adopted people appear to incorporate new information and relationships into their lives. Some adopted people incorporate their search findings and birth relatives into a single narrative with their adoptive selves in which the gaps get filled. Others see themselves as having two stories:

> In contrast to this assimilation of knowledge from the past into current lives is the reaction of those adoptees who come to regard themselves as having two life stories; that which they would have had with their real parents, under their real name, where they were really born; and that which they have had instead. (p. 72)

Long-term impact of a reunion

There has not been much formal study of reunions over the long term. However, reunions and their aftermath have been described autobiographically by those involved. These highly personal accounts underline how reunion relationships change with time and how it is misleading to see the actual reunion as the endpoint of a search (Lifton, 1979, 1983; Wadia-Ells, 1996; Iredale, 1997; Feast *et al.*, 1998). The authors of these stories identify themes rather than statistically significant facts. For example, Iredale (1997) and Gediman and Brown (1991) identify themes of loss, attachment and personal identity in their stories about reunion:

> Everyone in the adoption triad deals with the issue of loss, because the experience of loss is the fundamental ground upon which the event of adoption is built. For the birth mother it is the loss of her baby; for the adoptive parents the loss of the ability to reproduce. For the adoptee there is the separation from and loss of the first mother.
>
> (Gediman and Brown, 1991, p. 3)

In her book, *Journey of the Adopted Self*, Lifton (1983) describes the search as a healing experience for both adopted people and birth parents, healing the trauma of their initial loss.

These accounts emphasise that the reunion is the starting point of a long process of readjustment. There are many choices for the adoptive person to make and these choices are made within the context of two families – the adoptive family and the new birth family. There may be different expectations and hopes from the different participants. There may also be the issue of rejection, both the initial rejection and possible rejection after a new relationship has been established. There may be many conflicting emotions with which to deal, including feelings of anger and sorrow.

Sanders and Sitterly (1981) write from their own experiences, both as people who have had a reunion and as founders of Independent Search Consultants. They recognise that there is a wide range of aftermath experiences. However, for most adopted people the sense of control and choice after reunion is one of the most important achievements. They argue that adopted people may have felt that they had no control over their past but they can have control over their future.

Feast *et al.* (1998) present a collection of experiences from all sides of the adoption triad: birth parents, adopted people and adoptive parents. The book emphasises the impact adoption can have on identity and self-worth. It also seeks to provide an insight into the experiences of searching and reunion both from the emotional and the practical side.

Transracial adoptions

Very little is known of searching in the context of transracial adoption, either in research terms or in relation to official data collection. There has been no ethnic monitoring of adopted people seeking access to their birth records. It is therefore impossible to know whether transracially adopted people are more or less likely to search than either their White or ethnic minority counterparts adopted into ethnically matched families. In a study of The Children's Society's records, Feast and Howe (1997) found that 11% of adopted people seeking information about birth relatives were Black African/Caribbean or of mixed ethnicity. Lack of statistics for comparison make this figure difficult to interpret, but given that the adoptions involved would have taken place no later than the early 1970s, this figure seems to show a significant level of interest in searching. In the USA, Feigelman and Silverman (1983, p. 113) found that transracially adopted people were more likely to show interest in searching than White adopted people, although this finding was based on parental views. The authors argued that parental encouragement was a crucial factor, noting that when this was lacking (as in the case of most Colombian children adopted inter-country), the children were reported as showing minimal interest (1983, p. 138). Shireman (cited in Simon *et al.*, 1994, p. 93) found greater interest by Black children in their birth families in same-race placements compared with those adopted transracially.

Qualitative research on transracially adopted people's experiences of searching is even thinner on the ground, essentially restricted to autobiographical accounts. Such research could clearly cast light on some of the key issues related to the controversy surrounding transracial and same-race adoption. In particular, it would be valuable to know whether and in what ways searching by transracially adopted people is different from that of other adopted people. To what extent are they searching for a racial or cultural identity as well as for birth relatives? Feigelman and Silverman (1983, p. 219) claim such a connection when they write: 'The transracial adopted person who attempts to contact his or her birth parents is affirming a racial identification as well as a family tie' and the link is also confirmed in autobiographical accounts (Feast *et al.*, 1998, pp. 57–61). It would also seem important to know more of the role played by physical difference in transracially adopted people searching, given the wider finding that such difference can influence adopted people's sense of belonging to their adoptive families and act as a motivation towards searching for birth parents (Schechter and Bertocci, 1990, p. 68; Hoopes, 1990, p. 161; Hollingsworth, 1998).

While sharing many of the challenges faced by those transracially adopted domestically, people adopted inter-country may have to confront the additional obstacles of distance – geographical, cultural, legal and administrative – in pursuing their search (Ngabonziza, 1988, p. 39; Hill, 1991, pp. 21–2; Carstens and Julia, 1995, p. 31). Nevertheless, there is increasing evidence of people adopted inter-country returning to their country of origin searching for relatives or wanting to experience the place where they were born.

Discussion

A major criticism of many search and reunion studies is that sample sizes tend to be relatively small and sometimes biased. Pacheco and Eme (1993) note several potential sources of bias in their research and argue that these are common to the majority of adoption studies. For example, adopted people who have had more positive experiences of reunion are often more likely to volunteer to participate in research, skewing the results towards reports of good reunions. Adopted people who initiate the reunion may have different experiences to those who were first contacted by a birth relative. Pacheco and Eme (1993), Sachdev (1992) and Silverman *et al.* (1988) speculate that reunions initiated by birth parents might not be experienced as positively as those initiated by adopted people themselves. Many study samples of adopted people who have searched or had a reunion have been obtained from support organisations that help people search or counsel them about a reunion.

Adopted people who have not searched are a difficult population to access. Approaching them raises a number of difficult ethical issues, including the possibility that they do not know they are adopted. In the USA, it is not always easy to obtain even basic data, including how many legalised adoptions have actually taken place. As a result, many studies that seek to identify the characteristics of searchers do not have a comparison group of non-searchers. Although the results have value and interest, it is difficult to know whether the characteristics of adopted people who do search are different from those who do not, or whether they are common to all adopted people, whether they search or not.

To date, most studies into people's experiences of the search and reunion process have been either American or Canadian. In the USA, access to birth records varies considerably between the 52 states. Overall, the process there is more complex and adopted people generally have to overcome many hurdles before gaining access to records. The experience of British adopted people is set within a different tradition of adoption, and although it is likely that many of the findings of the North American enquiries will apply equally well this side of the Atlantic, there is a need to carry out search and reunion studies in the UK, the results of which can then be compared and contrasted with those conducted elsewhere in the world.

CHAPTER 3

Methodology

Introduction

It is important for adoption counsellors to understand people's motivations and experiences so that they can prepare adopted people for their own search and possible reunion. With this in mind, The Children's Society made a decision to support a study by its Post Adoption and Care team into an area of adoption experience that is still relatively under-explored.

There is still the belief in many quarters that the majority of people who search for information and birth relatives must have had an unhappy or unsatisfactory adoption experience. Such assumptions affect adopted people's sense of guilt and adoptive parents' feeling of failure and inadequacy. Whilst Triseliotis' (1973) research conveyed the message that it was natural for adoptive people to want to know their origins, he also reported that 'the majority of adoptees searching for their origins, conveyed a picture of alienation and poor self image which they generally attributed to depriving experiences within the adoptive home' (1973, p. 91). It was the second half of this message that many adoption practitioners latched onto. Somewhat lost in the reading was the first part of the findings – that it was perhaps natural for most adopted people to want to search. As Triseliotis (2000) also points out, adoption is bound by culture, values, traditions, social, religious and other beliefs. These are not static and neither is the adoption experience. Some of the circumstances that motivated adopted people 30 to 40 years ago to search for their roots continue to be the same, but others have changed because the social context has also changed. Within a climate of secrecy it was a very determined person then who set out on a quest. Now the pressure is on those who do not search to do so (see Triseliotis, 2000).

It is now more than 25 years since Triseliotis carried out his ground-breaking study of 70 adopted people's search for identity and we were interested to see to what extent the modern search and reunion landscape resembled the earlier terrain. The present study set out to compare a group of adopted people who initiated a search for information and birth relatives with a group of adopted people who were contacted by a birth relative; that is, people who searched and people who were searched for.

We also wanted to find out what proportion of people are satisfied with receiving only factual information about their adoption compared to the number of people who want to search for and re-establish some form of contact with a birth relative. For example, of those who decide to search for birth relatives, how many are successful in locating them and what type of relationship, if any, is developed with the birth relative? Finally, we were interested to know what impact the searching and reunion process has on adopted people and how it might affect the relationship they have with their adoptive parents.

Aims of the study

The main aims of this comparative study were:

- To examine the reasons for searching given by adopted people.
- To investigate adopted people's experience and evaluation of the search process and its outcome.
- To compare the biographical characteristics and adoption experiences of adopted people who search (searchers) and adopted people who do not search (non-searchers).
- To compare the experiences of searchers and non-searchers who had contact with a birth relative.
- To compare searchers' and non-searchers' evaluations of their contact with a birth relative.
- To examine the long-term outcome of adopted people's restored relationship with a birth relative.
- To investigate the effect on adoptive parents of their adopted son or daughter having contact and restoring relationships with birth relatives.

Design

Data were gathered using a postal questionnaire which was sent to adopted people. Two separate questionnaires were designed to take account of the particular experiences of two groups of adopted people – those who had actively initiated a search for information and/or contact with a birth relative (searchers) and those who had not initiated a search but had been approached by a birth relative for information and/or contact (non-searchers). The two questionnaires contained common questions allowing direct comparisons to be made between the two groups. Searchers were asked 90 primary questions with many broken down further into a series of secondary and sub-group questions. Non-searchers were asked 74 primary questions, again with many broken down further into a series of secondary and sub-group questions. The questionnaires included both pre-coded, closed questions and a small number of open-ended questions. The open-ended questions allowed the respondent to express their views.

The questionnaires sought information about adopted people's biographical characteristics, adoptive family characteristics, adoption experience, reasons for searching, and search and reunion experiences. They also asked people to describe and evaluate the outcome of their search and reunion experience, including the effect, if any, on their adoptive parents. Non-searchers were also asked about how they felt about being informed of a birth relative's enquiry, how they responded, whether or not any form of contact was established, and whether a relationship developed as a consequence. The study did not collect information about adopted people's physical and mental health.

Qualitative, in-depth interviews were carried out with a large sub-sample of 74 adopted people who had completed one or other of the two questionnaires. The analysis of these data is not presented in the present report but will appear in a series of later publications. However, extracts from the interviews are used to illustrate some of the statistical findings. All names and identifying details have been changed to preserve anonymity.

The sample

A weakness of many earlier studies of the search and reunion process was the lack of a comparison group of adopted people who had not searched. In order to examine whether or not there were significant and perhaps meaningful differences in the character, history, and experiences between those who searched and those who did not, the survey design needed to sample a population of non-searchers as well as a population of searchers.

For the searcher group, the sample was gathered from all adopted people who had received direct information, advice, counselling and an intermediary service from The Children's Society between 1988 and 1997. At the time of the survey, therefore, adopted people would be at different stages of the search and reunion process. Whenever it was appropriate, the analysis controlled for these differences. The total population of the searcher group was 538. The group did not include adopted people who had opted to receive a counselling and information service from either the local authority or the General Registrar's office. Nine questionnaires were returned uncompleted. Eighty-seven of the 135 people who did not return the questionnaire were found not to be residing at the address to which the questionnaire had been sent. Of the 451 people who had actually received the questionnaire, 394 completed and returned it, giving a high response rate of 87%.

The design of the research required a comparison group of non-searchers – adopted people who had not, so far, expressed a desire to seek information or search for their birth relatives. As a group, non-searchers are difficult to locate and access. By definition, they are adopted people who have not approached adoption and information-holding agencies for knowledge about their background and origins. The identification of a group of non-searchers would allow comparisons to be made between those who decide to search for information and possible contact and those who do not.

The Children's Society's Intermediary Service for birth relatives provided access to adopted people who had shown no apparent interest in receiving information from their adoption records and/or wishing to contact their birth relatives. In effect, this group provided a population of non-searchers. The Society's Intermediary Service was started in 1991. A total of 131 adopted people (non-searchers) had been approached by the Society's Intermediary Service between 1991 and 1997, all of whom were sent a questionnaire. Eight non-searchers returned the questionnaire uncompleted. Forty-five non-searchers failed to respond, 17 of whom were subsequently found not to be living at the address to which the questionnaire had been sent. Of the 114 non-searchers who received the questionnaire, 78 completed and returned it, giving a response rate of 68%.

A total of 16% from both groups (searchers and non-searchers) did not receive the questionnaire because they had moved from their last known address.

Pilot study

A pilot study was used to test and refine the study's design and questionnaire. People adopted through the Society were not used for this exercise. Approaches were made to other adoption agencies and organisations, including NORCAP, the Post Adoption Centre (London), and the Catholic Children's Society (Westminster; Arundel and Brighton, Portsmouth and Southwark). The pilot involved a total of 51 people. Thirty-four adopted people were sent a questionnaire through the post and asked to complete and return it. A further 17 adopted people were invited to a meeting at one of the Society's offices. They were asked to complete the questionnaire. A discussion then followed in which people were asked to comment both on the questions asked and the impact they had on them as adopted people. The discussion and comments considered the questionnaire in terms of its clarity, user friendliness, length, and emotional impact. The pilot study resulted in a small number of refinements being made, but essentially the questionnaire was well received and emerged from the exercise largely intact.

Advisory panel and ethical issues

An advisory panel was formed to offer advice, comment and guidance on all stages of the research. It met on four occasions to discuss the progress of the study and proved particularly helpful on a number of ethical issues.

Adoption, searching and reunion is a complex and emotive subject for most adopted people. We were therefore conscious that receiving a request to participate in a study of people's search and reunion experience might provoke strong feelings and raise issues for some adopted people. Particular attention was given to how much information should be sent to adopted people about the study and its objectives. An information leaflet was designed to accompany the questionnaire along with a covering letter. People were encouraged to contact the Society's Post Adoption and Care Counselling Project if they felt in need of further counselling or advice following receipt of the letter and questionnaire. The distribution of the questionnaires was staggered so that the project could manage and respond to any requests for help. In the event, 12 requests were received.

Ethical issues relating to adopted people who had not initiated contact with the Society were inevitably more complex. The comparative nature of the study required a survey of adopted people who had not wanted information about or contact with birth relatives. There was a small number in the sample of non-searchers who had asked us never to be in touch again following our initial contact about a birth relative's enquiry. Although small in number, we felt that the views of this particular group were important if we were to gain a full and representative view of the experiences of all non-searchers. It was decided to make an approach to this group of non-searchers with a carefully written explanation of why we had contacted them again.

There was also a small number of non-searching adopted people with whom we had not had direct contact, but who had been approached via their adoptive parents who had been informed of a birth relative's enquiry for information. In most of these cases, the adoptive parents had expressed distress caused by the counselling team's approach and had requested no further contact. Eleven adoptive parents fell into this category. A decision was made to write to them explaining why we felt it was important for their son/daughter to have an opportunity to participate in the research. The adoptive parents were asked to return a form indicating whether or not they would be willing for their son/daughter to be informed about the research so that a questionnaire could be sent to the adopted person either via them or directly. Eleven letters and reply slips were sent to adoptive parents. Seven replies were received, with five indicating that the adopted person was willing to receive the questionnaire.

Analysis

The questionnaires were coded and input into a database using the Statistical Package for the Social Sciences (SPSS). Statistical comparisons were made both between the two major comparison groups (searchers and non-searchers) and within each group. As the analysis evolved, new groupings were created to examine the strength of particular combinations of biographical and experiential characteristics in predicting whether or not an adopted person might search. The construction of these groupings is explained in the relevant chapters. Chi-square tests were used for examining distribution in all contingency tables; t-tests were used to test for significant differences between the means of samples.

Most of the findings are presented in tabular form with percentages (rounded up or down to the nearest whole number). The number of cases from which the percentage has been calculated is given at the base of each table allowing conversion of a percentage to an actual number if desired. Associations between variables have been presumed significant when a relationship occurs at a level beyond the 5% level of probability. In most cases, the actual probabilities are given to indicate to strength of the association. If a relationship between variables was not found to be significant, this is indicated by the abbreviation NS.

SEARCHING AND BEING SOUGHT

Amongst adult adopted people, there are those who have actively sought information about their origin and background and those who have not. The present study was able to investigate the experiences of several hundred adopted people who had sought information about their birth family and the circumstances of their adoption. Although a small number of these people ceased their search once they had received information, the majority went on to trace their birth relatives with a view to establishing contact and reunion.

Birth relatives can also initiate the search and contact process. The Children's Society offers an intermediary service for birth relatives wishing to make contact with their adopted relative. This service provided a means of contacting adopted people who had not initiated a search for a birth relative. Little is known about the experiences and reactions of adopted people who have been approached and contacted by a birth relative.

Part II looks at the experiences of adopted people who seek information about their adoption, including those who go on hoping to trace and make contact with their birth families. Their experiences are compared with those of adopted people who were sought and sometimes contacted by a birth relative.

CHAPTER 4

Adopted People who Search

Introduction

For most people the search process begins by contacting the agency holding their adoption records. In this and the following two chapters, we consider the characteristics of those who search. Seeking information about one's adoption and receiving information about birth parents triggers a range of feelings which are also examined. There is no single pathway through the search and reunion process and the chapter ends by outlining the main routes along which adopted people in the present study travelled.

Characteristics of those who search

In this study of 394 adopted people who contacted the Society seeking information about and possible contact with their birth relatives, the majority were placed for adoption in the 1960s and 1970s. This was a time when the typical placement was of a White baby with White adoptive parents. The peak year for adoptions in England and Wales was 1968 when 16,164 children were placed for adoption with 'strangers' – people to whom the children were not biologically related. The broad characteristics of adopted people in this study are typical of those placed around these times. Seventy-seven per cent of people were placed with their adoptive parents during their first year, 13% during their second year and the remaining 10% after the age of two.

Eight per cent ($n = 32$) were either Black, Asian or of mixed ethnicity. (In this book, the term 'Black', when applied to our sample, refers to those who described themselves as Black British, Black African-Caribbean or Black African in our questionnaire.) All but two of these 32 were placed with White adoptive parents. Of the two who were not placed with two White parents, one had an adoptive mother of mixed ethnicity and a White father, the other had an adoptive father of mixed ethnicity and a White mother.

A minority of adopted people were raised as only children (18%). The majority of people (56%) had brothers or sisters who were also adopted. About a third (35%) had siblings who were born to their adoptive parents.

The stability of the relationship between adopted people's adoptive parents was high. Only 5% of parents either separated or divorced whilst the adopted person was still a child and living at home. These rates appear to be lower than the general population, but direct comparisons are difficult. Divorce rates were lower in the 1950s and 1960s, the time when some adopted people were growing up. By the late 1980s, Wadsworth (1986) estimated that nearly half of all UK children did not spend the whole of their childhood and adolescence with both their biological parents. Many parents divorce or separate after their children leave home. A more likely loss was the death of a parent before the adopted person had reached the age of 18. One in seven (14%) of adoptive fathers and one in 14 (7%) of adoptive mothers died while the person was still living at home with their parents.

Many studies have shown that women are much more likely than men to use post-adoption services, including approaching agencies who can give them information about their adoption and help them search for their birth relatives. The present study adds further weight to this general picture in which women appear more prevalent in the world of post-adoption needs and services. For every two women who contacted the Society only one man made an approach. Moreover, women were likely to make their first contact at a significantly younger age (29.8 years) than men (32.3 years). In short, women were twice as likely as men to approach the Society, and at an age that was typically younger than their male counterparts.

Experiences of adoption

Other studies provide mixed messages about whether or not feelings of dissatisfaction with one's adoption are likely to increase the chances of searching and seeking contact with birth relatives. We shall be examining this issue in more detail in Chapter 10 when we compare adopted people who initiated contact with a birth relative (searchers) with those who did not initiate contact but were approached by a birth relative (non-searchers). Suffice it to say at this stage that a relatively high proportion of adopted people who contacted the Society evaluated their experience of being adopted with either mixed feelings (39%) or even negative feelings (9%). Nevertheless, this still leaves a slight majority (53%) who said that their experience of being adopted was either positive or very positive. Therefore, a feeling of dissatisfaction is unlikely to be the only or even the main reason for people wanting to search for information and seek reunion.

Seeking information

The reasons for seeking background information indicate some of the social and psychological needs associated with being adopted that first appear in childhood and continue to be present in adulthood. The availability of such information is affected by one or more of three things:

1. The information is not known by the adoptive parents.
2. There is reluctance to ask for information or enter into discussion with adoptive parents because it is felt to be a sensitive or anxiety-provoking topic.
3. Adoptive parents withhold information. In extreme cases, the fact of being adopted itself is never revealed to the adopted person.

Adulthood provides the adopted person with fresh opportunities to remedy their lack of knowledge. Contacting the agency that placed them is often the first step in this information gathering process. This chapter examines:

- the reasons for contacting the Society;
- whether or not the individual's adoptive parents were told of the contact and, if told, whether or not they were supportive;
- the outcome of the contact in terms of the quality and quantity of information obtained;
- the psychological impact and value of receiving the information.

Reasons for contacting The Children's Society

Adopted people were asked to give *one main* reason for contacting the Society as well as *all the reasons*. Table 4.1 shows that the three main reasons were: to satisfy a long-standing curiosity about origins; needing to know more about oneself; and wanting help and advice about how to search for a birth relative. Curiosity about one's origins stands out as the most frequently given reason: the psychological need to have more autobiographical information appears to be a strong motivating factor in the majority of cases. The distribution of these reasons did not vary according to gender, ethnicity, age at placement or type of adoption experience.

The psychological need for autobiographical information was even more strongly reported when people were asked to give *all* their reasons for searching (Table 4.1). The need to know more about one's origins, background, and self were given as reasons by most adopted people for contacting the adoption agency. Most people gave more than one reason for seeking further information about their adoption. Interestingly, women statistically gave more reasons on average than men (means = 4.5 v 3.9, $p < 0.01$). Adopted people who said that they felt different to their adoptive families *and* felt that they did not belong in their adoptive families also gave more reasons (mean = 5.0) for seeking background knowledge than those who did not feel different *and* who felt they did belong (mean = 3.6, $p < 0.01$).

The exact cluster of motivations varied for each individual. For some it was a need to meet and, more particularly, to see people to whom they were related and might physically look like. For others there was a need to know why they were adopted. A mixture of curiosity, feeling incomplete, and a need for background

Table 4.1 *Main* reason and *all* reasons for contacting The Children's Society

	Main (%)	All (%)
Long-standing curiosity about origins	41	82
Needed to know more about oneself	15	77
Wanting help and advice about searching for a birth relative	11	47
Birth of own child	8	25
Need for background information	6	69
Need for medical information	5	35
Miscellaneous	4	13
Death of adoptive parent	3	16
Experiencing difficulties in relationships	2	20
Saw information in the media which aroused interest	2	15
Nothing significant	2	5
Looking for information from birth relatives	1	33
Thinking of getting married/long-term relationship	< 1	4
Thinking about having a baby	< 1	6
	Total	100

n = 394

information generally drove most people to seek information and, in many cases, to go on to search. Partners, and often adoptive parents, were not only supportive but in many cases were said to be encouraging of the search process.

Searcher SUSIE

It was four or five years ago and I was discussing it with my partner, Les, and he said to me 'Have you ever thought of trying to find your blood mother?' And I think that everybody who is adopted, it always crosses their mind: 'I wonder if this bit's like her, or I wonder if that bit's like her?' I was about five or six months when I was adopted and I wanted to know what happened in that part of my life that nobody knew. Or just to ask the question, 'Why did you have me adopted? Why didn't she struggle?' Especially once I had my daughter, I thought, 'I couldn't give my daughter up. How could she give her child away?' And then my mum had a major clear out of her attic and she came across my adoption papers and she kept asking me if I wanted them and I said 'Yes' but then I conveniently kept forgetting to take them with me ... I kept leaving it because I think I didn't really want to know ... while I didn't have them I could accept my life the way it's been. Once I'd got them, you've got to read them ... It didn't really bother me until later on in life when I'd had my children and the oldest one had left home and so, as I say, she gave me the adoption papers and I came home and read them and that's when my partner said, 'Why don't we go and look – ask your mum to make sure she doesn't mind – and we'll see what we can find.'

Reaction of adoptive parents to adopted person's search for information

In cases where the adoptive parent was still alive, the majority of adopted people had told them that they had contacted the Society for further background information about their adoption. Adoptive mothers had been informed in 71% of cases. Nearly as many adoptive fathers (68%) and siblings, if present (58%), had also been told. However, 21% of adopted people told no-one of the contact. These various rates of informing parents were unaffected by gender, ethnicity, age at placement and people's evaluation of their adoption experience.

Of those who had chosen not to tell their adoptive parents of the contact, three types of reason were given for keeping them in the dark, at least at this early stage of the information seeking process. The first reason given below was the most frequently cited one.

Did not wish to upset one or both adoptive parents
'I didn't want to upset them.' 'I feel they would be very hurt.' 'I thought they would be heartbroken.' 'A painful subject for them.'

None of adoptive parents' business
'No need for them to know.' 'It's my affair.' 'None of their business.' 'This is between my natural mother and me.' 'I didn't feel the need to involve anyone else.'

Resistance by adopters to talk about background and birth relatives
'Adoptive parents made it clear that they didn't want to talk about it.'

Of those adopted parents who were told of the search for information, the majority were said to have been understanding and supportive, though mothers were slightly more likely than fathers to be broadly sympathetic. On the other hand, mothers were also more likely to be upset (31%) than fathers (17%). When told of the contact, a small number of adoptive mothers (8%) and fathers (3%) reacted with hostility. Gender, ethnicity and age at placement of the adopted person did not affect the rates of these reactions.

Searcher PETER
My parents said if I ever wanted to find my mother they'd always help me ... And they did. And really my father, he used to be a teacher and he likes to plan things out and does everything methodically, and he helped me. He dug all the forms out

which related to my adoption that he had, showed me all the information they had ... And then we thought, he said, 'Well the best way is to go up to Catherine House.' So one day that's where we went, my wife, my dad and me all went to London on the train, to look through all the things.

The outcome of the contact in terms of the information obtained

For most people, the information obtained from contacting the Society and seeing their adoption records was both new and helpful. Seventy-nine per cent of people felt they received a substantial amount of new information, leaving only 21% who said that no or only a little extra knowledge had been gained as a result of their visit to the adoption agency.

Most people described a number of benefits about receiving new information from their adoption records (see Table 4.2). Learning more about their birth mother and the circumstances surrounding the reasons for the adoption were the most frequently cited gains.

Table 4.2 The good things about receiving new information from the adoption records

	%
Learned more about my birth mother	76
A better understanding of why I was adopted	68
Filled in gaps in information	57
Gained information to help with a search	52
Learned more about my birth father	50
Improved sense of personal identity	45
Finding other birth relatives	40
Finding out my birth mother would have kept me if she could	35
Finding out medical information	24
None	1

n = 386 (8 cases missing)

Searcher HEATHER
As I got to my teens, I thought I might search one day. When I was 18, I applied for the information that was around my birth, but then I decided not to do any-thing about the searching immediately after that. I kept a diary in my teens and I must have had some massive crisis at one stage about being adopted because I wrote pages and pages, and I was scared my mum and dad would find out so I Tippexed it out ... I was probably feeling a bit unloved, but I know

all teenagers go through that, and I know I wasn't unloved ... In a sense, getting the information had sorted out that immediate crisis – about who I was and where I came from – because I really had no information at all. I didn't know how much I weighed, the hospital where I was born, what my name was, anything like that, and that was, in a way, quite enough to deal with at the time. I wanted to know more about my birth parents, but I think it was really more about me, more than thinking about the reasons why it never worked out and why I was adopted ... the sheet I got was fairly basic information, but at the time it was enough.

Inevitably, the experience of contacting the agency about one's adoption records was not all good news. Negative feelings about receiving the new information centred around its limitations. Just over half of people felt that there were still questions that remained unanswered. In 15% of cases, people said that the new knowledge differed in some ways from that given by their adoptive parents. A small but not insignificant number of people felt that the new information was either distressing (14%) or not pleasant in some way (6%). However, overall the number of good things about the contact far outweighed the bad for most people.

Psychological impact of new information about the adoption

The main effect on 60% of people upon receiving the new information was to contemplate beginning a search for their birth relatives (see Table 4.3). Knowing more about one's birth mother increased compassion and understanding in 43% of cases. For most people, the impact of being given knowledge about their adoption was said to be a positive experience. Only 13% said

Table 4.3 Effects of receiving new information about the adoption

	%
Became more interested to begin search for birth relatives	60
Feeling more compassionate towards birth mother	43
Feeling more compassionate towards birth father	14
Information was satisfactory and sufficient	14
Discovered that birth relatives had tried to make contact	13
Upset upon receiving the new information	13
Did not like the information received	5
The new information put off the search for birth relatives	4

n = 370 (24 cases missing)

that the new information had upset them. Four per cent of people said they had put off their desire to search for a birth relative as a result of their visit to the agency.

Pathways through the search and reunion process

Of the 394 adopted people who contacted the Society, 58 had decided to stop once they had received background information about their adoption. Of the remainder, 255 had gone on to establish contact with one or more of their birth relatives. A further 62 people were still trying to trace their birth relative

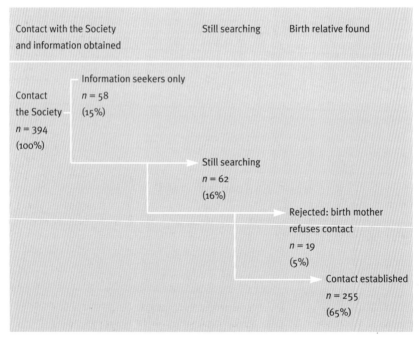

Fig. 4.1 Adopted person initiated contact: pathways and outcomes.

with a view to making contact – their search was still in progress. This left 19 people who had wanted contact and to meet with either their birth mother (17) or their birth father (2) but were rejected by her or him. In these cases, no contact was made with any birth relative. This 'rejected' group represented 7% of all those who had searched for, located and wanted contact with a birth relative.

Those still searching had characteristics similar to those who did manage to locate their birth relative. Some differentiation was observed within the large group of adopted people who did have contact with one or more of their birth relatives.

- A number of adopted people ceased contact with their birth relative after only one contact.
- Some people were accepted by one birth relative but rejected by another – theirs is therefore a 'mixed' experience in terms of outcome.
- Some maintained the contact for only a short time before ending the relationship.
- A small number of birth relatives refused to have any further contact with the adopted person after one or two meetings.
- For the majority, the initial reunion led to a relationship with the birth relative, which, although in some cases slowly petered out, lasted long enough for both parties to have got to know each other reasonably well.

In practice therefore, once a reunion had been achieved, adopted people's contact with birth relatives can range from only the briefest of meetings to a long-term secure relationship. Some people ceased contact with their birth relative after a couple of years. In contrast, some adopted people were still in contact with their birth relative ten or more years later.

It has to be borne in mind that at the time of the survey, different adopted people had been in contact with the Society for different lengths of time, ranging from less than a year to well over ten years. Where appropriate, we have controlled for length of time since initial contact. However, all contacts and reunions continue to evolve over time. For example, some of those classi-fied as 'information seekers only' in this study will in all probability go on to search and seek reunion with a birth relative at some future date. Being rejected by a birth mother, say, might well spur someone to look for their birth father.

Summary

For the majority of people, contacting the Society was described as a positive experience. The overwhelming need of most adopted people was to find out more about three things:

- the reason for their adoption *(reason)*;
- information about their own pre-placement history and background *(roots)*;
- information about their birth relatives, particularly their birth mother *(relationships)*.

Most adopted people felt they received a good deal of new information which they found helpful. Nevertheless, although the new knowledge was valued, a sig-nificant number of people still wanted answers to further questions. The way forward for most people, therefore, was to begin a search for their birth relatives. A small number of people found the new information distressing.

Of the 70% of adoptive parents who were told about the search, most were understanding and supportive. However, this did not mean that they might not feel upset. Only a small minority of parents felt hostile to their son or daughter's contact and search for information (8% mothers, 3% fathers).

At the time of the survey, 15% ($n = 58$) of adopted people, having received information about their adoption, had decided not to search for a birth relative, at least for the time being. The remaining 85% had decided to search for and seek contact with one or more of their birth relatives.

CHAPTER 5

Information Seekers Only

Introduction

Fifty-eight (15%) out of the 394 adopted people surveyed who sought information about their adoption had decided to take the search process no further. The impact and outcome of the visit to the Society to examine their adoption records was investigated.

Information seeking may be only a phase in the adoptive person's life – an early stage of the searching process. Many adopted people who describe themselves as 'information seekers only' at a particular point in time eventually go on to seek contact and reunion. Nevertheless, 'information seekers only' require investigation. They are people who occupy a midway point between a state of non-searching and a full activated search. They can therefore shed light on the thought processes, and life stages, that adopted people may go through before an actual reunion.

Information seekers only: characteristics

Those who sought information only and had chosen not to search for a birth relative at the time of the survey did not differ in any significant way from those who had chosen to search and seek reunion in terms of their age at placement, ethnicity, mean age when they first contacted the Society, and their evaluation of their adoption experience. However, there were significantly more women in the group of 'information seekers only' compared to the full 'search and reunion' group (78% *v* 64%).

Reasons for not pursuing search beyond information-gathering stage

When information seekers were asked for their *main* reason why they decided not to search for a birth relative, no one reason stood out (Table 5.1). Not wishing to upset adoptive parents (19%) and feeling that the time was not quite right to search (19%) were the main reason given by equal numbers of people.

Table 5.1 Main reason for not pursuing a search for birth relatives

	%
Interested but don't wish to upset adoptive parents	19
Wanting to wait until the time is right	19
No wish to complicate life	13
Not enough time/money to pursue a search	13
Interested but afraid of rejection by birth family	13
Interested but afraid contact might upset birth family	9
Not interested	6
Other/miscellaneous	6
Information received has satisfied curiosity	2
Afraid to find out information which may be unpleasant	0
People close not aware of the adoption	0
Total	100

n = 58

Searcher   DUNCAN

I was hoping for a bit more information – I'm very envious of that category where the birth relatives have come forward to look, that's the easy way, isn't it? It makes it a lot easier. That's the one thing that stops me, even now... I don't know what her situation is.

I just had thoughts of this nice cosy family and this letter coming through the door and maybe the husband opening it and... it's a shame, it would be lovely if there was a way of doing it... or finding out without actually making contact. I've always had these visions of standing across the road and just seeing her walk out or something.

Searcher   ANN

I'm working full time and looking after Oliver, life's just so busy anyway – you don't have a lot of time to – I don't know, there might be time later on when things aren't quite so hectic.

'Information seekers only' were also asked to give *all* their reasons for not pursuing a search. The mean number of reasons people gave was 3.4, suggesting that in practice individuals were trying to deal with a range of thoughts and feelings about whether or not to search for and seek reunion with a birth relative (Table 5.2). In fact the majority of this group (68%) said that they thought they would be likely to search sometime in the future, but either the time did not feel right or they were anxious that they might upset either their adoptive parents or their birth relatives. Twenty-six per cent said they did not know whether they would search at some later time. Only 6% said they definitely would not search at some future date. It seems, therefore, that the majority of information seekers are likely to evolve into full searchers when they feel the time might be more suitable or propitious. Not feeling ready emotionally, and the wish not to upset either adoptive or birth parents appears to lie behind most people's current decision not pursue the search further.

Table 5.2 All reasons for not pursuing a search for birth relatives

	%
Wanting to wait until the time is right	49
Interested but afraid of rejection by birth family	44
Interested but don't wish to upset adoptive parents	42
Interested but afraid contact might upset birth family	42
No wish to complicate life	36
Not enough time/money to pursue a search	31
Other/miscellaneous	15
Information received has filled the gaps	13
Information received has satisfied curiosity	11
Afraid to find out information which may be unpleasant	6
People close are not aware of the adoption	2
Not interested	7

$n = 58$

Searcher   RODNEY

There's no easy answer and you know I wouldn't like to feel that I was doing something that was opening a can of worms. And I suppose I also have to think about my family and would I want to do that to us really... and do I really want to hear that she doesn't want to contact me. I'm not sure that I do.

Yes – and then as I say, I don't think you can take it lightly, I don't think you can march in on somebody's life and say, 'Here I am', however curious you might be, because curiosity isn't a good enough reason is it?... Obviously if I was confident that she would like to meet me and that it would all go swimmingly and it wouldn't have any repercussions... negative repercussions, then you'd do it. But I think the bottom line is 'Could I really go through the rest of my life not having seen or possibly met the person who brought me here in the first place?'... I'm not really sure that I can. But there's a lot going on in my life at the moment and maybe there'll come a point where I feel that it's something I should do.

Searcher RITA

*I don't think I'll achieve anything except more hurt, I suppose that's what I'm fright-
ened of, being hurt again. Not just by my adoptive mum but by my natural mum as
well. It is too late – 31 years have gone by and have I been forgotten about? I can't just
turn up and intrude in somebody else's life. I really don't think I will – but it hurts
knowing that I can't take that step – I do, I really do want to find her, but I'm just frightened of being hurt – that's what stops me, so I just carry on with my own family and
think I'm lucky with what I've got.*

Outcome of receiving information from adoption records

Most adopted people reported various benefits as a result of receiving information about their adoption, origins and relatives. Most people said that
important questions had been answered about their background (71%). Even
so, 28% of people still felt some disappointment that the records held so little
information about their birth parents. However, reviewing the experience
overall, 80% of people said that receiving information had been a positive
experience. Only 12% of information seekers disagreed, saying that they did
not think the experience had been a positive one. The remaining 6% felt
uncertain about whether it had been a positive experience. Most adoptive parents (68%) who were aware of the search for information were said to have
reacted positively, though a quarter appeared to have reacted negatively to the
news that their son or daughter had sought information about their adoption
and birth parents.

Psychologically and emotionally, 'information seekers only' described a range
of feelings as a result of receiving new information. Around a third of people felt
more relaxed, more secure and more complete as a person. A third of people
(36%) said they felt sad as a result of their visit. Sixteen per cent said they felt
more angry having seen their adoption records. However, the strongest claim,
made by 47% of people, was that they felt unchanged as a result of receiving the
new information.

In an attempt to explore in what ways people felt they had changed or not,
they were asked to describe how the information had affected their lives, if at all.
Answers fell into the six broad categories given below.

No impact
'Nothing has changed.' 'My life has not changed.'

Positive impact on self and identity
'Added a new depth and a sense of perspective to my sense of identity.' 'Feel
more confident about myself.' 'Process helped me understand myself.' 'I could
make sense of the deep seated feeling of not belonging.' 'I felt that I existed and
finally had a history.'

Negative impact on self and identity

'Made me more curious but also confused.' 'Once I found more information I feel more hurt and rejected.'

Better understanding of reasons for being placed for adoption

'I really understood why I was adopted and how lucky I was to be with my family.' 'Process helped me understand myself and perhaps forgive birth mother.'

Triggered a desire to search

'Now have a timetable of events.' 'Now have more information to help me search.'

Positive impact on relationship with adoptive parents

'Going through process made me feel more sympathetic to adoptive parents.' 'Stronger emotions towards my adoptive parents.'

Searcher LEANNE

I feel a bit more confident in myself – I used to think, 'Oh, they've just given me away' and now I think, 'Oh what a good thing they did give me away!' so probably I feel a bit more confident in myself ... it's just really knowing more you're able to make a better judgement of what their lives were like and why I was adopted, whereas before I probably just thought, 'Oh, she just had a baby and it was a mistake and she didn't want it.'

Searcher JOCELINE

Funnily enough, I was thinking the other day, I'd actually like to push it a bit further now, especially now I've got Lewis and I've sorted myself out. I'm a lot straighter... but I would actually like to push further and try and find my mum – I don't know how to go about it but I wouldn't mind doing it. Even for Lewis, the only blood relation I've got is Lewis – OK, he's got a grandad and grandmother but you know it would be nice to find out a bit more for him, also for myself now.

At those times [when I first got the information], I couldn't deal with any more upset. At that time I was having enough upset anyway and the last thing I needed was another upset on top, whereas now I'm fairly happy with my life as it is now. I can deal with it if she said, 'I don't want to know you' or she wasn't alive any more or... I could deal with it now, because you know I've got Lewis – I've got family.

Summary

The majority of 'information seekers only' approach the search task with some hesitation, anxiety and concerns. These feelings focus on a desire not to upset their adoptive parents or themselves. Although 81% of people said that the overall experience of receiving new information was positive, the rates of reported gains were relatively modest. For example, 38% said they 'felt more complete as a person'; 30% felt their emotional outlook had improved; 47% said they felt emotionally unchanged. More positively, 71% said that the information had helped answer important questions about origins and background. A search sometime in the future was definitely contemplated by 68% of the information seekers only group.

The overall picture, then, is of a group of people who are tentative – people who seem to be feeling their way forward with some caution. Certainly, for most people, the information helped explain the reasons for the adoption. The background information provided was appreciated. But only about a third of people in this group felt that it had had a positive impact on their sense of self and identity. Receiving information appears to act like dipping a toe in the water of possible contact and reunion. Some people experience the water as warm and inviting and are encouraged to go forward with the search process. Others are not sure how to assess the experience. They imagine they will plunge into the search process at some future date but feel that the time is not right at the moment. A third, small group (6%) find the exposure unsettling or disturbing. They said they did not intend to search in the future.

CHAPTER 6

The Experience of Searching for Birth Relatives

Introduction

Having received information, 85% of adopted people then went on to search for and seek contact with one or more of their birth relatives. The chapter identifies which birth relative was sought, and describes the speed of the search process and the feelings that it engendered.

Birth relative for whom the search initially started

Even before receiving information from their adoption records, searchers already had some idea about which birth relative or relatives they wanted to find: 75% of people said they had set out wanting to find their birth mother; 40% mentioned that they would like contact with a birth brother or sister; 38% said they had also decided to search for their birth father. The most ambitious hoped to find their birth mother, birth father and birth siblings (11%). However, once the search was underway and given the background information they were receiving, in practice the birth mother was the first person for whom 91% of adopted people first decided to search.

Expectations and feelings before starting to search

A range of motives drove people to seek contact. The most common included wanting to know more about the background to the adoption, to 'complete the jigsaw' and to see who one looked like.

Searcher DELLA
I wanted to meet up for some information-type purposes – to see what I looked like, missing piece, that kind of thing. Curiosity and like completing the picture.

Searcher ANGELA
I was going through a very traumatic divorce, very, very traumatic and I felt very much at the time like I needed to relate to somebody who was my blood, who might understand my thinking. And I felt a very strong desire to belong to other people who I could identify with to help me go through a dreadful traumatic time ... and then a few years later my mother died, which again reinforced this wanting some-

body else who was physically the same as me or who I could identify mentally with, and that's what really prompted me because I knew I couldn't do it with my mother alive because I didn't want to feel I was betraying her in any way.

The most frequently cited hope expressed about the outcome of the search process was that happiness would increase (see Table 6.1). However, a cluster of worries and anxieties around the possibility of failure or rejection occupied a significant number of people.

Table 6.1 Expectations before starting the search process

	%
Would be happier as a result of the search	60
Worried about being rejected	53
Worried that the search would be unsuccessful	50
Thought they would look like me	38
Hoped to develop meaningful relationship with birth relative	35
Thought they would be like me	23
Thought they had been waiting for me to contact them	20
Thought the birth relative would be pleased to be contacted	14
Would find the birth relative quickly	11

n = 336

Most people described a mixture of feeling nervous (66%), excited (52%) and unsure (41%) in anticipation of the search. Although a small number of people said they set about the task in a calm, even matter-of-fact frame of mind, the majority said they were in a heightened emotional state. A small number said they felt some disloyalty towards their adoptive parents. Although some feared rejection, others felt charged with determination, even anger, feeling that they had a moral right to be seen by their birth relative.

Searcher SUSIE
I wanted to do the contacting myself. Because ... I don't know ... I didn't want her really to have a choice ... I was going to meet her no matter what by this time. It took me four years to do it and I didn't want to put myself in a situation of meeting my blood mother or father and being rejected. I wasn't going to give her a chance to reject me, because at the end of the day, all I wanted was answers to my questions. I think everybody that's adopted already feels slightly rejected and a rejection like that must be another rejection ... There was no intention of having a relationship whatsoever, because I've got my parents, my

parents have always been there for me, and if they hadn't been behind me ... I wouldn't have bothered.

Speed of beginning the search and outcome

Most people began to think about their birth parents with increasing frequency during their adolescence. However, in practice this rarely translated into a full search. Many of those who finally did search seemed to go through a fairly long and slow process that typically involved a number of stages, including awareness of and reflection on being adopted, information seeking, assimilation of the information, search, contact and reunion. Although some people completed this process in a very short period of time, the majority had been thinking about getting more information and looking at their adoption records for a number of years. Upon receipt of the information, a number of adopted people accelerated the process and went straight into a search, while others felt immediately satisfied with the new knowledge and only went on to seek contact at some much later date.

Searcher DAVID

I started my search when I was 34 ... I nearly did it when I was a teenager, 16, 17. Got very close to it and I think I used to think, 'I'm going to find out.' But I'm glad I didn't, really, because I wouldn't have been able to handle it then. If I'd done it at 16, I'd have fucked up everything, no question about it. I'd have blown my adoptive parents away. I'd have screwed myself up ... Then every year after Christmas and my birthday I thought about doing it – and it took another 20 years to do it!

I've been married to Liz for nine years, so she always knew from the start ... well the Barnado's TV programme triggered it. That's when I first contacted The Children's Society ... A couple of other things also acted as a trigger. Having your own kids changes you, so I wanted to know for that. I had a silly heart scare a few years ago which ended up being just stress because of work, and well it would be nice to know as much for me as for my kids if there were any things that we needed to know about – like cancer, heart problems, you know. My dad, being of a rational mind, thought it was a good reason for doing it anyway ... After I'd seen my file, I showed it to my parents. I think they were touched by the gesture of putting it all in front of them. I didn't want them to think I was going behind their backs and that they weren't good enough and that I was looking for something else that maybe they hadn't been able to provide. It was never that. As I say, the programme triggered it and then it was just curiosity and in a way I just wanted to know ...

By nature I'm very committed to things. If I do them, I do them 100%. The best thing about visiting Laura, the counsellor at The Children's Society, and initiating the search was that it enabled me to move on to the next step. Prior to meeting her, it was unknown. There were just these two people out there who I'd had some infor-

mation on for a long time, but never really taken any further. The meeting and then the search filled in a lot of blanks.

Within six months of receiving information from their adoption records, 88% of adopted people who intended to search had in fact begun the process. In practice, 65% started their search immediately. The exception was to delay the search process.

Not surprisingly, the birth mother was the relative most likely to be found first (see Table 6.2): 41% of searchers looking for their birth mother found her within one month. Within three months 60% had found her.

Table 6.2 Outcome of the search for the birth relative

	%
Found birth mother	73
Found birth sister/brother	51
Found birth grandparent(s)	28
Found birth father	24
Found that birth mother had died	8
Found that birth father had died	8
Not able to trace any birth relatives	3
Birth father denied paternity	3
Birth mother denied maternity	0.3
Other outcomes (predominantly found aunts, uncles and cousins)	10
(still searching)	(13)

n = 325 (11 cases missing)

Searcher SALLY
My partner at the time encouraged me to look for her and I was involved with people who were into personal development but I didn't ever have a burning thing to find her ... and it just happened so quickly actually. I mean I found her so incredibly quickly. It was like, 'Oh, I'll start thinking about this, maybe start looking' and then in about a day I'd found her. So it happened quicker than I'd expected really. I just looked up her name in the phone book ... And then either I rang her or she rang me, I can't remember, and then we met like a couple of days later.

Similar stories were told about searching for birth fathers: 33% found him within a month, while 53% had made contact within three months. And with birth mothers and birth fathers often came birth brothers, sisters and grandparents. For example, 58% of those who had contact with their birth mother also found themselves meeting brothers and sisters. In contrast, 8% of people managed to trace their birth mother only to learn that she had died. A similar proportion who searched for their birth father discovered that he had already died.

Searcher ARNOLD
I knocked on the door where my birth mother had once lived and was told she had died three years earlier ... I have mixed feelings. I was a bit disappointed ... But I dusted myself down, accepted the fact. Nothing I could do about it. I'm reasonably happy with the situation.

Several people found and had contact with more than one birth relative: 16% had contact with their birth mother, birth father and birth siblings (Table 6.3).

Table 6.3 Outcome of first search resulting in contact with more than one birth relative

	%
Birth mother and birth siblings	42
Birth mother and birth father	20
Birth father and birth siblings	18
Birth mother, birth father and birth siblings	16

n = 325 (11 cases missing)

First contacts with birth mothers were most likely to be by letter or telephone (91%). Only 9% went straight for a face-to-face meeting. Most people used an intermediary (78%) to establish their first contact. The remaining 22% made contact directly themselves.

Searcher HAZEL
Once I found her, I went for it. Because the more I thought about it, the more scared I got and I thought, 'No, I can't wait, I've got to do it.' I phoned her up. I got to the last digit of the number and I thought – I put it down six times – and I thought, 'No, I'm going to do it this time' and eventually I phoned her up and she came on the phone ... And I said, 'You don't know me, you know me as Helen Jones' and it went absolutely quiet and I said, 'Hello, are you still there?' And she went, 'Oh my God!' So she said, 'How are you?' and I said, 'I'm fine' and she said, 'I've been waiting. I thought this day might come' and she asked how long had I been looking and I said, 'A long while.' And she said, 'Are you married?' and she started off asking me questions and I said, 'I've got questions to ask you' and she said, 'How about coming up here to meet me – come to my house.' And so we arranged to meet the following week at her home, which frightened me even more ... So I went up and met her, it was quite an experience, because she's not how I

thought she would be. She doesn't look how I thought she would look. She's quite a nice lady.

Having established contact with their birth mother, many adopted people then went on to meet their mother's other children (i.e. siblings and half-siblings), her parents (i.e. maternal grandparents), and in a small number of cases their birth father if the birth mother agreed to facilitate contact with him.

Summary

Most people set out to find their birth mother. There was a widespread hope that a successful search would improve feelings of happiness. Sixty-five per cent of adopted people began their search immediately after receiving information from their adoption records. Feelings of anxiety, nervousness and excitement typically accompanied the search process. Some uncertainty and a degree of fear of rejection were also present in many cases. Sixty per cent of searchers had found their birth mother within three months. In many cases, finding the birth mother also meant having contact with birth siblings and birth grandparents.

Although most people pursued a 'fast-track' search strategy – immediate start and quick find – a significant minority either took matters more slowly or found that the search process was relatively slow. Around 10% failed to find or make contact with their birth relative either because they were dead, or, in a handful of cases, because they denied paternity or maternity.

CHAPTER 7

Non-Searchers and their Response to Contact Initiated by a Birth Relative

Introduction

At the national level, it remains very difficult to know what proportion of adult adopted people consult their adoption records and/or seek direct contact with one or more of their birth relatives. Although a growing amount is known about those who do search, much less is known about those who do not seek further information about their adoption or who do not actively desire contact with a birth relative. We were keen to seek the views and experiences of this non-searching group. One way of generating a sample of non-searchers was to contact adopted people who had been approached by one of their birth relatives. Since 1991, the Society has been offering an intermediary service to birth relatives enquiring about their adopted relative. A small number of birth relatives decide to initiate contact with the adopted person themselves. In most cases they can only gain access to the adopted person via an intermediary. The intermediary (usually an adoption agency worker) contacts the adopted person or their adoptive parents and explains that a birth relative has approached the agency seeking information. The adopted person is free to decide whether or not to respond to the enquiry. If they decide against making a response, the birth relative's request is not pursued any further and the relative is not given information that would enable them to make direct contact.

Adopted people who come to the attention of a counselling adoption agency because a birth relative initiates contact therefore represent a group of non-searchers. Their views and experiences might be seen as reasonably representative of all those adopted people who, at a point in time, had chosen not to search or seek reunion with a birth relative. In this chapter we concentrate on why non-searchers had decided not to search and how they reacted to the request for contact initiated by their birth relative. Seventy-eight adopted people who had been approached by a birth relative provided information about their experiences of being adopted and their views on being contacted.

Thinking about whether to trace a birth relative

Although nearly half (47%) of non-searchers said they had not thought about contacting a birth relative, 42% said that they had actually thought about searching even before their birth relative made their approach. In fact, 21% of the total sample of non-searchers said that they had actually taken some preliminary steps to try and locate their birth relative before being contacted by the Society on behalf of a birth relative. Even so, only 17% of non-searchers had heard of the Adoption Contact Register. Some examples of people in each of the above categories are given below.

Had never thought about it (47%)

Non-searcher LIZ

As I got older in my late teens, a few friends started to say to me, 'Aren't you inter-ested in finding out who your real parents are?' And I always used to say, 'No, not really. Why should I?' I was totally happy with my current family – so there wasn't a need as far as I was concerned … That's not to say that I might not have done as I've got older but there wasn't ever a time when I seriously thought about looking for her or finding out any more information.

Had been thinking about it (42%)

Non-searcher MOIRA

I did think about searching. I thought I'd do it when I was older, like when I was 18. And then when I reached 18, I thought, 'No, I'll put up for a little bit longer.' I never actually plucked up the courage to do it. I just didn't know where to start … but I did want to. And I didn't want to upset my mum and dad and I didn't want to be rejected by my birth mother.

Had taken steps towards it (21%)

Non-searcher JESSICA

When I was 18 I took that opportunity then to start trying to trace my natural mother. At the time you had to go through a social worker so that's what I did… On the second meeting with him he actually had a piece of paper with the details surrounding the circumstances of my adoption. I always remember it was rather impersonal and upsetting at the time. It just basically said my mother was 5ft 5ins, brown hair, brown eyes, an art student – the purportive father was blonde, 6ft – and that they regretted having to give me up for adoption but they did. And there was also a note about my mother, at the time when she was carrying me, that she had actually attempted to commit suicide – and it all sounded really quite traumatic and sad…

I decided then that it was just too big a thing for me to take on board and espe-cially as the circumstances seemed quite traumatic for my natural mother. I started thinking, 'Maybe it's not right for me just to turn up in her life so many years later' – so I thought I'd just leave it.

Reasons for not seeking information about the adoption

The *main* reason given by people for not contacting the Society about their adoption involved feelings for and about their adoptive parents. Typically, people said either that they considered that their adoptive parents were their real parents (34%) or that they did not wish to upset them (18%). This picture received further support when people were asked to give *all* the reasons why they had not searched for further information about their adoption or sought contact with a birth relative (see Table 7.1). About a third of people also said that they felt scared that the information might be either upsetting or unpleasant.

Table 7.1 *All* reasons for not seeking access to information from The Children's Society about birth and adoption

	%
Feel that my adoptive parents are my real parents	47
Did not want to upset adoptive parents	44
Scared that the information might be upsetting/unpleasant	31
Did not feel emotionally strong enough to begin a search	30
Never thought much about birth father	26
Feeling that there was no point as birth parents had already rejected me	
by placing me for adoption	23
No desire to learn more about background	22
No knowledge of how to begin the search	22
Never thought much about birth mother	21
Other people close to me might be upset	13
Did not have time or money	8
Did not want to go through a social worker	8
Taking own steps to locate birth relative	5
Thought one day my birth relatives would try and find me	5
Not many people know I'm adopted, so it would be difficult	4
Other/miscellaneous reasons	15

n = 77 (1 case missing)

Non-searcher MICHELLE
My parents, they did speak about it, like 'If you ever want to get in touch with your parents, you can. It won't hurt us.' Well, they said that. But I thought deep-down

that it could hurt them. And I always sat there and thought, 'Who do I look like?' But I've never had the actual guts to get up and do it, you know.

Non-searcher CHARLOTTE
My adoptive parents never brought up the subject of my adoption because I never brought it up – and they thought I didn't want to know – that I had no interest. And vice versa ... I didn't think it was a good idea to search ... I didn't know if I was protecting myself more than her [birth mother] or vice versa – a combination of the two I think. It was 'I want to know' but overridden by 'I don't want to know in case I don't like it' or 'She might not like it.' And always in the background, concern that I might hurt my adoptive parents who – they were marvellous and still are ... I'd never felt this need to understand and know about my 'roots'.

Feelings about an adoption agency letting adopted people know about a birth relative's interest

Seventy-six per cent of non-searchers felt that it was right for adoption agencies to let them know that a birth relative had approached them about trying to make contact. Only 6% said that they thought it was definitely wrong. The remaining 18% felt unsure about whether it was a good idea to be informed of the birth relative's interest. Less than one in ten people (8%) said that they would take action, if appropriate, to prevent a birth relative getting in contact with them.

Non-searcher CHARLOTTE
I think that adopted people should be aware of a birth relative's approach but they should be able to record their right to anonymity. So if a birth relative pitches up, they then have absolutely no right to approach the adopted person because they've said, 'I never want to be approached' but with the reservation that they could change their minds at any time ... it's all very well for people to say, 'Well you got our letter about your birth mother's approach and you could have said no'. But you can't! I'd say that I'm a very strong person and I couldn't resist it ... but if you could register somewhere and say, 'No, I never want to be contacted unless I change my mind at some stage, in which case I will let you know.'

Birth relatives who initiated the contact

The birth relative who was most likely to initiate contact was the birth mother (71%). However, nearly a quarter of all birth relative initiated contacts were made by a birth sibling (23%). Only 3% of contacts were initiated by a birth father. These proportions are very similar to those found by Mullender and Kearn (1997) in their study of birth relatives who have used Part II of the Adoption and Contact Register for England and Wales. In the present study, contact was typically made via the Society (94% of cases). The Society made the initial contact directly to the adopted person in 43% of cases or via the adoptive parent in 51% of cases. In the remaining cases it is not known who was initially contacted.

Non-searchers who agreed to contact with a birth relative

Non-searchers were asked for *all* the things they agreed to do when they learnt that a birth relative wanted to contact them. For those adopted people who agreed to some form of contact, an initial exchange of letters was most frequently preferred (51%). Thirty-one per cent were prepared to meet face-to-face without an exchange of letters or prior telephone conversation. Thirty-six per cent initially also said that they would like time to think about what to do.

Initial exchange of letters (51%)

Non-searcher MICHELLE
Well, it started off The Children's Society sent my mum a letter asking if I was still at the address. My mum said yes – sent a photograph of me. And then mum, or was it me, got a letter through saying that my birth mum wanted to get in contact with me. And I was, 'Oh dear! Oh no! What do I do?' I was so nervous. Very tearful! But I thought, 'Why not?' Then I wrote a letter back saying, 'Yes. I'll get in contact with her through The Children's Society but not giving our addresses yet' – not quite yet. We started writing to each other for about a year and then she wrote her telephone number on top of one of her letters and said if I wanted to get in contact I could... And then one night I phoned her and I said, 'Hello – is Julia there?' And she said, 'Yeah' and I said, 'It's Michelle.' 'Michelle?' she went. I said, 'Your daughter!' And that was it – cor! Screamed down my ear and she was excited. She started crying. That was it. I started crying ... so the week after that we went down and met each other.

Wanted time to think about it (36%)

Non-searcher MARTIN
It wasn't my natural mother who was looking for me; it was my half-sister – well what I thought at the time were two half-sisters looking for me – but it all came out it was one full sister and one half-sister ... I left it a while before I made contact with them – about 12 months – I sat back and really thought about it before I went ahead with it and wrote a letter back. I wanted a counsellor first and shortly after I got the letter I went to a counsellor and went through all the adoption papers. I'd calmed down a bit by then – I was just curious about everything ... my parents were a bit upset; they weren't entirely happy with it – but they went along with it.

Immediate face-to-face contact (31%)

NEIL
We met in November – so that was very fast by most standards, I'm told. We found a smashing place, and they gave us a room – and a lovely smart restaurant – which was lovely and quiet. There wasn't a great physical resemblance but we did a lot of talking. We had so much in common. We sat close together and held hands in the private room – a few tears on both sides. I sat closer to her than I did to my wife, I remember that – but I guess both partners were ready for that. It was a momentous, incredible day ... it really, really was.

Feelings triggered by the contact

A number of feelings were experienced by most people when they learned that a birth relative was seeking contact. Over 90% of people felt a mixture of two or more of the following emotions:

- surprise
- excitement
- shock
- curiosity
- anxiety

Typical feelings included: 'Frightened, excited, feeling of fate.' 'Surprised, nervous not knowing what to expect.' 'Excitement, intrigued and happy. I felt I'd been given another chance.' 'Excited, curious, surprised, anxious. Why now? I couldn't concentrate on anything.' 'Surprised, shocked and delighted.'

ALAN
My initial reaction was, 'Jesus Christ!' Well, anyone would, wouldn't they? You get a letter out of the blue: 'You are the youngest of four brothers ...' 'Oh jolly good!' You wouldn't be human if it didn't surprise you, would you? I only decided to see my brother when I knew my parents were happy about me going ... The last thing I want to do on any occasion would be to upset them in any way – no way whatever. They are more to me – they've been everything to me and still are.

BRIAN
The letter came direct to my mum and dad and as luck had it, we were staying with them ... Sunday morning it was, they said, 'Here you are, there's this letter, have a read of that.' It really was out of the blue. It shocked us all right down to the ground but if anyone from The Children's Society had appeared, knocking on the front door that day, dad would have torn them limb from limb, I think, because it really did upset everybody. But I've talked about since and I don't really think there's a different way of doing it – it's got to be done somehow – you can't have a complete

stranger turning up on your doorstep saying 'Hello'. But it was certainly very upsetting finding out, particularly for the parents.

Non-searcher JESSICA

My parents were upset. The thing is, I think, my mum's explained it to me since then – when she adopted me it was 1963 and it was a very solemn sort of procedure. She remembers going to the court and swearing that she would 'take this baby as her own' and that was that. They believed that the natural parents wouldn't figure at all. So she was genuinely really upset by it and I suppose, scared. She didn't know what would happen ... I think both my parents just felt as though they wished whoever it was would just keep their nose out of their lives and my life and just let things carry on. I did discuss it at length with them and I said really, even though I knew it was upsetting them, that if I didn't do it, didn't see her, it would be something that I may regret in the future. So then they said, 'OK then, if you really feel you need to go ahead with it, you must do, and we'll try and support you with that.'

A minority of people felt very angry and disturbed by the contact. Their comments included feeling: 'Angry, confused, upset, lonely, depressed, invaded.' 'Upset, shocked and protective towards my adoptive family.' Two people claimed to have felt nothing: 'No feelings.' 'Felt absolutely nothing.'

Non-searcher LIZ

I actually got a letter in the post, completely out of the blue ... I opened it and it started off – she'd been thinking about me and wondering where I was and that she gave birth to me 24 years ago ... I just read the first sentence and I knew who it was from, and it was just an enormous shock – very, very upsetting ... it just completely threw me. I wasn't expecting it all I suppose. So I was completely unprepared and it was very upsetting and I was really quite distressed by it – a whole range of emotions going through my mind thinking, 'How dare she do this!' So I then phoned my adoptive parents and told them what happened – and understandably they were pretty shocked as well and I went down to see them the next day.

So I thought about it for two or three weeks and talked it through ... I decided to write a letter back to her, saying how I felt – that I was quite angry that she'd contacted me in this way. I'd always been very happy and content with my life and had no reason for wanting to contact her and that my family were devastated by what she'd done. It was quite an angry letter really ... and 'there's no room for you in my life and I'd appreciate it if you didn't contact me again' ... Well about four years later, I suppose I'd moved on a bit and I started to soften towards her and think more of the positive things: 'I wonder what she does look like?' And then I started seeing this guy and he had a strong effect on me. He suggested to me, 'Don't you want to find out more?' And I started to think, 'Well, maybe I am at a stage in my life where I could cope' ... and eventually through an intermediary I wrote back to my natural mother.

Some non-searchers saw a counsellor and were shown their adoption records before pursuing the contact. This was generally felt to be helpful, but in some cases the new information was more than they had anticipated, both in quantity and quality.

Non-searcher MIKE

There was an awful lot of information there that I just didn't know about, I mean quite serious information. You know big things like my name, pictures of my mum, a letter from her ... I think with hindsight it might have been better to have known roughly what to expect. I didn't realise it would be as intense ... but it was information that I felt that I deserved as a human being. It was information that belonged to me.

Non-searchers who refused contact with their birth relative and/or agreed only to exchange information

Ten per cent (*n* = 8) of non-searchers chose not to have direct contact with their birth relative. In most of these cases, only a minimal amount of information was either received or given. Of the eight people in this category, half said that the main reason for their attitude was that they were not interested in exchanging information. When all reasons for not wishing to develop the contact were given, four people also felt they did not wish to complicate their lives. Other reasons included: no interest in having contact (one person); a feeling that the birth relative had no right to approach (two people); a feeling that adoptive parents would be upset (one person: 'adopted parents were devastated so I didn't want contact'); a belief that it was the wrong time (two people); and that too much was currently taking place in the adopted person's life (two people).

Overall, the birth relative's attempt at contact was not viewed well by non-searchers who refused contact. There were high rates of feeling angry and unsettled. On the other hand, six out of eight people said that nevertheless it felt good to know that their birth relative had not forgotten about them. It was not felt that the approach had filled in any gaps or improved a sense of identity.

Equal numbers of men and women made up this non-searcher no-contact group. All were placed as babies before the age of six months. All said that while growing up they did not feel different to their adoptive families and that they belonged. Their mean age at the time of their birth relative's contact (24.6 years) was significantly lower than the mean for that of the remaining non-searchers who did have contact (32.0 years). A little surprising was that although five out of the eight evaluated their adoption experience as very positive, the remaining three said they viewed it with mixed feelings.

The non-searchers who refused contact were asked to review the approach made by the birth relative via the Society. Though the numbers in this group are small, it was possible to recognise the following three themes in their reviews.

Reactions to request for contact with birth relative

Four people did not want any contact with their birth mother, birth father, birth siblings, or birth grandparents. Two people were not certain whether or not they wanted contact. One person did not want contact at present but did not rule it out on a future occasion. Nevertheless, two people said they did have questions to ask about their birth relatives. No-one felt that knowing that a birth relative had tried to make contact had improved the way they felt about themselves. Six out of the eight people said that they found the approach by the Society 'disturbing', with comments such as: 'The contact continues to upset my elderly adoptive parents.' 'The survey has rekindled feelings I've tried to bury but I'm aware they won't go away.' 'I didn't know birth relatives were allowed to make contact.'

Thoughts about birth family

Five out of the eight people in the no-contact group said they did not feel a conflict of loyalties between their adoptive and birth families. All eight people thought that they would be feel like a stranger with their birth family, and that they could never feel 'at home' with them. The general belief was that their birth family would be very different to their adoptive family. Six people out of eight felt uncertain whether or not their birth relatives would like them.

View of self

Everyone in this group said they felt secure, complete as a person, and had a broadly positive view of themselves. All but one person said that they could relate well with other people, had high self-esteem, and felt relaxed.

Non-searcher VINCENT
I don't think I feel fear but that doesn't mean that I'm not frightened. I just think one family is enough and I don't think I'd be a good deal for anyone – I don't want a social leper latched on to me – my life is too full now – something would have to give and I can't see the point of going for a weekend miles away to visit a total stranger who I'm never ever going to see again – just another person to send a Christmas card to.

Summary

There was a fairly even split amongst non-searchers between those who said that they had not thought about searching and those who said that they had actually thought about searching but had done nothing about it. Loyalty and other feelings for their adoptive parents appeared to be the main reasons why most people had decided against searching. About half of non-searchers said that they felt that their adoptive parents were their 'real parents' and nearly as many said that they did not wish to upset them by contemplating a search.

A third also felt worried that further information about their adoption might either be unpleasant or upsetting.

Three-quarters of non-searchers felt that it was right for adoption agencies to let them know that a birth relative had made an approach seeking contact. Only a tenth said they would take definite action to prevent a birth relative making direct contact. Six per cent said they felt it was definitely wrong that a birth relative should be able to contact them, either directly or through an intermediary. The most likely birth relative to try and make contact was the birth mother (71%). About a quarter of contacts were made by a birth sibling. Whereas contact by a birth mother usually carried a complex, often difficult emotional agenda involving issues of loss and rejection, contact by a birth sibling was viewed more equably by both the adopted person and his or her parents.

The majority of adopted people (90%) contacted by their birth relative did agree to have contact, although some needed time to think about matters before finally saying yes. Most people made their first response by letter or telephone. Only later did a face-to-face meeting take place. Birth siblings and birth grandparents were often met for the first time only after a face-to-face meeting with the birth parents had been arranged. We shall compare the experiences of non-searchers and searchers who had contact with and met their birth relatives in Chapters 13 and 14.

PART III

SEARCHERS AND NON-SEARCHERS COMPARED

There has long been a debate about whether or not adopted people who search for birth relatives differ in significant ways from those who do not search. In particular, speculation has centred around possible differences between the two groups in terms of biology and biography and the experience of being adopted (happy or unhappy, quality of relationship with adoptive parents etc.). Although it has been less clear how or why biography might affect the desire to search, it has been suggested by some that adopted people who view their experiences of adoption as less than satisfactory might be more inclined to search for and seek reunion with their birth parents. However, direct comparisons between those who search and those who do not have rarely been made. The design of the present study was able to build in a comparison between the two groups allowing us to investigate whether or not significant differences exist between adopted people who initiate a search (searchers) and those who do not (non-searchers).

In Part III we compare the two groups in the following seven areas:

- biographical characteristics
- telling and openness
- adoption experiences
- difference and belonging
- rejection
- contact and reunion
- the reunion experience: impact and evaluation.

CHAPTER 8

Biographical Characteristics

Introduction

In this chapter, we begin by comparing searchers and non-searchers in terms of a number of basic biographical characteristics: gender, ethnicity, age at placement, and composition of the adoptive family (including siblings). Personal characteristics and the characteristics of the situation into which the adopted child is placed have been seen as possible factors influencing both the adoption experience and the likelihood of searching.

Gender

The ratio of women to men in most surveys of adopted people's approaches to post-adoption services for information, counselling and searching is typically 2:1. The present survey confirms the tendency of adopted women to be much more active in seeking help, advice and information from adoption agencies and to be twice as likely as men to search for their birth relatives. However, birth relatives interested in seeking contact show no gender bias for the adopted person being sought, male adopted people being as likely to be searched for as female (see Fig. 8.1). However, the birth relative most likely to initiate a contact was a birth mother (71%), followed by a birth sibling (23%). Unfortunately the gender of the birth sibling seeking contact is not known. Only 3% of contacts were initiated by birth fathers.

Ethnicity

ETHNICITY OF THE ADOPTED PERSON

The relatively low proportion of adopted people of Black, Asian and mixed ethnicity in the study probably reflects the time when majority of the adoptions in this study took place (see Table 8.1). It was relatively unusual to place Black children and children of mixed ethnicity for adoption in the 1950s, 1960s and early 1970s. The majority of Black children placed in this sample are of mixed ethnicity, with less than 2% of the total sample having both parents who were Black or Asian.

Table 8.1 Ethnicity of adopted person

	Searchers (%)	Non-searchers (%)
White/European	92	97
Black/Asian	2	0
Mixed ethnicity	6	3
Total	100	100

Searchers n = 394; non-searchers n = 78; NS

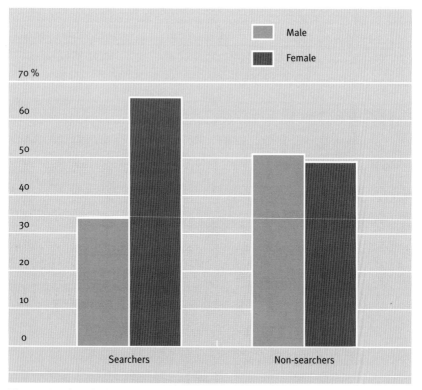

Fig. 8.1 Gender of adopted person seeking or being sought. Searchers n = 394; non-searchers n = 78; $p < 0.005$.

ETHNICITY OF ADOPTED PERSON'S BIRTH PARENTS

The majority of adopted people had two White European parents. In the case of children of mixed ethnicity, the birth mother was more likely to be White than Black or Asian. In the case of non-searchers, all contacts initiated by birth mothers were by mothers who are White. In the case of searchers who described themselves as of 'mixed ethnicity', all 24 people said that their birth mother was White European and their birth father was either Black African/Caribbean or Asian. Two adopted people from the searchers group described themselves as White but reported a Black African/Caribbean or Asian birth father (Table 8.2).

Table 8.2 Ethnicity of adopted person's birth parents

	Searchers		Non-searchers	
	Mother (%)	Father (%)	Mother (%)	Father (%)
White European	98.0	90	100	97
Black African/Caribbean	0.5	4	0	1
Asian	0.3	3	0	0
Mixed ethnicity	1.0	3	0	1

Mothers: searchers $n = 378$ (don't know/missing = 22); non-searchers $n = 72$ (don't know/missing = 6).
Fathers: searchers $n = 338$ (don't know/missing = 56); non-searchers $n = 67$ (don't know/missing = 11)

Age of adopted person when they first contacted or were contacted by the Society

The mean age of adopted people (searchers) when they first contacted the Society was 30.7 years. Again, we see a significant gender difference, with men, on average, delaying contact until age 32.3 years compared to a mean age of 29.8 for women at time of contact. Interestingly, the mean age at contact of those approached by a birth relative (non-searchers) is very similar to that of searchers (see Table 8.3). Equally difficult to interpret is why birth relatives who initiate contact tend to approach adopted women at a mean age which is four years younger than that for adopted men.

Thus, for searchers, when we add gender differences to age at first contact, men are not only less likely to search, but they are more likely to begin their search at an older age. For adopted people who are searched for by a birth relative, although men and women are equally likely to be contacted, women are approached at a significantly younger age than men.

Table 8.3 Age of adopted person at first contact

	Searchers (mean age in years)	Non-searchers (mean age in years)
Men	32.3 (SD = 8.9 y)	33.3 (SD = 9.3 y)
Women	29.8 (SD = 9.3 y)	29.3 (SD = 8.0 y)
All	30.7 (SD = 9.2 y)	31.3 (SD = 8.9 y)
	($p < 0.02$)	($p < 0.05$)

Adopted person's age at placement

The high proportion of people adopted as babies in the survey reflects adoption practice in the 1950s, 1960s and early 1970s when there were relatively few placements of older children. For example, 77% of searchers and 84% of non-searchers were placed for adoption before they were one year old. There is a slight non-statistical trend towards birth relatives being more likely to search for a child placed in infancy than for a child placed after the age of one year.

Age at leaving adoptive parents' home

The mean age for leaving home for both searchers and non-searchers was 20 years. The main reasons for leaving home were similar for the two groups. For example, 28% of searchers first left home to start college, compared to 21% of non-searchers; 27% of searchers and 23% of non-searchers left to get married; 14% of searchers said they left because they needed independence compared to 25% non-searchers. Starting college, getting married and needing independence accounted for 68% of the main reasons given by searchers and 69% of the main reasons given by non-searchers.

Adopters and their families

ADOPTERS

The poor quality of an adoptive parents' marriage or the death of an adoptive parent during the adopted person's childhood might be factors influencing whether or not an adopted person is likely to search. In our sample, rates of separation and divorce amongst the parents of both searchers and non-searchers were low (less than 5%). The death of a parent was more likely than the divorce or separation, with one in 14 mothers and one in seven fathers dying while the adopted person was still living at home. However, no differences in rates of either adoptive parent mortality or marital instability were found between the search and non-search groups. The study therefore provided no evidence that the loss of an adoptive parent through either death or divorce was more likely to trigger a search.

SIBLINGS

The sibling composition of the adoptive families of those who searched and those who did not showed no statistically significant difference (see Table 8.4). Taking the absence of any children born to the adopters as a possible (but not a necessary) indicator of infertility, adopted children of infertile adopters were just as likely to be searchers as non-searchers. Similarly, the presence of children born to the adopters appeared to have had no influence on whether or not an adopted person decided to search.

Table 8.4 Birth and adopted siblings

	Searchers (%)	Non-searchers (%)	
1 or more adopted siblings	56	63	NS
1 or more siblings born-to adopters	35	28	NS
No siblings born-to adopters	65	72	NS
Adopted person an only child	18	18	NS
1 or more siblings born-to adopters after placement	16	19	NS

Searchers n = 394; non-searchers n = 78

Summary

In terms of adopted people's broad biographical and family characteristics, there were few differences between searchers and non-searchers. No statistical differences were found between the two groups for:

- age of placement
- ethnicity
- sibling composition of the adoptive family
- stability of the adoptive parents' marriage or death of an adoptive parent while adopted person was still living at home.

The only significant difference between those who searched and those who did not was related to their gender. Adopted women were twice as likely as men to initiate a search. Moreover, the mean age at which they first began their search was significantly lower than that for men (29.8 years v 32.3 years). In contrast, those who were contacted by a birth relative were as likely to be men as women, although there is the curious finding that the mean age of women when they were first contacted was significantly lower than that of men (29.3 years v 33.3 years).

CHAPTER 9

Telling and Openness

Introduction

The ways in which both parents and children handle the fact and facts of adoption have long been thought to be highly relevant features of the adoption experience. For example, good and bad practices about how and when to tell children that they are adopted have been thought to affect both children's adjustment and whether or not they are likely to search. By examining the adoption experiences reported by both searchers and non-searchers, it is possible to see what effect, if any, these matters might have on adopted people's wish to search.

Disclosure and discussion

A range of issues and experiences were explored with adopted people about when and how they were told of their adoption. The age and manner in which adopted people are told about their backgrounds are possible factors that might influence whether or not they search.

Most people said they had always known that they were adopted, or at least known from a very young age. Parents handled this in a variety of ways. Some built it into the fabric of the relationship in a low-key way so that being adopted felt normal and not an issue. Others might 'tell' as a one-off event leaving the adopted child with the feeling that adoption was a sensitive issue which, though important, was one which parents found difficult to handle.

Searcher HELEN

I've always known, as early as I can remember. My parents were as open insofar as they told us about being adopted and they had a little story book about how their children were adopted, how special we were that we were adopted but they didn't really talk about it as we got older. Our feelings about it weren't discussed. We didn't really know any information about ourselves ... it wasn't really discussed.

The 'telling' experiences of both searchers and non-searchers were broadly similar. For example, the number of searchers and non-searchers who had either always known or been told before the age of five that they were adopted were similar (68% *v* 65%), and the proportion who said that they had never been told of their adoption by their parents was the same (3%) for both searchers and non-searchers (see Table 9.1).

Table 9.1 Age of the adopted person when their parents told them that they were adopted

	Searchers (%)	Non-searchers (%)
Always known/< 5 years	68	71
> 6 years	29	26
Never told	3	3

Searchers *n* = 382 (12 missing); non-searchers *n* = 72; NS

Searcher ARNOLD
The adoption was open in that I knew about it but they felt that my mother had neglected me and they had 'saved' me and they really had no wish at any time for me to me to become involved in my previous existence. Although they were open to tell me all they knew, which wasn't a lot, it would have upset them very much if I'd have done anything while they were alive.

Searcher LINDA
I found out when I was 11 ... it was by accident at school. We were just about to sit the eleven plus and I was always in the top grade. Teacher went off to the office and there were two boys, and all our records were piled up on the desk ready for the exam the next day, and they decided they would go and look through, which they did. They came across and yelled out to me, 'I didn't know you were adopted.' And I didn't know myself. And even then I didn't know what the word meant ... I recall coming home, opening the gate and coming in. Mum was standing there doing the ironing and I said, 'Mum, what does adoption mean?' And you can imagine what happened then. Mum said, 'Where did you hear this?' and I said, 'School.' She said, 'I must get on the phone and get dad home from work.' ... I was sat down much later on and was told, 'Yes, I was adopted ... I was chosen.' And when you're that age you think that's something wonderful, that makes you feel someone very, very different.

The survey results showed no difference between searchers and non-searchers in terms of how openly the adopted person felt parents had discussed the adoption (Table 9.2), whether the adopted person felt comfortable asking for information (Table 9.3), and how much information was given or available (Table 9.4). However, although no differences were found between the two groups, what is noteworthy is the high rate of ignorance and discomfort reported by both searchers and non-searchers alike when it came to talking about their adoption with their parents. Only around 40% of all adopted people said they felt that their parents were generally willing to discuss the background to the adoption. For example, although Melissa said that she had always known that she was adopted, 'it was never really a subject for discussion. I don't think I ever raised it, and I was never told that much. All I was told was "Your mum was really young".'

A significant exception to this relatively low rate of parental openness was reported by transracially placed adopted people of Black, Asian and mixed ethnicity, 67% of whom said that their adoption was openly discussed ($p < 0.01$).

Less than a third of adopted people said they had felt comfortable asking their parents for information about their birth family and origins. Over 50% of adopted people said they were given either no information or only a little about their adoption.

Table 9.2 Adopters discussed background to the adoption

	Searchers (%)	Non-searchers (%)
Yes	40	43
Sometimes	25	30
No	35	26

Searchers n = 392 (2 missing); non-searchers n = 76 (2 missing); NS

Non-searcher JESSICA

My parents didn't really want to discuss it with me any further when I asked for details, so when I was about nine or ten I rummaged through their bedroom and found various original birth certificates and court cases – the official papers for my adoption ... As long as I can remember I wanted to know more. My parents weren't very forthcoming when I spoke to them. They didn't want to divulge anything else about the adoption. I don't think they knew much though, to be honest. But they knew more than they told me, I've since found out.

Table 9.3 Adopted person felt comfortable asking for information about their birth family and their origins

	Searchers (%)	Non-searchers (%)
Yes	29	26
Sometimes	19	27
No	51	47

Searchers n = 390 (4 missing); non-searchers n = 73 (5 missing); NS

Table 9.4 Amount of background information given by adopters about the adoption

	Searchers (%)	Non-searchers (%)
None	18	16
Very little	38	45
Fair amount	28	28
A lot	16	12

Searchers n = 391 (3 missing); non-searchers n = 76 (2 missing); NS

Non-searcher MARTIN

I always knew I was adopted. They were open that I was adopted but they never told me the details – but then I never asked. I didn't like to ask ... I just felt it was in the past, and that's where it had to stay ... They also destroyed all the adoption papers as well, eventually. That was their way, you know, thinking it would never come up again.

However, when the issue of telling is approached from a different direction, significant differences between the two groups were found. For example, 60% of non-searchers felt that their adoptive parents had given them all the background information they had compared to only 50% of searchers ($p < 0.01$). The remainder in each group said either that their parents had not given them all the information they had or they did not know if they had or not.

The amount of information received by the adopted person is partly reflected in the degree of satisfaction felt with the level of information provided by parents. Significantly fewer searchers (48%) felt either very satisfied or satisfied with the level of information they were given than non-searchers (64%). Within the searcher group, those of Black, Asian or mixed ethnicity showed statistically higher rates of satisfaction with the level of information given (67%) than those of White European ethnicity (47%, $p < 0.05$). When satisfied people from all groups were asked to describe the reasons for their satisfaction, answers typically mentioned the belief that adoptive parents had told them everything they knew: 'My parents were totally honest and open'; 'Nothing hidden, always felt special'; 'Parents had limited information and did their best; didn't want to hurt parents.'

Thirty-one per cent of searchers and 18% of non-searchers said they were *dissatisfied* or *very dissatisfied* with the level of information given, a significant difference ($p < 0.05$). The different rates of dissatisfaction between the two groups would be consistent with the idea that adopted people who felt dissatisfied with how much they know about their origins and background are more inclined to search for information and seek contact with birth relatives. Reasons given for feeling dissatisfied ranged widely, though evasion and discomfort on the part of adoptive parents featured most often. Typical comments included: 'Adoptive mother lied to me about circumstances of adoption'; 'Made to feel uncomfortable about discussing roots'; 'Documents stolen, so no information available'; 'My father was dying in a coma. GP told me when my father died. I was 41 and it was a shock!'; 'My mother told me no one wanted me.'

Searcher ANGELA
Adoption was not talked about at all. I sensed my parents just didn't want to talk about it at all. They were just being protective towards me and ... any questions that I asked they weren't always talked about. If I asked, they would just say, 'Well, you don't need to know about that' or they 'didn't know'.

Although the majority of adopted people knew their birth name before contacting the Society (83% of searchers, 71% of non-searchers), the slightly lower rate found for non-searchers is statistically significant ($p < 0.05$). People discovered their birth names in a variety of ways ranging from being told by their adoptive parents to tracking down their birth certificate or adoption records. A small number learned of their birth name when secretly rummaging through their adoption papers as a child. One person discovered her birth name from reading her medical records at school. Children placed at older ages might remember their birth name (if it had been changed) from when they were younger.

Thinking about birth relatives while growing up

The majority of adopted people, whether searchers or non-searchers, thought about their birth relatives during childhood and adulthood at some time. The number of people who thought about their birth relatives either sometimes or a lot increased from childhood into adolescence and through into adulthood. Table 9.5 suggests that not only the number who thought about birth relatives increased with age, but also the frequency increased with age. Fifty-seven per cent of adult searchers said they had been thinking about their birth relatives a lot.

Table 9.5 Frequency of searchers' thoughts about birth relatives

	Thought about birth relative		
	A lot(%)	Sometimes (%)	Never (%)
During childhood	33	55	12
During adolescence	50	47	2
During adulthood	57	41	1

$n = 378$

Searcher ESTELLE

My birth mother had written a letter that I was supposed to read when I was 18, but I remember when my parents went out one weekend and I wanted to find the letter, and I had to find it that weekend, and I found it when I was 15 ... Ever since I found the letter I was thinking about her and it was then that I realised that adoption didn't necessarily mean rejection ... But I was thinking about her between the ages of 15 and 18 pretty much constantly ... I knew that I had to find her in order to feel happier inside as well. I got quite desperate to find her round about 15, I think because I wasn't getting on with my mum ... I was in my room a lot thinking about my natural mother. And I was writing to her then as well. I wasn't actually writing to her, but I wrote about three letters to her, imaginary letters as if she was going to respond and as if I had met her and told her all about myself.

Searcher CLARE

When I was about five or six and my dad had upset me I remember shouting at him, 'My real mummy and daddy wouldn't do that' and he went absolutely berserk, absolutely mental. I remember it terrified me and I never mentioned it again. I didn't bring up my adoption ... it was something censored ... but when I was about nine or ten and I started thinking an awful lot about 'what did my mother look like'. I was convinced that she lived in our town where I grew up and that there was some sort of conspiracy going on and that perhaps my parents knew who she was ... and so I started looking at everybody I came into contact with which upped my suspicion, and almost selecting who I'd like to be my mother and panicking if I thought the woman next to me in Waitrose was actually my mother!

These trends are matched by non-searchers, but the numbers thinking about their birth relatives and the frequency of their thoughts occur at significantly lower rates than those for searchers. For example, the proportions of non-searchers saying that they *never* thought about their birth relatives in childhood were 33% in childhood, 22% in adolescence, and 22% in adulthood (compared to 12%, 2% and 1% respectively for searchers). Significantly more searchers therefore appear to become preoccupied with thinking about their birth relatives, particularly their birth mother, from late childhood onwards.

Non-searcher FIONA

I didn't really think about my biological mother when I was growing up. I once thought it would be nice for somebody to point out my birth mum – say in a supermarket: 'Look there she is' – so I could see if I looked like her, just to have a peep to see what she looked like but no desire – 'When I'm 18 I'm going to track these people down.' In my mind they were my biological parents and that was it.

Non-searcher MIKE
*I think as you get older being adopted becomes more of an issue ... because I sup-
pose I started to wonder the usual things like where I was from, what my parents
were like. I remember starting to think about it when I was 13, 14. I remember thinking on my birthday, I think I was probably 14, I just remember thinking about my
mum on my birthday, wondering what she was doing, sort of thing. And from then
on, as I got into my early twenties, I started thinking about it a lot more.*

For searchers, at all stages, women were more likely than men to have thought
about birth relatives 'a lot'. By adulthood, 99% of both sexes were giving their
birth relatives some thought, at least sometimes and in some cases a lot.

There was a non-statistical tendency for those placed transracially to be
slightly more likely to think about their birth relatives 'a lot'. For example, 63%
of transracially placed people thought about their birth relatives a lot during
their adolescence compared to 48% of those in same-race White placements.
This difference disappeared by adulthood with White same-race and transracially placed people equally likely to think about their birth relatives 'a lot' (58%
v 58%). However, there are a number of interesting differences in the *main* thing
thought about. People placed transracially were statistically more likely to think
about whether or not their birth relatives looked liked them or they looked like
their birth relatives as their main thought (61%) than same-race White adopted
people (33%). This is hardly surprising given the often striking contrast in looks
between themselves and their adoptive families.

THINGS THOUGHT ABOUT BIRTH RELATIVES WHEN GROWING UP

Searchers and non-searchers thought about very similar things while growing
up. The most common *main* thought was to wonder why they were given up by
their birth parent. Forty-three per cent of searchers and 54% of non-searchers
wondered whether they were like their birth relative, either physically or in
terms of personality. Proportionately twice as many searchers as non-searchers
wondered whether their birth relative might wish to be contacted.

When asked to report *all* the things thought about while growing up, nearly
all categories were mentioned by most searchers and non-searchers. However,
overall, rates in each category of reason for searchers tended to be slightly higher
than for non-searchers (see Table 9.6). The most pronounced difference between
the two groups was whether or not the adopted person ever wondered why they
were placed for adoption. Seven out of ten searchers compared to under a half
of non-searchers said they thought about why they were placed for adoption by
their birth parents.

Table 9.6 All things thought about when growing up

	Searchers (%)	Non-searchers (%)
Why they placed me for adoption	70	48
What they looked like	86	83
Whether they would want to be contacted	77	52
Whether I looked like them	80	74
Whether they were alive or dead	72	60
What their personality was like	77	64
Whether they had other children	70	71
Other reasons	16	18

Searchers n = 288; non-searchers n = 78

Summary

The majority of adopted people in the survey had thought about one or more of their birth relatives while growing up. There was a great curiosity by adopted people about whether they looked like their birth relative. More specifically:

- Most people (67%) felt they had either always known that they were adopted or were under the age of five when first told by their adoptive parents.
- A majority of both searchers (70%) and non-searchers (74%) did not feel comfortable asking their adoptive parents for information about their birth families and their origins.
- Fifty-six per cent of searchers and 61% of non-searchers felt that they were given either none or only a very little background information about their adoption by their adoptive parents. Reasons varied and included parents not knowing very much about the background details themselves, and parents choosing not to give all the information they had.
- Non-searchers (64%) were more likely to feel satisfaction with the amount of information received from their parents than searchers (48%).
- Most searchers and non-searchers thought about one or more of their birth relatives while they were growing up.
- Over 80% of both searchers and non-searchers had wondered what their birth relatives looked like, and whether they might look like their birth relative.
- Searchers (70%) were more likely than non-searchers (48%) to wonder why their birth mother placed them for adoption.

CHAPTER 10

Adoption Experience

Introduction

Coping with the meaning of adoption requires both adopted children and adoptive parents to consider issues of integration and differentiation. Kirk (1964) was one of the first to point out that adopters are faced with conflicting obligations. They are required to integrate the child into their family, with an emphasis on acceptance, belonging and sameness. But they are also expected to tell their child that they are adopted, with its unavoidable emphasis on difference. Kirk called this the 'paradox' of adoption which both parents and children have to try and resolve. There is, then, a potential tension between integration and differentiation. Many parents and children, of course, resolve the paradox smoothly and without too much difficulty. Difference is acknowledged but does not affect a sense of belonging and being loved and accepted.

However, a number of studies have also noted that not all adopters and their children resolve this tension quite so successfully. For whatever reasons, the adopted person feels different to the adopted family. This feeling of difference can be experienced in a variety of ways. For many, it is a relatively benign experience that does not affect their feelings of belonging and being loved. For others, it feels more troubling. A sense of difference introduces uncertainties about feeling they really belong in their adoptive family. Although this may not necessarily affect feeling loved by and love for their adoptive parents, it is experienced as unsettling. In a minority of more extreme cases, these feelings of difference are associated with very unhappy experiences of feeling not loved and feelings of not belonging.

The present study provides an opportunity to explore some of these issues from a long-term adult perspective. We asked adopted people about their experiences of being adopted. Two kinds of analysis and comparison have been made. The first involves examining the range of adoption experiences reported by adult adopted people and seeing whether issues of difference and belonging featured in their accounts. The second allows a direct comparison of the adoption experiences of adopted people who had initiated contact with a birth relative (searchers) and those who had been contacted by a birth relative but who had not themselves sought contact (non-searchers). This comparison throws some light on the question of whether adopted people who seek information and search for birth relatives experience their adoption differently to those who have not been actively searching or seeking reunion with a birth relative.

Feelings of difference

Adopted people were asked questions about whether they felt different to their adoptive family, were treated differently by their extended adoptive family, or were treated differently by people outside the family when growing up as a child.

ADOPTIVE FAMILY

Fifty per cent of searchers said that they felt different to their adoptive family when they were growing up (see Table 10.1). This was twice the rate reported by non-searchers where only 27% said that they felt different, a statistically significant difference. The most common and glaring differences for many people were physical dissimilarities.

Table 10.1 Feeling different to adoptive family when growing up

	Searchers (%)	Non-searchers (%)
Yes	50	27
No	44	68
Don't know	6	5

Searchers $n = 394$; non-searchers $n = 78$; $p < 0.001$

When the searchers and non-searchers who said that they did feel different were invited to elaborate their answers, seven types of 'feeling different' were identified ($n = 218$).

Positive (4%)

'I had a sense of being special. My parents were very old.' 'I felt slightly different in a positive way.' 'Knowing I was adopted made me feel special.' 'I always felt lucky, strong and confident.'

Non-specific (10%)

'Just felt different.' 'Felt like a shoe that didn't fit.' 'Felt loved and accepted but different.'

Physical and psychological (46%)

'No physical resemblances and a lack of physical love.' 'I looked different. I had a different personality and outlook.' 'Felt different racially.' 'Different personality; I was more demonstrative.' 'My character was very different.'

Treatment (21%)

'Birth child received preferential treatment.' 'Birth sibling was spoilt.' 'Treated their own daughter as favourite.' 'I was always compared to their real son.' 'Never felt accepted by my adoptive mother.' 'I was the awkward one. I could never please her.'

Not belonging (16%)

'Always felt that I never belonged, even though I was loved.' 'Felt I didn't belong.' 'Odd one out.' 'I was always an outsider.' 'Never felt related.' 'Didn't fit in. More attention to the dogs than me.'

Incomplete (1%)

'Felt incomplete; didn't look the same.' 'I felt something was missing. I wanted children of my own.' 'I felt there was something missing.'

Old parents (2%)

'Parents were old and old-fashioned.' 'Age gap; my parents were much older than my friends' parents.'

Searcher BETH

I looked different and I knew I was different. My parents are blue-eyed and I was a lot darker. There were certainly no physical resemblances. They didn't draw these to my attention. I don't remember it being mentioned. I think I was very conscious of it more than anybody else. Just me.

Searcher ISOBEL

I'm mixed race, so it's pretty obvious that I looked a bit different ... We've always been brought up as a family but I am different to them in character ... I was quite out-going and did a lot of tennis when I was younger – I was quite sporty, active, lots of friends, going out, trying to get to parties whereas, for example, my older sister who's not adopted was more quiet.

Feeling different is not necessarily experienced as a negative state, but it does provide some support for the suggestion that many of those who search feel more conscious of their difference than many of those who do not search. And feeling different is often an internally generated and individual state and not one caused by parents who more often than not are described as warm and loving.

Searcher HELEN

My parents were very loving. Not in a demonstrative way, but we always knew we were loved and they wanted the best for us ... It was when I was a teenager I became very aware of being adopted. Particularly not looking like anyone in my family. All my friends were saying, 'Oh, I wish I was adopted' and I was thinking, 'I wish I wasn't, I wish I looked like somebody.' Those sort of feelings came more into play as a teenager. I was aware when I was younger but not quite in the same ways.

The biggest category of 'feeling different' (of those who said they felt different) is based on feeling different physically and/or psychologically (46%). Personality and temperamental differences were as likely to be mentioned as physical differences. Being treated differently, and negatively, was the second most frequently reported reason for feeling different. The major division in this category was being treated differently (and unfavourably) to siblings born to the adoptive parents or simply being treated negatively by an adoptive parent who in most cases was identified as the mother. Not belonging was the third most common reason for feeling different within the adoptive family. Eighty-five per cent of adopted people who said that they felt different to their adoptive family when growing up gave as their main reason feeling physically different, feeling psychologically different, being treated differently, or feeling that they did not belong.

Although the percentage of adopted people 'feeling different' in this sample is certainly high amongst the searchers (50%), it must be noted that 68% of adopted people who had not initiated a search but had been contacted by a birth relative (non-searchers) said that they *did not feel different to their adoptive family* when they were growing up.

ADOPTIVE FAMILY AND FEELING DIFFERENT: GENDER, ETHNICITY, AGE AT PLACEMENT AND FAMILY COMPOSITION

Interestingly, there were significant differences between the rates of 'feeling different' between men and women in the searcher group with more women (55%) reporting feeling different to their adoptive families than men (40%, $p < 0.02$). No differences in the rates of these feelings between men (28%) and women (26%) were found in the non-searcher group. Rates of feeling different were significantly higher for those who described their ethnicity as Black, Asian or 'mixed heritage' compared to those who described themselves as White/European (71% v 48%, $p < 0.01$).

Searcher GARY
The paradox was that I was adopted and these parents were making me feel special. There was a lot of showing me off, because I was a cute kid. When I was younger and I was having to deal with racism, with feeling like a piece of shit. I didn't fit in and I wasn't equal to these people and generally feeling alienated and having this negative self-image. There was an incident when I was younger of scrubbing myself, trying to scrub myself clean as it were. And there were a lot of incidents like that which caused me to have a lot of insecurities. Yeah – lack of self-worth. There was a lot of that all the way through so it did cause major psychological problems, which I'm still now working out and working through in order to grow and be fully whole.

Rates of feeling different to the adoptive family amongst searchers were not affected by the age when the adopted person was placed with the family. However, a significant difference was observed in the non-searcher group with 69% of those placed after the age of two years saying that they felt different to their adoptive family compared to only 18% of those placed before the age of two ($p < 0.01$). Rates of feeling different were not affected by (i) presence of siblings born to the adopters (although a non-statistical trend was observed, 58% feeling different when non-adopted siblings were present v 46% feeling different when there were no non-adopted siblings present, $p = 0.1$); or (ii) the presence of other adopted children in the family. However, when the *number of siblings born to the adopters* is considered, a significant difference did emerge between those who felt different (mean number of birth siblings = 0.64) to those who did not feel different (mean number of birth siblings = 0.47, two-tailed $p < 0.05$). This difference holds up even when age of placement is taken into account. For example, for children placed before the age of two, those who did not feel different to their adoptive families had a mean number of 0.47 siblings born to their adoptive parents, while those who did say they felt different had a mean number of 0.65 siblings born to their adoptive parents. These findings lend partial but not unambiguous support to the idea that the presence of children born to adopters slightly increases the likelihood of adopted children feelings different to their adoptive family.

EXTENDED FAMILY AND FEELING DIFFERENT

Adopted people were also asked whether they felt that people in their extended family treated them differently because they were adopted. Again, there was a modest but significant difference between searchers and non-searchers, with 68% of searchers and 82% of non-searchers saying they did not feel that they were treated differently by their extended family ($p < 0.05$).

Searcher PETER
My adoptive parents were brilliant ... they loved me and treated me as their own all my life and I've never been anything but their son ... but I did feel treated unequally by my grandparents, and this hurt. I mean there is always that stigma at the back when you think you're different. My grandparents actually treated me different. My brother, who was younger than me and my parents' natural child, was actually spoilt more than me, although my parents did everything to discourage that, it was still there ... My grandparents would always offer him things and I was sort of left out which, well it is upsetting, to be honest with you.

Within the search group, 32% of those placed transracially felt they were treated differently by their adoptive extended family compared to 17% of White same-race children ($p < 0.05$). However, for both searchers and non-searchers, there were no significant differences in rates of being treated differently by the extended family in terms of (i) gender, (ii) age of placement, (iii) presence of siblings born to the adopters (though there was a non-significant tendency towards feeling different if there were birth siblings present), and (iv) the presence of other adopted children.

When being treated differently by extended family members was reported, comments fell into one major category – that of being treated differently and unfavourably by extended family members who did not see or accept them as part of the family: 'They didn't treat me as real family.' 'They didn't have any photographs of me in their house but did of their other grandchildren.' 'I was left out of the family tree.' 'My father's mother cut him and us out of her will.' 'Little things said like "she's ungrateful considering she's adopted".'

Three adopted people said that they were treated differently, but here the discrimination was felt to be positive: 'I was made to feel special and spoiled rotten.' 'Felt like someone special and very loved.'

FEELING DIFFERENT AND THE OUTSIDE COMMUNITY

Outside the family, most adopted adults felt that people did not treat them differently because they were adopted. Only 14% of searchers and 5% of non-searchers felt that they were treated differently outside the family, a non-significant difference. Those who felt they were treated differently mentioned racism, teasing, bullying, and being pitied. No differences emerged in terms of (i) gender, (ii) age of placement, (iii) presence of children born to the adopters, and (iv) presence of other adopted children. Within the search group, 29% of people who described themselves as either Black, Asian or of mixed ethnicity said that they felt people outside their adoptive family treated them differently compared to only 13% of those who described themselves as ethnically White European ($p < 0.01$). Nearly all Black, Asian and mixed ethnicity children experienced racism on a regular basis during childhood. White adoptive parents tried to protect their children as best they could, but it was said to be difficult for them to fully understand what it was like to be on the receiving end of racist remarks and behaviour.

Searcher ESTELLE
There were only four Black kids in the school John and I went to … I just stayed in at weekends and I wouldn't go out with my friends at night. I just felt there was no point because I was too dark and things like that … I realised when I was in my teens 'cos I knew that there had to be more to life than just coming home and crying and then just doing your homework … I did get an awful lot of support from my family … I don't know whether I blamed them, because I sort of did, I think, for adopting me and bringing me to this community that was obviously quite hostile to some people. So I sort of blamed them and that's why I was rude to them and everything. But then I felt grateful that they wanted to do something about it, you know, by going to school – but then that just made it worse.

The majority of adopted people felt comfortable – most of the time – talking about their adoption with people outside the family (63% always, 29% sometimes, 8% never). Again, there were no significant differences in this matter between searchers and non-searchers. Nor were there these rates affected by (i) gender, (ii) age of placement, (iii) ethnicity, (iv) presence of children born to the adopters, and (v) presence of other adopted children.

Feelings of acceptance and belonging: relationships with adoptive parents

The quality of the relationship the adopted person feels they have with their adoptive parents can be used as a measure of the emotional integration and sense of belonging they felt they had with their adoptive families. Differences between searchers and non-searchers might suggest possible motivating factors, causing some people to seek information about and reunion with their birth relatives.

The survey asked people about their feelings of being adopted and the quality of relationships they felt they had with their adoptive parents. We were particularly interested to see if there were any differences between searchers and non-searchers, although the study also looked at people's experiences with reference to their gender, ethnicity, age at placement and family composition.

FEELING HAPPY ABOUT BEING ADOPTED

Although the majority of adopted people (68%) said that they felt happy about being adopted, significant differences were observed between the searcher and non-searcher groups (see Table 10.2). Adopted people who initiated contact with a birth relative were less likely to feel as happy about being adopted than those who had not actively initiated contact. Eighty per cent of non-searchers agreed or strongly agreed that they felt happy compared to only 65% of searchers. More marked still, almost twice as many non-searchers (59%) as searchers (31%) expressed the strongest sentiment, saying that they strongly agreed that they felt happy being adopted.

Table 10.2 Felt happy about being adopted

	Searchers (%)	Non-searchers (%)
Strongly agree	31	59
Agree	34	26
Uncertain	20	11
Disagree	8	3
Strongly disagree	7	1

Searchers $n = 371$ (23 missing); non-searchers $n = 76$ (2 missing); $p < 0.001$

Rates of happiness in both groups appeared unaffected by (i) gender, (ii) age of placement, (iii) ethnicity, (iv) presence of siblings born to the adopters, and (v) presence of other adopted children.

FEELING LOVED BY ADOPTIVE MOTHER AND ADOPTIVE FATHER

Although most adopted people in both groups said they felt loved by their adoptive mother (78%), significant differences were found in feelings of being loved by one's adoptive mother between searchers and non-searchers (Table 10.3). Seventy-seven per cent of searchers, but a much higher 91% of non-searchers agreed or strongly agreed that they felt loved by their adoptive mother.

Table 10.3 Felt loved by adoptive mother

	Searchers (%)	Non-searchers (%)
Strongly agree/agree	77	91
Uncertain	9	5
Disagree/strongly disagree	14	4

Searchers n = 387 (7 missing); non-searchers n = 78; $p < 0.02$

Rates of feeling loved by one's adoptive mother were unaffected by gender, ethnicity, presence of siblings born to the adopters, and presence of other adopted siblings. However, although age of placement did not influence the distribution of feelings amongst non-searchers, there was a small but significant difference when age of placement was taken into consideration amongst searchers. Those placed after the age of two were less likely to feel that they were loved by their adoptive mother than those placed before the age of two (29% v 12%, $p < 0.05$). Although the trend is similar for non-searchers, their smaller numbers means that it is not possible to establish significance.

Results are similar for adoptive fathers, with 83% of searchers and 89% of non-searchers feeling loved. Overall rates were high and no differences were found between searchers and non-searchers. Rates were unaffected by gender, ethnicity, presence of siblings born to the adopters, and presence of other adopted siblings. Age of placement did not influence the distribution of feelings amongst non-searchers, but there was a small but significant difference when age of placement was taken into consideration for searchers. Those placed after the age of two were slightly less likely to feel that they were loved by their adoptive father than those placed before the age of two.

FEELINGS OF LOVE FOR ADOPTIVE MOTHER AND FATHER

Overall, 83% of adopted people agreed/strongly agreed that they loved their adoptive mother. Significantly more non-searchers than searchers expressed the strongest agreement with this sentiment (76% v 57%, $p < 0.05$), though these differences become less pronounced amongst those who disagree with the sentiment. Gender, ethnicity, and presence of siblings born to the adopters had no effect on the distribution of feelings but age of placement and presence of other adopted siblings did. For both groups, those adopted after the age of two were slightly less likely to say that they agreed/strongly agreed that they loved their adoptive mother compared to those adopted before the age of two (searchers: 72% v 85%, $p < 0.05$; non-searchers: 70% v 92%, $p < 0.05$). For searchers, the presence of other adopted siblings seemed to *increase* feelings of love for adoptive mothers. Eighty-eight per cent of those with adopted siblings said they loved their adoptive mother compared to 76% who had no adopted siblings ($p < 0.01$).

Overall, 85% of adopted people from both groups agreed/strongly agreed that they loved their adoptive father. Although rates of agreement were slightly higher for non-searchers, the differences between the two groups did not reach significance. Gender, age of placement, ethnicity, presence of siblings born to the adopters, and presence of other adopted siblings had no affect on the distribution of feelings of love for adoptive fathers.

FEELINGS OF BELONGING IN THE ADOPTIVE FAMILY

Overall, 70% of adopted people agreed/strongly agreed that they felt they belonged in their adoptive family (Table 10.4). However, marked significant differences were observed between searchers and non-searchers, with fewer adopted people who initiated contact reporting they felt they belonged in their adoptive families (68% v 85%).

Table 10.4 Felt I belonged in my adoptive family

	Searchers (%)	Non-searchers (%)
Strongly agree	44	71
Agree	24	14
Uncertain	14	6
Disagree	10	6
Strongly disagree	9	3

Searchers n = 386 (8 missing); non-searchers n = 78; $p < 0.001$

Gender had no effect on the distribution of feelings of belonging reported by non-searchers. However, amongst searchers, fewer women than men said they felt they belonged in their adoptive families, a small difference but one which was statistically significant (64% v 77%, $p < 0.05$). A surprisingly high number of women searchers (21%) said they disagreed or strongly disagreed with feeling that they belonged in their adoptive family

Age of placement, the presence of siblings born to adopters and the presence of other adopted children had no effect on the distribution of feelings of belonging. Being White and same-race placed showed a slight, non-statistical trend towards higher rates of feeling one belonged to one's adoptive family compared to those placed transracially (71% v 56%).

Non-searcher LIZ

I was five or six years when my parents told me I was adopted ... They must have done a good job of telling because I don't remember being upset or any negative feelings at all. I think I was made to feel quite special in a way. My father used to say, 'You were chosen – we always wanted a girl.' I always felt part of the family. I never felt different as such ... I have very happy memories of my childhood.

Searcher NINA

I mean I didn't have a happy childhood ... There was always a sense of you've got to be grateful because we adopted you ... And the feeling grew throughout my teens that this family would never belong to me, as opposed to at the beginning vague feeling of uneasiness that I don't belong anywhere ... that I didn't fit in, that I've never fitted in.

FREQUENCY OF CONTACT WITH ADOPTIVE MOTHERS

In cases where the adoptive mother was still alive, non-searchers were more likely not only to be still in contact, but the frequency of their contact was more likely to be higher (see Table 10.5). For example, 87% of non-searchers were contacting their adoptive mother either by telephone or in a face-to-face meeting at least once a week compared to a rate of 72% for searchers.

Table 10.5 Frequency of contact with adoptive mother where still alive

	Searchers (%)	Non-searchers (%)
Once a week or more	72	87
About once a month	13	3
Less than once a month	4	5
Never	10	5

Searchers $n = 299$ (6 missing); non-searchers $n = 62$; $p < 0.05$

Evaluation of adoption

Although the majority of adopted people in both groups evaluated their adoptions positively, significant differences emerged between searchers (53%) and non-searchers (74%). The higher rates of positive evaluations expressed by non-searchers is a possible factor in explaining their decision not to initiate a search for information about or contact with birth relatives (see Table 10.6). Conversely, the higher rates of mixed and negative evaluations expressed by searchers might explain why some at least go on to search for information or seek contact with a birth relative. Even so, it must be remembered that a slight majority of searchers evaluated their experience of being adopted positively. A negative evaluation alone therefore does not explain the desire of this sub-group to search.

Table 10.6 Evaluation of being adopted

	Searchers (%)	Non-searchers (%)
Very positive experience	27	55
Positive experience	26	19
Mixed feelings	39	22
Negative experience	6	1
Very negative experience	3	3

Searchers n = 388 (6 missing); non-searchers n = 78; $p < 0.001$

People were asked to expand on their evaluations by writing a few lines of commentary and explanation, examples of which are given below.

POSITIVE EVALUATIONS (53% SEARCHERS, 74% NON-SEARCHERS)

Those making positive evaluations typically commented that they felt loved, wanted and secure: 'I was given to the best possible adoptive parents'; 'Lucky to have been brought up in a loving family'; 'Had a normal happy childhood and did not need for anything more in life'. A few people felt that being adopted had probably given them various kinds of advantage that they might not otherwise have enjoyed: 'Learned that I would have probably had a hard life otherwise.'

Searcher   BETH
I had a very happy upbringing. I was raised by two people who obviously very much wanted a child … I don't think it registered particularly that I was different to anybody else.

Non-searcher   BRIAN
Ideal, I suppose. Nice house, lovely big garden … dad and I fishing, me looking for fossils in rocks. It was ideal. Can't fault my childhood at all! I had a lovely childhood.

Searcher   LINDA
I was very much loved, very much wanted. I was given a great deal of love,

encouraged to achieve what I could, but was never pushed to do something I really couldn't do.

MIXED FEELINGS (39% SEARCHERS, 22% NON-SEARCHERS)

Those with mixed feelings broadly felt positive, but they did report one or more negative features: 'I'm not against adoption, but my parents were incompatible'; 'I'm not unhappy with life, but adoption does leave scars'; 'Good middle class upbringing, but emotionally sterile'. Many others mentioned that although they felt loved, they also felt 'incomplete' in some way: 'Feel like a piece of the jigsaw is missing'; 'Felt happy but never felt whole'; 'I was loved but never felt part of it.' A number had mixed feelings about their adoption because of being placed transracially, though transracially placed children in general were no more likely to feel negative than children in same-race placements.

Searcher MARIA

It's almost as if because there's supposed to be a natural bond between mother and child, and I think when you're adopted you feel as if you've been rejected, even if you haven't necessarily been completely rejected, it's almost as if you've been pushed away and you think that you weren't good enough ... Your mother doesn't know whether or not you're going to be any good or whatever, you know, intellectu-ally or something. So you feel as if no matter what family you're with, you have to show them that you were worth adopting and that's what I've been doing, I've been trying to get as many qualifications and things as I can, just to say I am worth all the money that you've invested in me.

NEGATIVE EVALUATIONS (9% SEARCHERS, 4% NON-SEARCHERS)

Negative evaluations were made by people who had experienced unhappy adop-tions: 'I always felt like an unpaid servant. I never felt loved'; 'I felt I was a substi-tute for the real thing'; 'I have spent my whole life feeling different.' A small number of adopted people had extremely negative experiences: 'I had a talent in music that was rigorously encouraged to the point of violent treatment'; 'I hated every minute of my adoption'; 'I had a very lonely childhood; no affection, no cuddles, no praise, no friends made welcome.'

Searcher ELEANOR

My adoptive father died when I was about six, which left a dreadful mark. My adop-tive mother was having an affair pre his death with someone who wasn't sterile. So it's all a bit complicated but she subsequently had a baby by her boyfriend before my dad died ... and then after his death, said boyfriend was around for a long time but wouldn't marry my adoptive mum because of me. I was a spanner in the works of their nice little ideal family – so I spent most of my adoptive childhood having a pretty rough time ... I had a hateful relationship with my sister. I don't think I've ever felt like that about somebody – it was awful ... And I hated him [mother's boyfriend, sister's father] with a passion, because he made me feel so outside ... I have no contact with my adoptive mother now.

Gender, ethnicity, and presence of siblings born to adopters had no significant effect on adopted people's evaluation of their adoption. Amongst searchers, the presence of other adopted children significantly increased rates of feeling positive (58% v 46%, $p < 0.05$). This hints at the possibility that the presence of other adopted children might act as a protective factor in adopted children's psychosocial development and family integration. Also amongst searchers, age of placement influenced people's evaluation of their experience. Those placed after the age of two were less likely to view their adoption experience as either very positive or positive compared to those placed before the age of two (38% v 55%, $p < 0.02$).

The age at which one was first told about one's adoption did not appear to significantly affect whether or not the adoption was assessed as a positive experience. For example, 55% of searchers told before the age of five compared to 48% of those told after the age of five evaluated their adoption positively.

Summary

Forty-four per cent of searchers and 68% of non-searchers said that they did not feel different to their adoptive families while growing up. When feelings of difference were reported, they were greatest within the immediate adoptive family, becoming less pronounced as the adopted person moved out into circles beyond the family home. Adopted people who actively sought background information and searched for birth relatives reported higher rates of feeling different in all three social domains (the adoptive family, the extended family and the outside world) than adopted people who had not initiated a search or sought reunion with a birth relative.

Proportionately more adopted people who had been placed transracially felt that they could discuss their adoptions openly and comfortably with their adoptive parents than White children placed in same-race families. On the other hand, amongst the searchers, more transracially placed people than White same-race placed people said they felt different to their adoptive families (71% v 48%), and were treated differently by their extended families (32% v 17%) and by people outside the family (29% v 13%).

Significant differences in the rates of feeling happy, loved, and loving were observed between searchers and non-searchers, with non-searchers more likely to describe their feelings and experiences positively. These differences were reflected in the proportions who said they felt they 'belonged' in their adoptive family.

When asked to take an overall view of their experience of being adopted, non-searchers were more likely to answer that it was a positive experience: 74% of non-searchers evaluated their experience as either very positive or positive compared to 53% of searchers.

A number of 'within group' differences were also observed, mainly for the searcher group:

- Age at placement beyond two years was associated with slightly higher rates of not feeling loved by one's adoptive mother and father. Marginally more of these later placed people said that they did not love their adoptive mothers (28% said they either did not love their mothers or felt uncertain, compared to 15% of those placed before the age of two), but no differences were observed for feeling love for adoptive fathers. These feelings about parents were reflected in the final evaluation: 61% of those placed after the age of two, compared to 45% of those placed before the age of two, viewed their adoption either negatively or with mixed feelings.

- The presence of siblings born to the adoptive parents, including any born after the placement, did not appear to affect the evaluation of the adoption experience. However, the presence of other adopted children was associated with slightly higher rates of some of the positive feelings expressed about being adopted. These included feelings of love for one's adoptive mother and a tendency towards higher rates of feeling that one belonged in one's adoptive family. More people with adopted siblings (58%) than those who did not have any adopted siblings (46%) viewed their adoption as either very positive or positive.

CHAPTER 11

Difference and Belonging

Introduction

Research and practice has taken a keen interest in adopted people's feelings of difference and belonging in the context of their adoptive families. The previous chapter found that a majority (71%) of adopted people, even if they felt different to their adoptive families, felt that they belonged. Fifty-seven per cent of all adopted people in the survey evaluated their experience of adoption positively. However, there were differences between searchers and non-searchers. On the whole, non-searchers were more likely than searchers to say that they did not feel different to their adoptive family (68% *v* 44%) and that they felt they belonged in their adoptive families (85% *v* 68%).

To explore these matters of difference and belonging further, a two-dimensional framework was constructed. The majority of adopted people answered either 'yes' or 'no' when asked if they felt different to their adoptive family when growing up (see Table 10.1). Similarly, when asked if they felt they belonged in their adoptive family, people answered either positively or negatively (or that they felt uncertain) (see Table 10.4). These two dimensions – difference and belonging – generate four theoretical positions *vis-à-vis* the experience of being adopted (see Fig. 11.1).

Kirk (1964) and others believe the tasks of integration and differentiation (belonging and difference) are unavoidable and inherent in the experience of being adopted. It must be emphasised that 'feeling different' is not necessarily perceived or experienced as a negative state. Nor is it quite the same as the sense of difference explored by Kirk who examines the ways in which families dealt with the differences in being parented psychosocially (adoption) rather than biologically. The three adoption experience groups defined in the grid opposite suggest three different ways, described below, in which adopted people have experienced and handled these tasks of integration and differentiation.

INTEGRATED EXPERIENCE OF BEING ADOPTED

Adopted people who did not feel different to their adoptive family *and* felt they belonged in their adoptive family:

Searchers $n = 159$ (40% of all searchers)
Non-searchers $n = 52$ (67% of all non-searchers)

		Felt different to adoptive family	
		No	Yes
Felt belonged in adoptive family	Yes	Feelings of integration *Integrated experience of adoption*	Feelings of difference *Differentiated experience of adoption*
	No/uncertain	(Not significantly represented – theoretically unlikely position)	Feelings of alienation *Alienated experience of adoption*

Figure 11.1 Adoption experience groups

DIFFERENTIATED EXPERIENCE OF BEING ADOPTED

Adopted people who felt different to their adoptive family *but who also* felt they belonged in their adoptive family:

Searchers *n* = 85 (22% of all searchers)
Non-searchers *n* = 10 (13% of all non-searchers)

ALIENATED EXPERIENCE OF BEING ADOPTED

Adopted people who felt different to their adoptive family *and* that they did not belong in their adoptive family:

Searchers *n* = 105 (27% of all searchers)
Non-searchers *n* = 11 (14% of all non-searchers)

These three groups cover 89% of searchers. The remaining 11% said either they did not know whether they felt different to their adoptive family or, if they did not feel different, nevertheless were not certain whether they felt they belonged in their adoptive family. Ninety-four per cent of non-searchers are defined by the three groups.

Combining the various values of the two variables of 'feelings of difference' and 'feelings of belonging' offers an interesting way of exploring people's experience and evaluation of their adoption. This should not be too surprising, but it does suggest that adopted people's motives for searching might be affected in part by the psychological impact of their particular experience of being adopted. Hints of this are picked up in the distribution of the three adoption experience groups between searchers and non-searchers (see Table 11.1). The proportion of adopted people in the Integrated experience group is significantly higher amongst non-searchers than searchers.

Table 11.1 Distribution of the Integrated, Differentiated and Alienated experience groups

	Searchers (%)	Non-searchers (%)
Integrated experience	46	71
Differentiated experience	24	14
Alienated experience	30	15

Searchers n = 349; non-searchers n = 73; $p < 0.001$

The numbers of non-searchers placed in either the Differentiated ($n = 10$) or Alienated ($n = 11$) experience groups are too small for statistical purposes. Therefore only comparisons between searchers and Integrated non-searchers will be made. It will be noticed that when comparisons are made between searchers placed in the Integrated experience group and non-searchers placed in the Integrated experience group, non-searchers show a greater bias than searchers towards the more positive values of most adoption experience variables. This suggests that although 'Integrated' non-searchers and 'Integrated' searchers have been defined in the same way, non-searchers represent a more robust version of the Integrated adoption experience type. This may provide some support for why they have chosen not to search or seek information, at least at the time of the survey. This difference between searchers and non-searchers holds even when controlled for gender.

Information and openness

Adopted people who felt different and that they did not belong in their adoptive families (Alienated experience group) were consistently and significantly more likely than those in the Integrated and Differentiated experience groups to say that the amount of information and openness available to them about their adoptions was low. They were much more likely to register dissatisfaction with the way that being adopted had been handled by their parents.

Searcher MARTINE

They didn't give me that much information. They would just say, 'Well, you don't need to know about that' or they said they didn't know ... My parents made a very big effort to reimburse for the fact that I was in a children's home and always dressed me like a model. I always felt – I didn't feel I belonged, not because of the way I was treated but only because I was so different.

Whereas a slight majority of those in the Integrated experience group felt that their adoption was openly discussed by their parents, only a minority of the Alienated experience group felt this to be the case (see Table 11.2). There was no significant difference between the Integrated and Differentiated groups.

Table 11.2 Adoption experience groups and open discussion of adoption

	Searchers			Non-searchers
	Integrated (%)	Differentiated (%)	Alienated (%)	Integrated (%)
Yes	54	46	17	58
Sometimes	17	27	36	18
No	29	27	47	24

Searchers, Integrated n = 159, Differentiated n = 85, Alienated n = 105
Non-searchers n = 52
Searchers only: p < 0.001 (3 x 2 cells)

A similar pattern was found across most people's reviews of their experience of 'telling' and openness. For example, amongst searchers, significantly more of the Integrated group (46%) said they *always felt comfortable* asking for information about their adoption from their parents than either the Differentiated (25%) or Alienated (14%) groups. Even higher rates were observed for non-searchers who had an Integrated experience of adoption, 55% of whom said they always felt comfortable asking for information.

Non-searcher (Integrated adoption experience) LIZ

I don't actually remember being told. I just grew up knowing I was adopted and knowing my two brothers were my parents' real children and I was not ... They must have done a good a job of telling me because I don't remember being upset or any negative feelings at all. I think I was made to feel quite special in a way – I always felt part of the family. I've never felt different as such.

Similarly, while 67% of Integrated non-searchers and 63% of Integrated searchers thought that their parents had given them all the information they had, only 53% of the Differentiated and 33% of the Alienated groups thought the same. The result was that levels of satisfaction about the amount of adoption information received from parents differed significantly between the three groups. Eighty per cent of non-searchers and 64% of searchers in the Integrated experience group said they were satisfied with the level of information given. A slightly lower level of satisfaction was observed in the Differentiated experience group, 58% of whom said they were happy with the amount of information received. However, levels dropped significantly for those placed in the Alienated experience group with only 22% saying they felt satisfied.

Adoption experience

Not surprisingly, the three groups predict the way adopted people are likely to describe and evaluate their adoption experience. For example, people placed in the Integrated (97% of non-searchers, 94% of searchers) and Differentiated (87%) experience groups were highly likely to say that they felt loved by their adoptive mother. However, 'feeling loved by one's adoptive mother' fell to only 41% for the Alienated experience group. A similar pattern is seen in people's relationships with their adoptive fathers, though there is a slight increase across all groups towards the more positive sentiment. A similar distribution of feelings is found in the answers people gave when they were asked if they loved their adoptive mother and father. For example, 98% of Integrated non-searchers, 95% of Integrated searchers and 88% of Differentiated searchers said they loved their adoptive mother. In contrast, only 57% of those in the Alienated experience group said they loved their adoptive mother.

These sentiments translate into people's current levels of contact with their adoptive parents. For example, for those whose adoptive mother was still alive, the following rates of weekly contact were reported for each group:

Integrated adoption experience group (non-searchers): 91%

Integrated adoption experience group (searchers):   85%

Differentiated adoption experience group: 75%

Alienated adoption experience group: 55%

THINKING ABOUT BIRTH RELATIVES WHILE GROWING UP
At each stage in the life span, the Differentiated and the Alienated adoption experience groups said they thought more about their birth relatives than the Integrated group. The broad pattern is that people in all three groups think more about their birth relatives with age, but the numbers are always highest at any age for those in the Alienated group (see Table 11.3).

Table 11.3 Adoption experience group (searchers) and thinking about birth relative

	Integrated (%)	Differentiated (%)	Alienated (%)	
Childhood				
A lot	19	41	56	
Sometimes	62	48	43	
Never	19	11	1	$p < 0.001$
Adolescence				
A lot	34	55	73	
Sometimes	60	43	27	$p < 0.001$
Never	6	2	0	
Adulthood				
A lot	42	59	83	
Sometimes	56	41	17	$p < 0.001$
Never	2	0	0	

We have already found that women are more likely to think about their birth relatives than men, and that women are under represented in the Integrated group and over represented in the Alienated group. It is necessary to consider whether the high rate of people thinking about their birth relatives in the Alienated group is simply a reflection of the higher proportion of women in this group. Rates of thinking about birth relatives for both men and women increase across the three experience groups, being the lowest for the Integrated adoption experience group and highest for the Alienated adoption experience group. However, within each group, rates are always higher for women. This suggests that both gender and group type affect thinking about birth relatives. The group effect is stronger than gender alone. Group effect and gender may combine to produce high rates of thinking about birth relatives (e.g. women in the Alienated group) or subtract to produce lower rates of thinking about birth relatives (e.g. women in the Integrated group).

For example:

- The lowest rates of thinking about birth relatives in adulthood were found in men who did not feel different to their adoptive family and who felt they belonged in their adoptive family (Integrated adoption experience group): 30% said they thought about their birth relatives a lot.
- However, 80% of adult men in the Alienated adoption experience group said they thought about their birth relatives a lot.
- The highest rates of thinking about birth relatives in adulthood were found in women who felt different to their adoptive families and felt they did not

belong (Alienated adoption experience group): 84% said they thought about their birth relatives a lot.

- However, only 51% of adult women in the Integrated adoption experience group said they thought about their birth relatives a lot, which nevertheless is still a higher rate than for men in this group, only 30% of whom said they thought about their birth relatives a lot.

Generally, increasing age, female gender, and feeling different and not belonging to one's adoptive family (Alienated adoption experience group) each increase the likelihood of an adopted person thinking about their birth relatives at any stage in the lifespan prior to contact and reunion.

EVALUATION OF BEING ADOPTED AND ADOPTION EXPERIENCE

Positive feelings about being adopted were expressed much more frequently by the Integrated adoption experience groups (non-searchers 90%, searchers 78%) than either the Differentiated (54%) or the Alienated adoption experience groups (18%) (see Table 11.4). However, looked at in terms of negative feelings, very low rates of outright negative evaluations were reported by both the Integrated and Differentiated adoption experience groups. Twenty-three per cent of the Alienated group felt negative about their experience, with the majority of this group saying they had mixed feelings (59%).

Table 11.4 Adoption experience groups and evaluation of the experience of being adopted

	Searchers			Non-searchers
	Integrated (%)	Differentiated (%)	Alienated (%)	Integrated (%)
Very positive	46	25	5	71
Positive	32	29	13	19
Mixed feelings	21	41	59	10
Negative	1	5	13	0
Very negative	0	0	10	0

Searchers, integrated $n = 153$, differentiated $n = 85$, alienated $n = 105$
Non-searchers $n = 52$
$p < 0.001$ (3 x 2 cells)

Seeking information

Adopted people in the Alienated experience group typically gave more reasons for contacting The Children's Society than either those in the Differentiated or Integrated groups (means: 5.0 v 4.7 v 3.6, $p < 0.01$). Comparisons between the three searcher adoption experience groups also suggest that those in the Alienated adoption experience group felt that the impact of receiving information from their adoption records had been particularly positive. For example, these differences are particularly marked in the 'information seekers only' group who stopped their search after visiting the Society and seeing their adoption records. As a consequence of receiving the new information, Alienated information seekers only (n = 10) were more likely than people in either the Integrated (n = 25) or Differentiated (n = 12) adoption experience groups to say they felt more secure (A v I v D = 60% v 28% v 0%), more relaxed (70% v 28% v 17%), and more complete as a person (80% v 32% v 25%). The Integrated and Differentiated adoption experience groups reported a greater range of responses and outcomes. Information seekers only in these two groups were as likely to feel negatively about a particular feeling as they were likely to feel positive. However, 84% of the Integrated and 83% of the Differentiated adoption experience groups said the information received had been a positive experience overall. One hundred per cent of the Alienated adoption experience group said the overall experience was positive.

Information seekers only from the Alienated adoption experience group appear to derive the most satisfaction and benefits from the new knowledge. There are possible clues that the dissatisfactions they experienced in their adoption are more readily assuaged by the acquisition of new information. The outcome differences between the three groups did not appear to affect people's desire to search in the future where all three groups showed an equal interest in contacting birth relatives. Seventy-five per cent of the information seekers only from the Alienated adoption experience group said they would search in the future, compared to 73% from the Integrated group and 67% from the Differentiated adoption experience group.

Returning to the whole sample of searchers, the level of support and understanding given by parents was said to be high by those whose adoption experience was classified as either Integrated or Differentiated. For example, 76% of adoptive mothers of people in the Integrated adoption experience group were felt to have shown understanding and 64% to have given support to their child and their quest to search. In contrast, people whose adoption experience was classified as Alienated were much less likely to say they received understanding (43%) or support (42%) from their adoptive mothers. Mothers of those in the Alienated adoption experience group were also reported to show the highest rates of opposition to the search process, with 15% said to be hostile, compared to 9% and 1% of mothers of those classified as Integrated and Differentiated. These findings give a further sense that the quality of relations that adopted people feel they have with their adoptive mothers is an important factor in the adoption experience. It also appears to affect the character of the search process.

Summary

A continuum of behaviours, feelings and experiences appears to exist between people who report an Integrated adoption experience at one end, and those who describe an Alienated adoption experience at the other. Assessment of the adoption experience is more likely to be negative as the viewpoint shifts from the Integrated to the Alienated group. Integrated non-searchers report the most positive view of the adoption experience. Alienated searchers are most likely to evaluate their adoption either negatively or with mixed feelings.

However, there remains a question of causal direction. At least two possible lines of explanation suggest themselves. Unsatisfactory relationships with adoptive parents and family might make the individual feel alienated. Or psychological disquiets about being adopted, often coupled with feelings of being rejected by birth parents, might upset and adversely affect relationships with adoptive parents leading to feelings of alienation. Neither the survey results nor the qualitative interviews clearly resolve this issue. Indeed, it may be that both explanations are true. Any one case might be best explained by unsatisfactory family relationships, psychological disquiets about rejection and difference, or an interaction between the two.

Similar arguments might be used to explain positively evaluated, integrated adoption experiences. Satisfactory family experiences, psychological adjustment to and acceptance of being placed for adoption, or some benign interaction between the two might explain why many people describe their adoption as a positive, integrated experience.

CHAPTER 12

Adopted People's Experience of Being Rejected by a Birth Parent

Introduction

When thinking about initiating a search for a birth relative, most adopted people recognise that there is a risk that they might be rejected outright or fail to be given the information that they set out to find.

Rejection and loss run as themes throughout the adoption experience. Adopted children often wonder why they were 'rejected' by their birth parents in the first place. Although the idea of searching for a birth mother or birth father is often driven by strong feelings, running counter to these emotions is the fear that a successful search in adult life might simply lead to being rejected a second time. In cases where these fears run high, a search is unlikely to take place. Although most adopted people who do initiate a search are successful in contacting and being accepted by their birth parent, a small proportion of birth parents refuse to have any form of contact with their adopted child. Searchers experience this as rejection. There are also a few birth relatives who cease contact not long after having met the adopted person and this is also experienced as a rejection. A small number of adopted people are rejected by one birth parent but accepted by another. Theirs is a mixed experience of acceptance and rejection and we shall say a little about their experience. Overall, then, three types of rejection by a birth parent were reported by adopted people:

- Outright rejection
- Rejection after a short contact
- Rejection by one birth parent but acceptance by the other.

Searchers who are rejected outright by a birth parent

Nineteen (7%) of the 274 people who searched and found their birth parent suffered an outright rejection, the birth parent refusing to have any form of contact. In these cases, the adopted person also had no contact with any other birth relative. Seventeen people were rejected by their birth mother. The remaining two adopted people suffered a rejection by their birth father.

CHARACTERISTICS AND ADOPTION EXPERIENCES OF THOSE REJECTED OUTRIGHT

People who suffered an outright rejection did not differ significantly from those who searched and had contact in terms of their biographical characteristics or adoption experiences. Thirty-two per cent were men and 68% were women. Nine per cent of those rejected outright were placed transracially. Fifty-eight per cent evaluated their adoption positively. There was a non-statistical trend to be more likely to have been placed for adoption before the age of six months (67% *v* 53%). There was also a non-statistical trend for the rejected group to be more likely to say that they felt they belonged to their adoptive family (84% *v* 66%), although the experience of being rejected might have influenced the response to this question. The mean age of first approach to the Society was slightly older than the successful contact group (33.3 years *v* 30.1 years).

FEELINGS AND REACTION TO THE BIRTH PARENT'S REFUSAL TO HAVE CONTACT

The immediate feelings after rejection were predominantly ones of frustration, hurt and upset (see Table 12.1). For those who were rejected outright, it was difficult for them to understand why the birth mother did not feel as curious as they did.

Table 12.1 Feelings and reactions to the birth parent's refusal to have contact

	Initial feelings (%)	Feelings after some time had elapsed (%)
Frustrated	63	53
Upset	47	32
Hurt	47	21
Understanding	37	47
Angry	32	21
Shock	21	0
Accepted it	16	37
Depressed	16	5
Couldn't believe it	5	5
Relieved	5	5
Happy	0	0
Try not to think about it	(–)	26

n = 19

Searcher CLAIRE

I could acknowledge that it was difficult for her [birth mother], that she had two other children, that maybe her husband made it difficult as well – I could acknowledge that she probably had a really hard time of it because I assume that she went back to her parents and carried on her life as if nothing had happened. But I couldn't understand how you couldn't want to see or know, especially after having my children, I couldn't understand this ... when the opportunity was there for her not to take it.

Rejection was experienced as particularly hurtful and difficult to understand when the birth mother and birth father had subsequently married each other. Oliver's birth parents had eventually married, but they rejected contact with their adopted son.

Searcher OLIVER

It was horrible, it was the most horrible thing I could ever have experienced. It absolutely wrecked me, I just went to pieces for about four days, I just didn't leave the house, I just sat in and could not, could not understand it. Twenty-three years of thinking about, you know, a large proportion of my life thought was given over to it. I was just thinking the other day actually, even the smallest, tiniest little things would spark something off, you know I'd see someone and think, 'Do I look like that?' You know, 'Is that her, is that him?' And all the time it's there, it was there in my mind, my whole life, and when I got this call back I just, I was so not expecting it because I thought, 'Right, they're together, what is the problem?'

Birth parents who fail to give any kind of response can leave the adopted person feeling both confused and rejected. Anita, for example, did write to her birth mother but never received a reply: 'Although as I say I never expected to receive anything, knowing that she wasn't going to was, well, I suppose it was a rejection really. I know logically why she didn't and why she hasn't and it's probably just as well she hasn't but at the time it was a bit of a slap in the face.' For most adopted people, having steeled themselves to search for the birth parent, the outright rejection was initially hard to understand or accept. Anger was typically mixed with feelings of hurt.

Searcher ELAINE

When I think about it I get quite angry now and I don't think that's a very healthy emotion to feel towards them, because if I do ever meet them I don't want it to be like that – but they are forcing this upon me, they are creating this emotion within me and one part of me just wants to turn up on the doorstep now – just knock on the door – and another part of me is close to saying, 'Well, I've had enough, you'll never get the chance to meet me, it's your loss.'

A small proportion of those rejected continued to feel hurt and upset, even with the passage of time. However, most adopted people began to make some psychological adjustments to the pain of rejection. A sense of frustration tended to remain but gradually people said they began to develop some understanding and acceptance of their parents and the rejection.

Searcher SANDRA

I thought, 'Well sod you, it's your loss not mine' and I still believe it is. At the end of the day I've got my children, she hasn't got hers and that's her choice. I don't worry about things I can't change and I can't change her attitude, I can't change her feelings, so there's no point. No point getting yourself all worked up about it, getting upset, getting stressed about something that I can do nothing about ... I think you've got to be positive, me sitting here getting all depressed and moping about it is not going to change anything. I'm going to be the one suffering then, not her. So in actual fact although you might say it's a bad experience, it's brought reality home in that you don't think any more, you don't wonder any more because you know.

Searcher (rejected independently by both birth parents) TONY

No, no regrets. It was hard work emotionally whilst it was going on, it was certainly hard work when the rejection came again ... I don't regret it, if anything it's filled in a lot of blanks for me and I know a lot more about me ... Because I'm quite positive by nature and anything that happens in my life is pretty much down to me, I make things happen because I've had to. You want to believe, right until you get the final kick in the nose, that something will come of it ... My rationale is that I went as far as was acceptable to go, without causing more upset. A long time ago I learnt to handle it, it's put away and that's it.

REVIEW OF THE SEARCH AND THE EXPERIENCE OF BEING REJECTED OUTRIGHT

In a number of areas, adopted people who were rejected outright by their birth parent *did not differ* from those who did achieve contact in their review of the search/contact experience. For example, most rejected people (78% *v* 86%) felt that important questions had been answered about their background: 'At least some of my questions have been answered'; 'Interested to know history, but can't get over the rejection'; 'I'm glad I attempted to contact. Family may want to contact me in the future.' About half of both the rejected group and the reunion group said that having completed their search, they were more appreciative of their adoptive family. Only 19% of those rejected and 15% of those achieving reunion said they felt more angry.

However, *a number of significant differences did emerge* between those who were rejected and those who were not, although it should be noted that the experience of being rejected may well have influenced people's responses. Those in the rejected group were much more likely to say they felt disappointed (78% *v*

19%) and dissatisfied (67% *v* 10%) as a result of their search. Rejected people were slightly less likely to say that they felt more complete as a person (50% *v* 65%). In spite of these disappointments and setbacks, 32% of those rejected thought they would try another approach some time in the future.

Reviewing their experience, 90% of rejected adopted people said that they had no regrets about searching for and trying to make contact with their birth parent.

Adopted people whose birth parents cease contact after a short time

Of the 274 searchers who located their birth parent, 24 (9%) made contact only to have it terminated by the birth parent within a year, and often after only one or two visits. This was experienced as a form of rejection by the adopted person. Particularly difficult was when birth parents stopped contact for no apparent reason. For example, Fran said: 'The experience has left me feeling hurt, confused and a little resentful – no explanations were offered for her apparent change of heart. I feel my self-esteem has suffered.' 'Sometimes,' said Nadine, 'I feel a complete rejection would be easier to cope with than being ignored.'

People who had contact and then were rejected did not differ from the remainder of the contact group in terms of gender, ethnicity, age at placement, or age when they first contacted the Society.

However, there were a number of significant differences between the 'contact then rejected' group and the remainder of the contact group. Adopted people who were rejected after some form of contact were more likely to evaluate their adoption negatively (23% *v* 7%). They were less likely to say that they felt happy about being adopted (48% *v* 71%), loved by their adoptive mother (52% *v* 77%), or loved their adoptive mother (61% *v* 83%). There were non-significant trends for those who were rejected after contact to be more likely to say that they felt different to their adoptive family (70% *v* 55%), and less likely to say that they felt they belonged in their adoptive family (50% *v* 66%).

There appears, therefore, to be the possibility that adopted people who evaluated their adoption negatively were at slightly increased risk of being rejected by their birth parent after contact and reunion. This is in contrast to adopted people who had been rejected outright and therefore had never met their birth parent. People rejected outright were no more or less likely to evaluate their adoption or their relationships with their adoptive mother negatively or with mixed feelings than those who had not been rejected after contact.

REVIEW OF THE SEARCH AND SUBSEQUENT REJECTION BY THE BIRTH PARENT

In a number of areas, adopted people who had contact with a birth parent and then were rejected did not differ from those who had contact and were not rejected. The 'contact then rejected group' were as likely as those who had not been rejected to say:

- that important questions had been answered about their background (75% *v* 84%);
- that they were more appreciative of their adoptive family since contact (57% *v* 54%);
- that their birth family was very different from their adoptive family (80% *v* 82%).

However, a number of significant differences did emerge between those who had contact and then were rejected and those had contact and were accepted. Those in the 'contact then rejected' group were much more likely to say they:

- found it hard to cope with the intensity of their feelings (74% *v* 36%): e.g. 'After initial elation, felt bitter, confused and unloved';
- felt their emotional outlook had worsened (36% *v* 7%): e.g. 'More depressed. I have tried to commit suicide';
- felt a stranger with their birth relatives (55% *v* 17%);
- felt more 'at home' with their adoptive family (67% *v* 55%).

The 'contact then rejected' group were less likely to say that:

- they felt more complete as a person (41% *v* 65%);
- the overall contact experience had been positive (61% *v* 89%);
- they felt more 'at home' with their birth relatives (5% *v* 56%);
- overall, they felt satisfied with the outcome (30% *v* 76%).

Searcher PETRA
I wish that she had thought the process of contact through more clearly and had refused it at the start rather than starting it and suddenly ending it. I felt rejected – something I had not ironically felt before as regards my adoption.

Searcher CHLOE
My brother Tom decided, after years of searching for me, that I wasn't the little girl he had seen at three to four years old. I might add he had been searching for me for about 15 years. Contact stopped after three months.

Rejection by one birth relative and acceptance by another

Fifteen (5%) of the search and contact group had the experience of being rejected by one birth relative and accepted by another. Eight people were rejected by their birth mother but were accepted by their birth father and/or birth sibling. Seven people were rejected by their birth father but were accepted by their birth mother and/or birth siblings. The numbers in this group are too small to carry out much useful statistical analysis. In general, their personal characteristics and experiences of adoption did not differ from the broad group of people who had contact with their birth relatives. Their review of the contact experience did not differ from the larger contact group. The only exceptions were in answer to questions about whether they were happy with their contact with their birth mother or father. Predictably, in those cases where they had been rejected they reported that they were not happy with the contact with that birth relative.

The acceptance by one or more birth relatives appears to protect people from the negative impact of being rejected by another birth relative. This 'rejected and accepted' group appeared least upset about their rejection and in most respects did not differ from the larger contact group.

Summary

Searchers who suffered either an outright rejection or a rejection after contact without the compensation of acceptance by another birth relative were, not surprisingly, more likely to view elements of the contact experience negatively and unhappily. They were left with long-term feelings of frustration, disappointment and dissatisfaction. Even so, the majority had no regrets about making the search: they felt that some important questions had been answered.

Adopted people who had contact and then were rejected by their birth parent were significantly more likely to evaluate their adoption negatively and less likely to say that they felt loved by or love for their adoptive mother. For example, only 52% said they felt loved by their adoptive mother compared to 77% of people who had contact and were not rejected. The experience of achieving contact with their birth parent only to be rejected meant that this group was most likely to review the contact and reunion as emotionally upsetting: 74% said that they found it hard to cope with the intense feelings triggered by the rejection.

CHAPTER 13

Contact and Reunion

Introduction

In this and the following chapter we examine both the impact of contact and reunion with a birth relative and the long-term durability of the relationship. Again, we compare the views and experiences of those who searched and those who were searched for. For many adopted people in the study, at least five years had elapsed since they first had contact with their birth relative. Twenty-seven per cent of searchers and 22% of non-searchers first had contact with their birth mothers five years or more prior to the survey. This provides a long-term view of the post-reunion experience. However, we begin with an examination of people's experience of contact with their birth relative during the year after they first met.

Frequency of contact during first year

In all, 274 searchers located their birth relative. Ninety-three per cent of these people then went on to have some direct, usually face-to-face, contact. Ninety per cent of adopted people who were approached by a birth relative (non-searchers) also went on to have some kind of direct contact with them. For both searchers and non-searchers, rates of contact with birth relatives were highest during the year after they first met (see Table 13.1).

For example, 67% of searchers were having some kind of contact, either by letter, telephone or meeting, with their birth mother at least once a month during the first year of contact. For those who were in touch with either a birth sibling or birth father, rates of contact once a month or more were slightly lower (birth siblings: 59%; birth fathers: 48%).

In general, rates and frequency of contact with a birth relative were slightly lower for non-searchers. For example, 59% of non-searchers were having some kind of contact with their birth mother at least once a month during the first year of contact. Rates were a little lower for contact with birth siblings (56%) and birth fathers (40%).

Statistically, rates of contact with birth mothers, birth fathers and birth siblings during the first year by letter or telephone were no different between searchers and non-searchers. However, searchers had significantly higher rates of face-to-face contact with all three birth relative groups (mothers, fathers, siblings) than non-searchers. In particular, non-searchers were less likely to be having face-to-face contact with their birth relatives than searchers during the first year of contact: for example, whereas 47% of searchers were seeing their birth mothers at least once every three or four months, this figure dropped to 30% for non-searchers.

Table 13.1 Searchers and non-searchers: rates of contact with the birth relative during the first year

	Face-to-face		Letter/telephone	
	Searchers (%)	Non-searchers (%)	Searchers (%)	Non-searchers (%)
Birth mother				
Weekly	4	4	23	24
About once a month	15	9	44	35
Every 3 to 4 months	28	17	19	26
Once every 6 months or less	48	32	15	15
Never	4	39	0	0
		$p < 0.001$		NS
Birth father				
Weekly	1	0	17	20
About once a month	17	6	31	20
Every 3 to 4 months	16	0	13	13
Once every 6 months or less	57	41	40	47
Never	9	53	0	0
		$p < 0.001$		NS
Birth sibling(s)				
Weekly	2	2	19	24
About once a month	19	16	40	32
Every 3 to 4 months	30	14	21	17
Once every 6 months or less	48	40	21	27
Never	2	28	0	0
		$p < 0.001$		NS

Searchers: birth mothers $n = 216$; birth fathers $n = 72$; birth siblings $n = 136$
Non-searchers: birth mothers $n = 54$; birth fathers $n = 15$; birth siblings $n = 41$

Feelings about the contact experience

People reported a range of feelings when they first had contact with their birth relative. Most people thought the relationship was more like being a friend than a close relative. However, a substantial number did say they felt instantly connected. A minority said they felt distant and unconnected. Although not investigated in the self-administered questionnaire, feeling sexually attracted to a birth relative was mentioned explicitly by one adopted person in the following in-depth interviews.

SEARCHERS

Many people were intrigued by their physical likeness to a mother, sister or brother. There was a sense of being biologically and physically connected. People said they could not help staring. Eighty-two per cent of searchers described their initial relationship with their birth relative as feeling like a *friend*, *family* or *stranger*. The remaining 18% felt confused, rejected or elated by the experience.

The following quotes and case studies illustrate typical responses under each category.

Friend (36%)

'Felt like a friend who hasn't been seen for a long time.' 'Felt like a friend with her.' 'Easy to get on with, like a friend.'

Searcher   SARAH

I wanted to take Kate [counsellor] with me although I had Anna with me as well. Anna was eight months old. I wanted somebody else there ... When we went inside she [mother] just burst into tears and Kate said, 'What do you think?' and Vera said, 'Oh, she's beautiful.' I didn't cry a bit. I suppose I had prepared myself a long time before – I'd done all my crying years ago ... Vera wanted to be my mother again. I had to sit down and explain, 'I have a mother.' And she was sorry that she couldn't be there when I got married, she couldn't be there when I had my first two children, and shared experiences that she wanted to share with me but that's all in the past and we can't form a relationship on that. I'd rather be very good friends ... She couldn't take the place of my adoptive mother just like that. I said to her, 'That's not what I'm looking for.'

Family: instant connection (29%)

'Felt immediately that they were my family.' 'Felt like a daughter.' 'Felt a very strong bond immediately.' 'Felt like a son and part of the family.'

Searcher   BETH

First of all I had a letter from her and a picture. And I remember opening this letter and looking at this picture and my husband said, 'What's the matter?' And I said, 'You don't know. You take for granted that you know who you look like ... You cannot believe what this is like.' And that's the thing that sticks in my mind. I found who I looked like and I'd gone 30 years not knowing and all of a sudden ... And when I met her, I couldn't believe that I could look like somebody else ... there was a lot more depth to this than I realised at the time. So I do remember looking – and I remember the voice, and the mannerisms – it was weird … She certainly didn't feel like mummy, but the bond was instant. It was there, especially when somebody looks so much like you. That's the thing I probably latched on to the most: 'I looked like somebody.'

A few weeks later I met the other children … As the afternoon wore on, we went for a picnic … We could make each other laugh, we had so much in common and I thought, 'I've come home – these are my people.' I felt a closeness there that I'd never felt with my younger brother. For the first time I didn't feel different any more.

Stranger: emotional flatness or distance (15%)

'I felt like a stranger.' 'I expected an instant bond, but felt nothing.' 'Quite remote at first.' 'I didn't feel any bond.'

Searcher SALLY

I felt a bit nervous, but I didn't get 'Oh my baby' or anything like that. I mean neither of us were – ever have been – emotional with one another … I think I felt a slight bit of disappointment that she's just like this ordinary working class woman and she's not, you know, somebody special! Which I think, you know, I would have quite liked really … We got on well as you would meeting somebody socially and you could manage to spend a couple of hours with them. There was no like antagonism between us but it wasn't like this big connection, and there never has been really.

Emotional confusion (11%)

'Mixed feelings.' 'I felt confused.' 'It felt weird and confusing.' 'A combination of strangeness and connectedness.'

Searcher CLARE

I had an expectation that my birth parents would be both devastated by having given me away for adoption and I would actually see some devastation if you like. It sounds very horrible but I wanted to see some proof that I did matter, that I do matter … I feel very pompous but I wanted them to be aware of the seriousness of what had happened and that to be reflected in any relationship or meeting that we may have. And certainly with my father, I never felt that, till the day he died … and I was disappointed … I suppose having felt that my adopted family had failed in that respect, that surely my real family would at least have some remorse perhaps. I wanted them to make me feel better about being adopted and they didn't really … I found out about all my other brothers and sisters when I had arranged to meet him [birth father] and he'd kept me waiting for two hours on the station … And I was devastated because I had gone from feeling that was this sort of mistake that every- one would regret to realising he'd made millions of them. You know, he hadn't been devastated by giving me up and I meet all these other people who've actually had problems with him before I ever turned up … And then a year later I managed to find my birth mother and her family's pretty fucked up actually! ... And when I turned up I think it reawakened unresolved feelings that she hadn't dealt with for 19 years ... and consequently when I met her I felt I was responsible in some way for this woman going through these things. And all I could do having opened up this hornet's nest was to be supportive but I ended up feeling smothered by her, it ended being a really difficult relationship where I felt I had to tread carefully and cater for her needs and sensitivities at the expense of mine.

Rejection (7%)
'Natural father denied paternity.' 'I rejected them.'

Elation (3%)
'Liberation and felt in control.' 'Very happy and overwhelmed.'

NON-SEARCHERS
Similar feelings were described by non-searchers, as illustrated below.

Friends (54%)
'Felt more like a family friend.' 'Felt like a stranger with a strong link.' 'More like a distant friend.' 'Felt at ease with my birth mother but more as a friend.' 'More friend than family.'

Non-searcher MIKE
I mean obviously, it was a difficult day. It's more nerve-racking really. Twenty-eight years of not knowing who she is and thinking about it ... And it's the same for her, I mean she was nervous. I think we gave each other a hug and then we went down to the pub after about half an hour and it was fine. We got on well immediately. Difficult day, though.

Family: instant connection (11%)
'Brilliant – instant recognition.' 'Physical and spiritual connection.' 'Felt as if I'd always known my birth mother and that I had never been separated from her.'

Non-searcher MICHELLE
My husband took me. It was just a day. Just full of tears all day ... We are so alike. We get on so well. I said to her, 'It just don't seem like we've ever been apart' and it don't. We come out with similar comments. We sound alike. We are both bubbly. It's just so weird.

Emotional confusion (20%)
'Confused feelings.' 'I felt guilty because I didn't want further contact.' 'Felt odd with mixed feelings. Unsure if I felt a daughter or a friend.' 'Strained – we're from different backgrounds.'

Non-searcher LIZ

I wrote a very brief letter about my life and did refer to the fact that I was angry about the way she contacted me initially – but now three or four years had passed I realised that I felt stronger about making contact and it was just a better time for me generally. She wrote back and was obviously euphoric ... We wrote to each other about four or five times and it got to the point where I was really looking forward to getting her letters ... then we sent each other photos ... I really didn't want to just arrange to meet up with her. I said in the letter that 'I don't want to rush this; it is such a big thing for me that I just want to take it a step at a time and I hope you can understand this.' ... I think she felt that I wanted to be in control and she was very understanding of that. She never pushed it. She let me lead the whole way. It was my suggestion that we meet up ... That was probably the most nerve-racking experience in my life. We arranged to meet for tea but I just remember being very nervous about it. She was very nervous as well and I think we spent about three hours together ... it was quite awkward to start with but also very exciting as well – to see what you look like – terrible thing is, I can't even really remember what we talked about. I just remember afterwards feeling absolutely exhausted!

Emotional distance (15%)

'Felt indifferent.' 'I felt distant.' 'Felt we were strangers with very little in common.' 'I felt odd; she seemed a complete stranger who had given birth to me.'

COMPARISON OF SEARCHERS AND NON-SEARCHERS

Although both searchers and non-searchers were equally likely to describe the relationship with their birth relative as one of close friendship, searchers were statistically more likely to feel some kind of emotional connection and familial closeness with their birth relative than non-searchers (see Table 13.2). About one sixth of both searchers and non-searchers said they felt a stranger and distant with their birth relative.

Table 13.2 Description of feelings/relationship upon first contact with birth relative

	Searchers (%)	Non-searchers (%)
Friend	36	54
Instant connection/bond	29	11
Distance/strangers	15	15
Confusion	11	20
Other	4	0

Searchers n = 250; non-searchers n = 61; $p < 0.02$

The majority of searchers and non-searchers were struck and intrigued by physical similarities between themselves and their birth relative. Isobel, of mixed ethnicity, said, 'Quite a lot of it came down to looks with me', a sentiment echoed by the majority of both searchers and non-searchers. Most people said they just gazed and looked at the other, talking rapidly but taking in very little and remembering next to nothing of what was actually said. Mutual gaze seemed to characterise much of what took place on first encounter. A childhood of wondering who you looked like was matched by the fascination of seeing someone who actually did look like you.

Non-searcher JESSICA
We met up in a restaurant in Manchester – and that was very, very emotional, very charged emotionally. I remember being totally, totally dumbfounded. Both myself and my natural mother were at first – we both cried and both gave each other a big hug and we both spent a lot of time just staring at one another. I think we were both amazed at the similarity in our physical appearance ... it all just seemed so natural ... we were in this restaurant and it closed about three o'clock but the waiter realised that there was some sort of reunion going on and he said, 'Carry on and we'll clear up around you.' And we were there until about eight o'clock that evening when the next setting of people started coming in to eat. Time just flew! I can't really remember what we talked about now!

To sum up, the range of emotions people experience following contact and reunion is enormous and differs in complexity, depth and sentiment.

Adopted people who ceased the relationship with their birth relative after the first contact

Seven per cent of searchers ceased contact with their birth mother after only one meeting, letter or phone call. The figure was slightly higher for birth fathers and birth siblings at 10% and 12% respectively. The numbers involved are too small for much statistical testing. However, non-significant trends emerged suggesting that those who ceased the relationship with their birth mother after the first contact were more likely to be men than women, to have been placed for adoption after the age of two, and to be younger at first contact (27.1 years *v* 29.1 years).

Searcher ARNOLD
My birth mother had died three years previously and I'd found my half-brother who had also been adopted ... I took the bull by the horns and arranged to meet him at his home. I was terribly nervous before the meeting ... I took flowers for his wife and I also took a complete copy of my research for him ... I think

it's true to say I'd gone there with trepidation, not really certain what I was doing. And when he opened the door, one, I didn't actually take to him, and he also had a black eye. He'd gone down to a local pub with his son a few days earlier and had a fight with him. With his own son! ... I had an instant feeling that things were not right for a ready-made new family for me. I'm not a very tactile person, strangely enough, and having rejected him personally, privately at the door, it became worse when he cuddled me when I arrived there. So we sat down ... I gathered that he'd had a very, very hard upbringing and he did not like his adoption at all ... He'd not really had a settled working life at all from what I could tell and was in desperate need of care and finding something tangible in his roots, which unfortunately could have been me ... I spent about three hours there, the longest three hours ... I just could not really imagine opening up my family existence to someone who ends up having fights with his son. It just didn't seem right to me. The circumstances were not quite conducive to a future and I felt then that the only thing to do would be to end there and not to continue.

Adopted people whose relationship with their birth relative ceased within a year

By the end of the first year after initial contact, 15% of searchers and 10% of non-searchers were no longer seeing their birth mothers. In the case of searchers, a similar figure was observed for birth fathers, with 16% no longer in contact. The adopted person was as likely to cease contact as the birth relative. But whoever ended the relationship, most adopted people still reported that the reunion had been important and worthwhile.

Searcher HELEN

I found my birth mother within two or three weeks of beginning my search ... I then wrote a letter 'blah, blah, hope you didn't mind me writing'. Talked a bit who I was ... and then next day there was a message on my answerphone – and it was my mother – I didn't expect her to ring – that was a bonus because I'd actually recorded it, I've still got it – it was really tearful – just saying, 'It's Julia here, I've thought about you everyday for 25 years.' I was just so happy that I had contacted her. And she said she was writing to me and I got a letter from her and some photographs and that was amazing ... When I met her there were certain resemblances but you know how some people really look like their parents, it's not that at all. So that was a little disappointing in a funny way, because it was one of those big things ...We met outside the front door. It was a very, very emotional moment. We just kept looking at each other. It was really, really strange. It was like a magnet. I just kept looking at her and I suppose she just kept looking at me, noticing things. I noticed straight away that we had exactly the same eye colour. I felt very close. It's hard to describe the feeling. The only closest thing is when you're in love with somebody, it's that sort of tense feeling and closeness.

We met up again, fairly soon after and I said, 'Perhaps we could meet one evening?' But she cancelled it and that was it. It was obvious from the second meeting that we weren't going to be, you know, like people who get reunited and are always seeing each other. I didn't really want that. I always knew I didn't want a replacement family, so I wasn't looking for that but I had hoped that we'd see each other more often. So that's been a bit of a disappointment.

I know where I come from genetically. I've met her. The mystery has gone. The gains are the missing pieces, if you like, being put into place. And I suppose I do feel a loss insofar as I've contacted her and now I've lost her again ... It's better to do it because otherwise you'll always wonder, even though there are difficulties for me now – the rejection – I'm still glad I did it, because otherwise it's such a massive question-mark over your life. Overall, definitely it's been worth it.

Adopted people who decided to stop seeing their birth relative within a year after reunion gave a variety of reasons. Some saw their search and reunion as an information and identity quest and not a route to a relationship. Greta said she had no feelings for her birth mother: ' I found out what I needed to, so no need for fuller contact.' 'I wish I hadn't bothered,' said Trudy, 'but then again, I probably would have always wondered, "What if?"'

The majority of adopted people who ceased contact said they felt no emotional bond, felt like strangers or they just found managing the relationship with an additional family too difficult.

Searcher SYLVIA

I felt there was nothing emotional between myself and my birth mother. I felt confused. I expected to be drawn to my mother but found we had very little in common other than mutual curiosity. No bond appeared to be made between us.

Non-searcher JEMMA

Well after the first meeting we got on quite well, even though I didn't really speak to her – the whole situation was kind of ... because we'd wanted it for such a long time ... it was nice I suppose ... I was quite excited, I was quite positive about it, we all were. She actually came back to the town where we lived ... and we just met and I kept looking at her and I saw that I had her legs and I had her hands and we asked some questions that we wanted answered – and we got a bit of the background and that was all good. And at that time I saw something coming out of it – even though I still found it difficult.

Then after that I invited her to stay with me, I think it was two months later, for a few days. I suppose, because I was the only one with her, I had to talk to her and that's when everything really changed I suppose. She talked about what she'd been through – and she was basically just full of negativity – I found it really hard, I couldn't talk to her because every time I tried to talk about myself she just changed the subject and wanted to talk about herself. And she just wouldn't leave me alone, it was getting to me and I just needed a bit of space but she just wouldn't allow me to be by myself. She didn't really want to know about me or how I felt about ... how everything made me feel ... you know about my child-hood experiences, anything like that. All she wanted to do was make me feel really negative about life.

Contact experiences in the early years

Although a significant number of people ceased contact with their birth relative within a year or two of their first meeting, the majority were still maintaining some form of relationship: 76% of searchers and 77% of non-searchers who first contacted or had been contacted by their birth mother three years or more ago were still in contact with her. And after three years or more, 85% of searchers were still in contact with one or more of their birth siblings, and 70% of searchers were still communicating with or seeing their birth father.

Searcher ESTELLE

It's been a roller-coaster with my natural mother! 1994 we got on really well. 1995, she was just trying to steer me away from my family, the one that I'd always been with, and I suddenly found myself feeling very loyal to them, sort of ... I suddenly realised that she was just waltzing into my life and acting as if she's given me everything, but they were the ones who'd put me through university and everything. So I was backing them up and then she felt as if she was made to feel rejected and so she went back to St Lucia and wrote me a very hostile letter and then we exchanged hostile letters for a long time. And then in 1996 we were barely in contact at all. And this year, it's been the best year. It's almost as if we had to go through that phase to work out who we were and what boundaries we can't cross and things like that, and she's made me realise that I do want to have a friendship with her.

Frequency of contact five or years or more since the initial contact

Over time, there is a trend towards decreasing contact with birth relatives (see Table 13.3). For example, 37% of searchers and 45% of non-searchers who were first in contact with their birth mother five or more years ago had ceased all contact at the time of the survey.

Table 13.3 Five years or more since the first contact: rates of contact with the birth relative

	Face-to-face		Letter/telephone	
	Searchers (%)	Non-searchers (%)	Searchers (%)	Non-searchers (%)
Birth mother				
Weekly	3	6	16	25
About once a month	6	18	18	6
Every 3 to 4 months	16	6	16	6
Once every 6 months or less	35	6	13	18
Never	40	65	37	45
		$p < 0.03$		NS
Birth father				
Weekly	0	0	6	0
About once a month	11	0	23	0
Every 3 to 4 months	11	17	8	17
Once every 6 months or less	30	0	16	17
Never	49	83	47	67
Birth sibling(s)				
Weekly	3	3	15	13
About once a month	12	9	23	13
Every 3 to 4 months	19	27	14	19
Once every 6 months or less	37	21	23	6
Never	28	40	25	50

Searchers: birth mothers $n = 106$; birth fathers $n = 48$; birth siblings $n = 72$
Non-searchers: birth mothers $n = 17$; birth fathers $n = 6$; birth siblings $n = 16$

Overall, after five years or more since the first contact with the birth relative the following rates and frequency of contact were reported.

Birth mothers

- The proportion of searchers (34%) and non-searchers (31%) in weekly or monthly contact (all forms) with birth mothers were roughly equal.
- Non-searchers were more likely than searchers to have ceased face-to-face contact with their birth mother (65% *v* 38%).
- Non-searchers were more likely than searchers to have ceased all forms of contact with their birth mother (45% *v* 37%).

Birth fathers

- Proportionately fewer adopted people remained in contact (all forms) with their birth father than with their birth mother.
- Non-searchers were more likely than searchers to have ceased face-to-face contact with their birth father (83% *v* 49%).
- Non-searchers were more likely than searchers to have ceased all forms of contact with their birth father (67% *v* 47%).

Birth siblings

- The proportion of searchers (40%) in weekly or monthly contact (all forms) with their birth siblings was higher than for non-searchers (27%).
- Non-searchers were more likely than searchers to have ceased face-to-face contact with their birth siblings (40% *v* 25%).
- Non-searchers were more likely than searchers to have ceased all forms of contact with their birth siblings (50% *v* 25%).

Searcher SARAH

When I first met my father two years ago ... I rang my birth mother and said, 'Charles [birth father] is here for his father's funeral – I'm meeting him next Friday for dinner – do you want to come and have dinner with us?' She arrived an hour earlier and I could tell as soon as I arrived that I wasn't needed. The spark was there and they just had eyes for each other and I sat there like a gooseberry while they reminisced about the sixties. I was a bit upset because I thought this is the last time I see my father before he goes back to South Africa and why should she butt in ... neither of them were in a solid marriage so unfortunately I got them together at the 'wrong' or the 'right' time. So they're blissfully happy together now – she's over in Australia and they've got a house together and it's just one big fairy tale! I speak to them both every week ... Before he married my birth mother he wrote, 'For me to act as your father would be inappropriate and morally wrong but I hope that I can become a friend that loves you very much. If at any time you need a shoulder to cry on or a butt to kick I promise I will be there for you ...' Charles has always been a friend.

Contact rates with birth mothers and adoptive mothers compared

Contact rates with birth and adoptive mothers were compared for searchers and non-searchers who were still in contact with their birth mothers five years or more after their first reunion and whose adoptive mothers were still alive (see Fig. 13.1). In most cases, where the adopted person was in contact with both mothers, frequency of contact was more likely to be higher with the adoptive mother than with the birth mother. A similar pattern was found for non-searchers, but numbers are too small for statistical purposes.

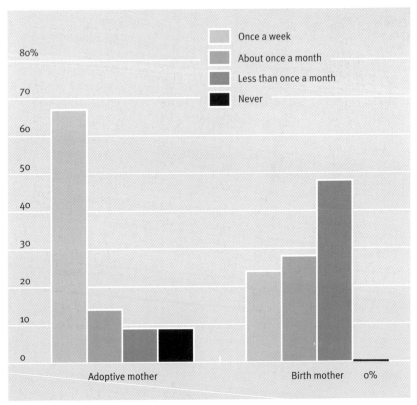

Fig. 13.1 Frequency of contact (all forms) with adoptive and birth mothers five years or more after reunion in cases where adopted person was still in contact with birth mother and adoptive mother was still alive (searchers only). $n = 60$; $p < 0.001$

Proportions of searchers and non-searchers remaining in contact with birth relatives

The general picture is one of a year-on-year drop in the number of adopted people maintaining contact with their birth relatives (see Table 13.4). This is most pronounced for relationships with birth fathers (53% still in contact with birth fathers compared to 76% for birth siblings and 63% for birth mothers five years after the initial reunion). However, for all groups, there is a sense that the attrition rate begins to plateau after seven or eight years. For example, five years after their initial reunion, 63% of searchers were still in some form of contact with their birth mother. The proportion dropped only a little to 57% for those still in contact eight years after their initial reunion.

However, the proportion of searchers maintaining contact over the long term is slightly higher than the proportion of non-searchers maintaining contact (see Figures 13.2–13.5, and Table 13.4).

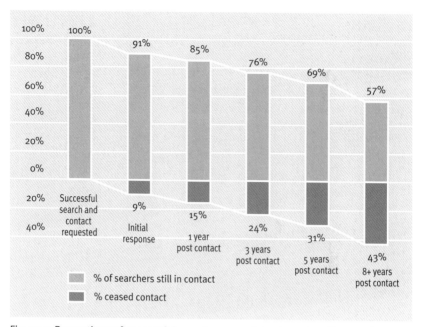

Fig. 13.2 Proportions of successful searchers remaining in contact (face-to-face, phone and/or letter) with birth mother over time.

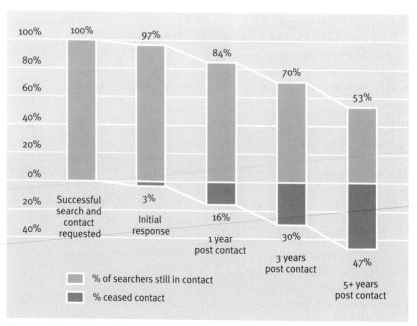

Fig. 13.3 Proportions of successful searchers remaining in contact (face-to-face, phone and/or letter) with birth father over time.

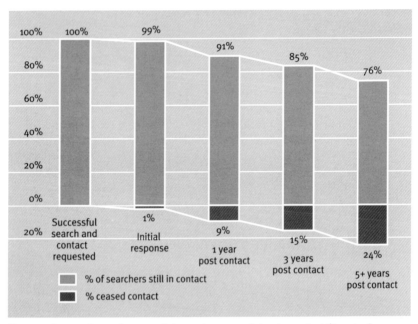

Fig. 13.4 Proportions of successful searchers remaining in contact (face-to-face, phone and/or letter) with birth sibling(s) over time.

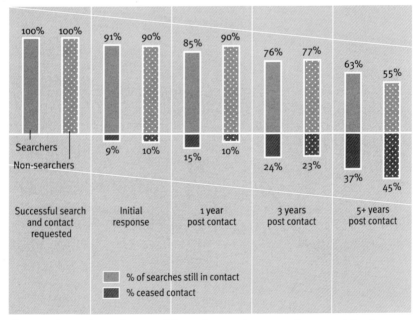

Fig. 13.5 Proportions of successful searchers and non-searchers remaining in contact (face-to-face, phone and/or letter) with birth mother over time.

Table 13.4 Proportion of searchers and non-searchers remaining in contact with their birth mother over time

	Initial approach (%)	Accept initial contact (%)	3 years post-contact (%)	5+ years post-contact (%)
Searchers	100	91	76	63
Non-searchers	100	90	77	55

For many adopted people, over the long term their relationship with their birth relative settled into a comfortable, familiar and regular pattern. Many people commented that the success of their relationship with the birth relative had not adversely affected their relationship with their adoptive parents; indeed some people felt they had the best of both worlds.

Searcher BRYNN

It's nine years since I first found my birth mum ... I can tell my natural mother an awful lot more that my adoptive mum, I suppose because she's more worldly wise. I can tell her anything and we have a lot in common, the way we talk, mannerisms, personality. It's actually a feeling of belonging in a way. Although I know I belong with my adoptive parents, and that will never be taken away or changed, it's still a nice feeling of belonging ... And it's laid the ghost to rest, so to speak. I see both parents about equally I suppose, but I do feel connected to my natural mum, no doubt.

Non-searcher LIZ

I feel we've got through all the difficult conversations ... and I've realised that we have so much in common it's unbelievable – not just the things we like doing and our lifestyles but the way we think – we just get on very well. I see her now as a friend. I still don't see her as my mum; she will never be my mum ... It's almost like I've got this whole new family and social circle, and it feels very comfortable.

Other adopted people, although they had been in a long-term relationship with their birth relative, felt that a number of issues continued to colour how they felt and behaved in that relationship. For some people, coming to terms with being given up for adoption remained difficult. Unresolved feelings affected a number of their roles and relationships.

Searcher RUTH

She came one Sunday morning ... And we talked for nine hours, non-stop ... and I think we held hands almost the whole way through. For that first year afterwards we had to have absolute regular contact, we had to see each other once a month

...There was a sense of loss because I hadn't seen her for so many years, a loss because of my own mum, but complete happiness because we were together and it had gone so well and it was more perfect – totally connected. And we still are after almost ten years. It's just settled into a normal family relationship.

I still have a constant battle with myself as to who I am. I thought when I met my mum everything would be in place, all my insecurities would go into check, my whole life would be sorted out and all it did was bring up more questions with less answers ... I couldn't do without her; she's my life and we will stay together but it throws up all sorts of other – you know, you start hearing about your family background ... It gives you a kind of completeness in one sense but whether it's just me because I'm such an insecure person ... I know a lot goes back to that initial rejection, that sort of thing, even as a child I had a sort of bad self-image and that just carried on through and despite meeting my mum and being completely accepted in the family, that still hasn't gone away...

I've got very odd thoughts about mothers and motherhood and mothering in general, because of my own experiences. It's actually a negative thought that I have because mums go away, mums leave you, mums die – even though in between I've had good experiences. But I've got to understand myself more. I've chosen at quite an early age not to be a mother. I know what a mum's role is but I haven't had a proper experience. I don't remember the mum I did have. And the mum I have now, we are like mum and daughter but we're also like friends and I don't have that childhood experience with her.

Meeting birth relatives provided most people with background knowledge and insights that they could have gained no other way. However, once some people had filled in the gaps and completed their 'story' they felt somewhat stuck with the relationship. A number of people said they felt obliged to continue seeing their birth relative, even though, at least as far as they were concerned, it had lost much of its appeal. A lack of shared history or strong feelings meant that the relationship had become a routine without much affection or satisfaction.

Searcher SALLY

[Sally is still seeing her birth mother ten years after they first met. However, she feels their relationship is somewhat mechanical and routine. She feels both bored and frustrated with it.]

We've got into this habit of just meeting in a restaurant near where I work for lunch every three months or so ... it was a bit like a chore really that we had to keep doing but it wasn't great fun for either of us ... this will sound really awful but, in some ways, if I never saw her again it wouldn't really matter to me ... You know I'd like to feel more cosseted by her. I suppose I'd like to feel more loved by her. But I don't feel that I have to respond, I'd just like to feel more loved by her ... I feel I've gained. I've gained information that helped me make sense of my feelings. So, I mean I'm glad I've done it and I'm really glad that I found her. But it's more to do with how it's affected me personally, internally, rather than a relationship with her.

Reasons for stopping contact with the birth mother

Year on year after the initial reunion, a small but steady number of people ceased contact with their birth mother. Death of the birth mother accounted for a small number of ceased contacts. More typically, either the birth mother stopped contact or the adopted person felt that the relationship with the birth mother had become an emotional strain.

SEARCHERS
Birth mother rejects further contact (50%)
'Birth mother rejected me – not sure why.' 'I told her I was pregnant and she wrote saying she never wanted to see me again.' 'She wasn't interested – it was her mother who is still alive who encouraged the adoption.' 'After our second meeting she was not interested in a relationship.' 'She stopped replying to my letters – I've no idea why.'

Adopted person ceases contact (36%)
'She was completely unreasonable.' 'I had enough of being blamed for her situation.' 'We had nothing in common. I didn't write and she didn't want me to phone.' 'No bond appeared; I saw no future in the contact.' 'She got on my nerves – too obsessive.' 'She was saying horrible things about my adoptive parents.'

Birth mother dead (11%)
'Mother died of cancer.' 'She died from alcoholism.'

Miscellaneous (4%)
'Unknown for definite.' 'Stopped after second meeting.'

NON-SEARCHERS
In contrast to searchers, when contact with the birth mother stopped in non-searcher cases, except in the event of death, it was always the adopted person who decided to end the relationship.

Adopted person ceases contact (93%)
'Emotionally draining; for her benefit not mine.' 'I felt guilty, but I felt no bond with birth mother.' 'She was screwed up.' 'She needed a family and I didn't need another mother.' 'Didn't like her letters; emotionally blackmailed. I had no feelings for her.' 'She was mixed up and pushed too much.'

Birth mother died (7%)

Reasons for stopping contact with the birth father

A similar picture emerges in cases where contact has ceased with birth fathers.

SEARCHERS

In 54% of cases the birth father ended the contact: 'I've never heard from him since the first contact; he puts the phone down.' 'He has stopped responding to my letters.' 'He was unprepared and asked me not to see him again.'

In 38% of cases, the adopted person chose to end contact: 'He became too interested; I felt I had nothing in common with him.' 'He became too possessive.' 'I did not like the way he treated my family.'

Contacted ended in 8% of cases because of the birth father's death.

Searcher BARRY

It was a couple of years after I'd found my birth mum I decided to look for my birth father ... Once I'd got a bit of information, I found him very quickly – less than a day! I left a message with his brother and my phone number and I told him I'd found my mum. So that evening, my father phoned me up ... Two days later he came down and stayed overnight and went back. So we met and I'm not sure what I made of him really ... I could tell he was my dad ... but he was very strange and a real spiv type, very strange, not comfortable ... I just felt totally different. I got on with him OK, and his wife, and they came to see us once more after that and they sent a con- gratulations card when Lisa was born but they got my wife's name wrong and I didn't contact him for a while after that and he didn't bother contacting me ...And that was the last time, six years ago now ... I suppose it would have been nice to have had a father who was, I don't know how to describe it, I mean he is in a way, without being too nasty, everything I wouldn't want to be.

NON-SEARCHERS

The number of non-searchers involved with their birth fathers was small, but in all cases where the relationship had ceased, the adopted person ended the con- tact: 'Even more screwed up [than birth mother].' 'I only wanted to exchange medical information. Told him how I was doing but nothing after that.'

Reasons for stopping contact with birth siblings

The reasons for stopping contact are slightly different for birth siblings. Amongst searchers, 52% of adopted people decided to end the contact: 'My curiosity was satisfied'; 'I found concept of new family hard to handle'; 'Stopped since stopped contact with birth mother.' Thirty-five per cent were rejected by the birth sibling: 'I was told to stay away from our birth mother'; 'Adverse reac- tion from birth sister.' Thirteen per cent of cases reported a variety of miscella- neous reasons for ending the contact: 'We stopped after our second meeting';

'The ones I met were too young.' The picture for non-searchers was similar, but numbers were very small: 'Nothing in common'; 'Took birth mother's side'; 'Didn't feel like a blood brother.'

Comparison of adopted people who continue contact and those who cease contact with birth mother

Both in the medium term (less than five years since original contact with birth mother) and long term (five years or more since original contact with birth mother), no significant differences were found between those who continued contact and those who ceased contact in terms of:

- age of placement
- gender
- ethnicity
- age at contact
- adoption experience group (Integrated/Differentiated/Alienated)
- evaluation of the adoption experience (positive/mixed feelings/negative).

Reaction of adoptive parents

In cases in which the adoptive mother was still alive, 67% of searchers and 78% non-searchers (who accepted contact from their birth relative) told their adoptive mother of their actions. A similar picture emerged for telling adoptive fathers. Most adoptive parents were supportive, although many were also worried and upset (Table 13.5).

Table 13.5 Reactions of adoptive parents to contact (if told)

	Adoptive mother		Adoptive father	
	Searchers (%)	Non-searchers (%)	Searchers (%)	Non-searchers (%)
Supportive	68	77	63	70
Worried	36	46	26	36
Upset	35	21	18	14
Angry	12	7	10	9
Don't know	3	2	15	11

Searchers: adoptive mothers $n = 179$; adoptive fathers $n = 158$
Non-searchers: adoptive mothers $n = 44$; adoptive fathers $n = 42$

Searcher BETH

I 'phoned my mum and I said' 'Are you sitting down because I've got something to tell you, but I'm not pregnant!' I said' 'I've got to the point now where we have got my birth mother's address.' And it did hurt my mum terribly but she said, 'I knew, I always knew you would do it – it was only a question of when.' And you say lots of things to reassure somebody but it doesn't really make any difference – she was very hurt. She kept thinking she'd failed in some way. 'Was it because we moved?' she asked. I said, 'No. I can't actually say why. But I had to do it. You're not adopted. You don't know.' I did feel bad, but adopted children, I think, subconsciously grow up being 'pleasers' ... and for the first time in my life I was being really quite selfish and doing it my way ... but I did feel bad.

Non-searcher JESSICA

I think deep down, my adoptive mum wanted me to meet my natural mother and my half-brother and either not like them or say, 'Right, I've met them now. That's it. I'm just going to carry on with my life.' And of course, I was actually saying, 'I've met her. I've met the family and I'd actually like to have some sort of relationship with them in the future' and so my mum was really upset about it, which I could totally understand ... With time it's got better. But for the first two years, it was very difficult ... I didn't want to exclude my parents by not telling them about when I'd see my natural mother – I thought I need to include her, but she didn't want to be included ... she just wanted to pretend they didn't exist ... But gradually over time things have got better and now I'm able to say, 'Oh, I just spent the evening with Carol' – say it conversation without my mum slamming the phone down or bursting into tears. I suppose after all this time she's realised that I'm not going to run away and my mum's my mum and Carol's my natural mother but she's more like a friend than a mother. My relationship with my mother is unique but there's room for lots of people in your life if you allow it.

- Most people said that the contact did not *initially* affect their relationship with their adoptive parents. Sixty per cent of searchers and 64% of non-searchers reported that their relationship had not changed. However, 28% of searchers and 26% of non-searchers did say that they felt the contact had placed the relationship with their adoptive parents under some strain. Eight per cent of searchers and 6% of non-searchers said that the relationship had actually improved as a result of the contact.
- For those adopted people who *remained in contact with their birth relative for at least a year*, 21% of searchers and 15% of non-searchers said that the relationship with their adoptive parent had actually improved; 61% of searchers and 72% of non-searchers said that it remained unchanged. This left 10% of searchers and 9% of non-searchers saying they felt their relationship with their adoptive parents continued under some strain as a result of the contact with the birth relative.

Non-searchers, even though they had not initiated the contact, still had to make a decision about whether or not to see their birth relative. In most cases, people felt very aware of their adoptive parents' feelings and position. They wanted support from them but they were equally anxious to reassure their parents that wanting to see their birth relative was not a threat to their relationship with them.

Non-searcher MICHELLE

I spoke to mum and dad and said, 'Would you mind if I went to see her?' Mum and dad said, 'No. It's up to you. It won't upset us.' But I think deep down, my dad – I was daddy's little girl – I think he thought deep down that I was going to go back to her. But he knows I wouldn't. No – I like it down here too much!

Summary

- In response to the initial contact, most adopted people felt one or other of two feelings predominated: (i) a feeling of interest and friendship, or (ii) a feeling of instant family bond and connection. Searchers were more likely than non-searchers to feel an instant family bond (29% *v* 11%).
- One year after initial reunion, 15% of searchers and 10% of non-searchers had ceased contact with their birth mothers.
- Five years or more after the initial reunion, searchers (63%) were more likely than non-searchers (55%) to have remained in contact with their birth mothers.
- Five years or more after the initial reunion, searchers (62%) were more likely than non-searchers (35%) to have remained in face-to-face contact with their birth mothers.
- Five years or more after the initial reunion and in cases where the adopted person was still in contact with their birth mother (searchers only), 67% were in weekly contact with their adoptive mother compared to 24% who were in weekly contact with their birth mother.
- Contact over time and at any point in time was more likely to be more robust, sustained and frequent with adoptive parents than birth parents. Contact with adoptive parents was also more likely to be more robust for non-searchers than searchers. For most adopted people, parent–child relationships established in childhood appear to be more durable than those formed in adulthood.

CHAPTER 14

The Reunion Experience: Impact and Evaluation

In all, 255 searchers established some form of direct contact with one or more of their birth relatives. Seventy non-searchers approached by a birth relative agreed to have some form of contact with them. Both searchers and non-searchers were asked to review and comment on the outcome of the contact and reunion experience. People's reunion experiences are examined in the following five areas:

- Emotional impact
- Family relationships
- Impact on self, identity and wellbeing
- Overall evaluation of the reunion.

Emotional impact

Although many people said they found some of the feelings triggered by the reunion experience difficult, only a minority evaluated this negatively. So, for example, although 39% of both searchers and non-searchers said they found it hard to cope with the strong feelings generated by the contact, only 10% and 14% respectively felt that their emotional outlook had actually worsened. A minority of people (17% of searchers and 16% of non-searchers) reported feeling more angry as a result of the reunion. In most cases, people did not feel that the emotional impact of the reunion was either too great or too distressing.

No differences in emotional impact were detected between searchers and non-searchers, or those placed transracially and those not. However, women were significantly more likely than men to say that they found it hard to cope with the intensity of feelings triggered by the initial reunion (46% v 26%). They were also slightly more likely than men to say they felt more angry as a result of the contact (21% v 16%). Similarly, people who evaluated their adoption negatively and people classified as 'Alienated' in terms of their adoption experience were much more likely to say that as a result of the contact they (i) found it hard to cope with the intensity of their feelings, and (ii) felt more angry. People who had evaluated their adoption negatively were also more likely to report that their emotional outlook had worsened since the reunion. For example, 53% of the 'negative' evaluators said they found it hard to cope with the intensity of their feelings compared to only 29% of the 'positive' evaluators. And 35% of the negative group said they felt more angry since the contact compared to only 13% of the positive group.

Interestingly, it appears that people who experienced their adoption positively and felt integrated with their adoptive families were much less likely to report feeling emotionally upset as a result of their reunion. In contrast, people who either viewed their adoption negatively or felt a degree of alienation while they were growing up were at greater risk of both finding it hard to cope with the feelings triggered by the contact and for those feelings to be negative. Of course, we need to remember that about half of the adopted people sampled evaluated their adoption positively and only about a tenth viewed their experiences negatively. For the large majority of adopted people the reunion was therefore experienced as emotionally satisfying (71%).

Family relationships

Those who had experienced a reunion were asked about how it had impacted on relationships with both their birth and adoptive family.

BIRTH FAMILY

While around half of adopted people said that they felt 'at home' with their birth relatives, a quarter were not certain and a quarter were definite that they did not feel at home. Searchers were statistically more likely to say that they felt at home with their birth relatives than non-searchers (51% v 34%, $p < 0.03$). People placed transracially were less likely than those placed in same-race White families to feel at home with their birth relatives (23% v 54%, $p < 0.02$).

Searcher ANGELA
My birth mother has made me feel very welcome but I also know that she doesn't want me to get too involved so the fact I perhaps see her perhaps once or twice a year – birthdays and Christmas – I think that's the way she wants it. I've actually seen my step-sister, Sheila, two weeks ago. She came and spent the day with us and she said, 'Joan's still very, very undecided as to how far she wants this relationship to go ...' she's nearly 80 years old and I don't think she wants the rest of the family to know about me ... Meeting Sheila was lovely because she's warm, friendly and we have similar taste in clothes – the first time we met we were wearing something almost identical, which was lovely ... but two of my half-sisters don't want to meet me. They don't want anything to do with me – Joan told me that.

However, although half of adopted people said they did not feel at home with their birth family, this did not necessarily mean they felt like strangers. Only 21% of people said that actually felt like a stranger with their birth family. The only biographical grouping that showed a statistically higher rate of feeling like strangers were those who had been placed transracially, 35% of whom felt like strangers with their birth relatives compared to 19% of those who had same-race placements.

ADOPTIVE FAMILY

The majority (60%) of both searchers and non-searchers said they felt more at home with their adoptive family. Thirteen per cent said they were not certain, leaving 27% who did not agree that they felt more at home with their adoptive family. The adopted people most likely to say they felt more at home with their adoptive family were those who had evaluated their adoption positively (76%) and those whose adoption experience was classified as Integrated (70%).

Searcher SUSIE

As far as a relationship is concerned, it's me really, because she [birth mother] would have more involvement in my life. She would like to be – not a mum because she knows that she would never be my mum now. She'd like more involvement ... and although Wendy's my blood mother, she's not my mum. My mum is Jean, because she's always been there for me, she's always picked me up when I've been down, looked after me when I've been ill. So that's what you call a mum. Not some-body that's actually had you, given birth to you. So, I see her [birth mother] once every six to nine months and she phones me about once a month. I feel part of my blood mother's family to a certain extent, and I fit in very easily, but I have my own family, like my parents, my brothers and I feel part of that ... I've had 40-odd years with my mum and dad and my brothers and memories of holidays, Christmases and birthdays and bad times with them as well but we've all stuck together. I haven't had that with Wendy's family ... My loyalty is one hundred per cent with my family here. I couldn't have asked for a better life even if they were my blood mother and father.

Searcher TINA

As for my adoptive mother, she's been completely hopeless about the whole thing: 'I don't want to know about that bloody woman, why should I know about her, what's she ever done for you. Don't ever mention her name to me again.' And she's never asked about her. She's never wanted to see a photo of her and assumes that because she's blotted it out of her mind therefore I can't be seeing her again. As far as she's concerned, it's a selfish thing – 'She gave you to me; she can't come back on the scene now.' I have such an appalling relationship with my adoptive mother anyway, it doesn't really matter ... I probably feel closer to my natural mother than I do to my mother, because three years of therapy and three years of Prozac and my bloody awful childhood has made me realise that, you know, I've got no relation-ship with my mother.

Those least likely to say they felt more at home with their adoptive families were those who had evaluated their adoption negatively (25%) and those whose adoption experience was classified as Alienated (31%). A similar picture emerged when people said whether or not they appreciated their adoptive families more since the contact and reunion. Fifty-four per cent of adopted people felt their appreciation had increased, with those evaluating their adoption positively (65%) and those whose adoption experience was classified as Integrated (60%) or Differentiated (63%) showing the highest rates of increased appreciation. Non-searchers were more likely than searchers to feel a conflict of loyalties between their adoptive and birth families (41% *v* 30%), though overall 55% of people said they felt no conflict of loyalties.

A few adopted people kept their two families apart; they had no wish for them to meet or connect. However, in many other cases, adoptive and birth parents did meet. Some parents got on extremely well, and continued to have contact. In other cases the meeting was more cautious and less relaxed.

Searcher BETH

My parents met my birth mother and my half-siblings. They stayed two or three hours and that was enough. They won't ever have to meet them again, but at least when I talk about them by name, they'll know who they are ... They got on fine but I don't think it would be a good idea to try to make them friends. They've only one thing in common at the end of the day and that's me.

Searcher BARRY

My mum and birth mum first of all had a talk on the phone, and that was quite emotional I think. I think mum was sort of thanking her for me and she was thanking mum for looking after me and bringing me up. And then the first Christmas my adoptive mum did a photo album, a selection of photographs, right from as a baby right the way through to an adult, and gave it to her as a Christmas present, which she's still got ... and they still keep in touch.

Impact on the self, identity and wellbeing

Searchers were more likely (55%) to say that they felt more relaxed after the contact than non-searchers (34%). Overall, 42% of people said that they felt they could relate better to others since they had met their birth relatives. This improvement in the quality of interpersonal relationships was statistically most pronounced in those classified as Differentiated (52%) and Alienated (57%) and least marked for those in the Integrated group (36%).

Searchers were also more likely than non-searchers to say that their self-esteem had improved since their contact (46% *v* 30%, $p < 0.03$). Adopted people classified as Alienated and Differentiated were more likely than those in the Integrated group to feel that their self-esteem had improved (55% *v* 53% *v* 35%, $p < 0.05$). The story is similar for raised security and feeling more complete as result of the contact. Searchers were significantly more likely than non-searchers to say that they felt more secure since the contact (51% v 31%, $p < 0.04$), and more 'complete as a person' (61% v 44%, $p < 0.05$). Those classified as Alienated in their adoption experience were also slightly more likely to say they felt more complete as a person than either those classified as Integrated or Differentiated (67% v 58% v 57%, A v I v D).

Most people felt that the contact affected them emotionally and psychologically. Only 25% of adopted people said they felt 'unchanged'. However, non-searchers were more likely to claim they did not feel different as a result of the contact (37% v 21%, $p < 0.02$). Men (32%) and those whose adoption experience was classified as Integrated (36%) were also more likely to say that they remained unchanged by the reunion: 46% of male searchers whose adoption experiences were classified as Integrated said they felt unchanged as a result of the contact.

Non-searcher BRIAN

I first met my brother Phil about six or seven years ago now ... Well, it was a big shock to the system meeting my older brother and then later on my even older brother Jim ... and next weekend I'm going to see my birth mother ... But in a way it's worked out, I'm glad it's happened because every single one of us gets on absolutely famously and have done from the very first instant we met and Phil gets on and thinks the world of my adoptive mum and dad ... but it's got to have an effect on me. For the majority of my life I've been quite happily going along, knowing I was adopted. It was no big deal. I was quite happy with my life. Then all of a sudden, without me asking for it, I got a whole damn family jumping out of the woodwork. And I don't know how it's affected me but it's like a hell of a lot to suddenly take on ... At one stage I thought I weren't handling it all and I was in half an inch of losing my wife and baby. I was pushing my parents away from me, inadvertently upsetting them. Some sort of insecurity in me, I think, or maybe I kept it inside me for too long and the bubble just burst and I had all the emotions all over again.

The contact also allowed the individual to say whether or not they felt more complete a person as a result. Strong statistical differences emerged between searchers and non-searchers: 61% of searchers compared to 44% of non-searchers said they more complete as a person as a result of the contact ($p < 0.001$). Similarly, those placed in White same-race placements were more likely than those placed transracially to say that they felt more complete as a person since they had met their birth relatives (63% v 44%, $p < 0.05$).

Searcher ANGELA

It just makes you feel that you belong to something because I used to very much feel as I was growing up, especially when I was going through traumatic times, like

I'd just been plonked on the earth – a mystery – no past at all that you can relate to – I'd constantly think, 'Why do I think this way, surely there's something else, someone who understands about this or that?' So you feel isolated and cut off. I'm sure that's one of the reasons why wanting to find birth parents is so important because it makes you have a beginning, middle and an end.

Overall evaluation of impact of contact and reunion

For most people, the contact and reunion experience was viewed positively. For example, the majority of both searchers (83%) and non-searchers (81%) concluded that the contact had answered important questions about their backgrounds. Similarly, 72% of searchers and 71% of non-searchers said that overall they felt satisfied with the contact.

All of this translated into most people feeling that overall their reunion had been a positive experience (85% of searchers and 72% of non-searchers). Proportionately, slightly fewer women (81%) than men (93%) felt positive ($p < 0.03$). Only 6% of searchers and 10% of non-searchers felt that it had not been a positive experience.

When asked to comment on how, if at all, their life had changed since they had been in contact with their birth relative, people's responses fell into four major categories (see Table 14.1).

Table 14.1 People's comments on their life changes since contact with a birth relative

	Searchers (%)	Non-searchers (%)
Improved sense of identity and wellbeing	51	36
Extension to family and busier social life	11	0
No change	24	40
Emotionally upsetting and negative experience	14	24
Total	100	100

The four categories are given below with quotes illustrating each.

Improved sense of identity and wellbeing (48% of searchers and non-searchers)

'Felt at peace.' 'Feel more content with myself as an individual.' 'Understand why I tick better and feel more complete.' 'I now feel that I belong.' 'Now have a positive self-identity.' 'Feel more alive and I enjoy every minute.' 'I know where I came from and why.' 'Fulfilled now that pieces of the jigsaw are in place.' 'Life is more full now I know my background and I feel better about myself.'

Searcher SUSIE

Well, it's changed my personality. I'm more laid back now. I'm not so frustrated. I don't go off in a tantrum, because all the questions that were unanswered as a child and teenager and right up until my late thirties, things that have been going on in my mind, the questions that I've wanted to ask – it's all been answered now ... I'm at ease; I feel more at ease within myself for knowing. My [adoptive] parents say I'm not so uptight any more!

Non-searcher MICHELLE

Knowing that she wanted me. Knowing that she never forgot about me. To find things about my background and who I look like, that was the main thing ... It really worked out really well and we really get on. I think I'm very lucky.

No change (27% of searchers and non-searchers)

'It has not changed my life.' 'I haven't changed.' 'Not changed life very much but happy to have met my birth mother, though now quite glad of the distance.'

Emotionally upsetting and negative experiences (16% of searchers and non-searchers)

'I feel more confused.' 'It's hard to ignore and I have never come to terms with it.' 'I feel angry, rejected and sad.' 'I feel more depressed and have tried to commit suicide.' 'I feel more insecure and unsure.' 'Feel more confused.' 'Bad enough being rejected but twice feels awful.' 'I feel insecure and find it difficult to trust people in close relationships.' 'Painful – I had a breakdown but some questions answered.' 'I'm confused emotionally.' 'Nervous breakdown, fallen out with adoptive parents and I still feel angry.' 'I have moments of feeling torn to shreds.'

Extension to family and busier social life (9% of searchers and non-searchers)

'A lot more new friends.' 'Have acquired an extended family.' 'Now have a wider circle of friends and acquaintances.' 'Now have a very busy social life.'

Summary

Most adopted people, irrespective of the quality or duration of the contact with their birth relatives, evaluated the reunion experience positively. Throughout, searchers were marginally more likely to assess the outcome as positive, though rates of satisfaction were high for both groups. Eighty-five per cent of searchers and 72% of non-searchers said that overall the reunion had been a positive experience. Nevertheless, 14% of searchers and nearly a quarter (24%) of non-searchers said that the contact and reunion experience had been emotionally upsetting and negative. Searchers (61%) were more likely than non-searchers (44%) to say that they felt 'more complete as a person' since the reunion.

Sixty per cent of adopted people (searchers and non-searchers) said that they felt more at home with their adoptive family. This did not necessarily mean that they felt uncomfortable with their birth family – indeed, about half of all adopted people who had achieved a reunion said they felt at home with their birth family. In cases where adoptive and birth parents met, the outcome was generally seen as successful. Seeing their two sets of parents together seemed to give many adopted people a deep sense of pleasure and satisfaction.

Transracially Placed Adopted People

Introduction

Knowledge and beliefs about the value and acceptability of placing children transracially vary according to the position and perspective of the observer. Research findings have painted an equivocal picture of transracial adoption in terms of outcome. In basic developmental terms, the broad psychosocial prospects of children placed transracially appear on a par with White children placed in same-race placements (Rushton and Minnis, 1997; Thoburn *et al.*, 2000; Howe, 1997). They do as well in the education system, they are no more likely than white adopted children to develop behavioural problems (all else being equal), and they develop equally good emotional and cognitive competences. However, there is acknowledgement that in terms of identity and cultural location, many people of Black African/Caribbean, Asian or mixed ethnicity who have been raised by White adoptive families do experience additional confusions and difficulties. Thoburn *et al.* (2000) suggest that people's personal biographies interact with their adoption and ethnic identities in ways which are both complex and dynamic.

Therapists, counsellors and post-adoption support workers report particular concerns around adjustment and identity associated with those who have been placed transracially. Although they work clinically with self-selecting populations, with the result that generalisations can only be made with caution, they do alert us to some of the potential disadvantages of being placed transracially. Adoption workers have been amongst the most outspoken against the wisdom of Black African/Caribbean or Asian children being raised by White families. Some have argued that across the psychosocial spectrum of development, transracial placements are damaging to the wellbeing of Black African/Caribbean, Asian and children of mixed ethnicity where one parent is not of White European origin.

The findings of the present study of the outcomes and experiences of adults placed transracially are complex and the results can be interpreted in a variety of ways. The major limitation of the study is the very small number of transracially placed adults in the non-searcher group. Of the 78 non-searchers who responded, only three (4%) experienced a transracial placement. Not only was this proportion half that of searchers (8%), but in absolute terms it meant that we were dealing with very low numbers of transracially placed non-searchers (three non-searchers compared with 32 searchers). In practice, this means that we cannot realistically use the non-searcher group as a comparison to see whether or not transracially placed people who search are in any way significantly different to those who do not. All the following findings are therefore based on an analysis of transracially placed searchers only. We simply do not know how representative they are of transracially placed people in general. It must therefore always be borne in mind that their experiences, motivations and characteristics might be true only of transracially placed people who search and might not apply to non-searchers.

Numbers and characteristics

Thirty-two adopted people who sought information about or wished to have contact with their birth relatives described themselves as either Black (16%) (i.e. Black British, Black African-Caribbean or Black African), Asian (3%), mixed Black ethnicity (Black African/Caribbean–White: 50%), or mixed Asian ethnicity (Asian–White: 31%). These 32 people represented 8% of the total sample of searchers. All but two of the 32 were placed with White adoptive parents. Of the two who were not placed with two White parents, one had an adoptive mother of mixed ethnicity and a White father, while the other had an adoptive father of mixed ethnicity and a White mother.

Of the 24 children of mixed ethnicity, in all cases their birth mother was White. The remaining eight people said that both their birth parents were either Black, Asian or of mixed ethnicity.

The distribution of the sexes was the same as that for same-race White placements with a ratio of 2:1 women to men (68% women, 32% men). Those who had been placed transracially were twice as likely as White same-race children to have been placed after the age of two (24% v 13%, $p < 0.05$). The mean age at placement was 10.8 months for White adopted people and 16.3 months for adopted people of Black, Asian and mixed ethnicity.

Table 15.1 Ethnicity and number of siblings born to the adopters

	0 (%)	1 (%)	2+ (%)
White adopted children	68	20	12
Black, Asian and mixed ethnicity	36	15	49

White $n = 360$; Black, Asian, mixed ethnicity $n = 32$; $p < 0.001$

Significant differences were found in the number and type of siblings between those who were transracially placed and those who were not. White adopted people in same-race placements had a mean number of siblings of 1.22. This figure more than doubled for those placed transracially who had a mean number of siblings of 2.68. In other words, it was much more likely for Black, Asian and mixed ethnicity children to be with families where there were not only siblings but more of them, particularly siblings who were the birth children of the adoptive parents (see Table 15.1). Indeed, the difference in the greater likelihood of a transracially placed child having at least two siblings who are the birth children of the adopters is highly significant (49% v 12%).

Telling and openness

In the total sample, 68% of all searchers said that they had always known, or certainly known from a very young age, that they were adopted. Transracially placed people were slightly more likely to report that they had always known or known from a young age that they were adopted (79%) than same-race placed White people (64%) but this difference did not reach statistical significance. Parents of those placed transracially also tended to be more open about the adoption. A number of respondents added wryly that being black in a White family meant that it would have been difficult for their parents to conceal the fact that they were adopted.

Similarly, those of Black, Asian or mixed ethnicity showed statistically higher rates of satisfaction with the level of information given in childhood by their adoptive parents (67%) than those of White European ethnicity (47%, $p < 0.05$).

Searcher KERRY
I used to have this little pink file – with my name on it ... I used to get it out quite a lot actually. I don't know how they got the information but there were a few bits of paper saying what my name was before I was adopted and what my mum was called and how old she was and how tall she was and what she was doing at the time and why she gave me up ... When I used to feel down, I just used to get it out and read it.

While less than 40% of those placed with same-race White families felt their parents were always open to discussion about their adoption, 67% of transracially placed adopted people of Black, Asian and mixed ethnicity said that their adoption was openly discussed ($p < 0.01$).

Searcher VALERIE
I didn't really have any strong feelings about the fact that I was adopted, because it seemed quite normal for me, that was my situation. I remember when I was a child when my father used to put me to bed I always used to ask 'tell me the story about me.' And he'd give me the story about me, in a fairy tale type of way. So I always knew I was adopted.

Adoption experience

ADOPTIVE FAMILY, EXTENDED FAMILY, THE OUTSIDE COMMUNITY AND FEELING DIFFERENT

Adopted people placed transracially were much more likely to say that they felt different to those around them while growing up. This was true both within and without the immediate adoptive family. Adoptive parents were said to be very supportive when individuals experienced racism, but people gradually realised that in practice there was little that parents could do to prevent it.

Searcher MELANIE

I didn't realise until I was older that other people didn't have the same upbringing. One thing I did think, I thought all Black kids came from homes because the other Black children that I saw around – a couple of Black boys were from Barnardo's, myself – it was only when I was seven or eight that I realised Black people came from Black families. I thought Black people lived in Africa or India and ones who lived over here were adopted. I used to read lots of book like A Little Princess *and* Orphan Annie *– all those books; anything that had displaced children in it. I used to identify with that.*

Searcher GARY

There was an incident when I went to primary school and then when I went to high school. I got into fights all the time, getting the cane week in, week out, but it was purely self-defence. And then it got so bad that it was seriously disrupting my education and so the headmaster asked to see my parents. But race wasn't discussed, even though it was the major thing for me ... I don't believe my parents are racist – not at all – but they found it difficult to get their heads round the fact that other people out there, even teachers, were racist. They had no understanding of racism or prejudices and the effects that has.

When asked to say whether or not they felt different to their adoptive family when growing up, adopted people who described their ethnicity as Black, Asian or mixed were much more likely than those who described themselves as White European to say that they did feel different (71% v 48%, $p < 0.01$). Similarly, 32% of those placed transracially felt they were treated differently by their adoptive extended family compared to 17% of White same-race children ($p < 0.05$).

Not surprisingly, physical differences were the most sharply felt. However, for some, more pervasive feelings of psychological difference began to be felt, formed more generally by an awareness that being Black in a White community was an experience that was beyond the comprehension of White parents, no matter how supportive and understanding they might be.

Outside the family, 29% of those who had been placed transracially compared to only 13% of those who had had White same-race placements said that they felt they had been treated differently by people in the community ($p < 0.01$). Nearly all Black, Asian and children of mixed ethnicity experienced racism on a regular basis during childhood. White adoptive parents tried to protect their children as best they could, but adopted people said it was difficult for their parents to fully understand what it was like to be on the receiving end of racist remarks and behaviour.

Searcher HEATHER

I think if I had been brought up in an area with Black people or the schools were mixed or something like that … I truly think that would have helped. Just to know that you walk down the street and you might bump into somebody that was the same colour as you. I could go for flipping weeks in the area my mum lived and not see any other Black people. And I think it's important for the parents that are going to adopt these children to have knowledge, an understanding, you know. Love is great but it's not everything. It really isn't everything because I had all the love I could possibly ask for but I'm not all right.

Ninety-three per cent of those placed transracially thought about what their birth relatives might look like when they were growing up, a slightly higher rate than those who placed in White same-race placements (85%, NS).

Searcher DEE

It became more difficult and more unpleasant around puberty and wanting to know what I would look like when I was older, wondering whether I had half-brothers and sisters because she [White birth mother] was only very young when she had me … wondering whether she'd told them about me, suspecting that she probably didn't, suspecting there was a great deal of shame around my existence and so on. And feeling like wanting to trace or find out something. I used to say to friends: 'I don't want to meet her. I just want to see her walking down the end of the street so I can see what she looks like, I've seen her – flesh and blood – and she's a reality.' That just chokes me up.

LOVE AND BEING LOVED, HAPPINESS AND BELONGING

Although being placed transracially certainly meant that people were more likely to report feeling different to their adoptive family while growing up, this feeling did not translate into an increased likelihood of feeling unhappy, unloved or negative about one's adoption.

Sixty-five per cent of all searchers said that they felt happy being adopted. Rates of happiness did not differ between those who were placed transracially and those who were not. Similarly, rates of feeling loved by and love for one's adoptive parents were unaffected by ethnicity.

However, being White and same-race placed showed a slight, non-statistical trend towards higher rates of feeling one belonged to one's adoptive family compared to those placed transracially (71% *v* 56%).

Searcher MELANIE
Most of the time I felt I belonged and other times I felt quite clearly that I wasn't part of the family. Physically, definitely physically. When I was younger it was just mainly the physical differences when I didn't feel I belonged, because my interests were different, my capabilities very different. I was singing and dancing and doing all those kind of things. My family, they were very White, blue-eyed, very pinky. Overweight a little bit – and what I can do is nothing that any of them can do.

Searcher DANNY
I felt I totally belonged. I mean from what my mother says to me now, for the first six months I was very, very quiet and I'd just sit in a corner and do what I wanted to do by myself, but after that I was totally integrated with the family ... My extended family accepted me fully. I think it helped the fact my brother was already adopted ... Yeah, I couldn't have been luckier, really, I couldn't have been.

The distribution of transracially adopted people varied significantly between the three adoption experience groups (searchers only). Of the 32 transracially placed people, 45% fell into the Alienated group (compared to 29% of White same-race), 34% into the Differentiated group (compared to 23% of White same-race), and 21% into the Integrated group (compared to 48% White same-race) ($p < 0.02$).

EVALUATION OF BEING ADOPTED
In the total sample of all searchers, 53% of searchers described their adoption experience as positive and 39% said they had mixed feelings. Ethnicity and being placed transracially did not significantly affect these rates with 50% saying they felt positive about their adoption and 43% reporting mixed feelings.

Like many other adopted people in this study, those who had been placed transracially talked about how being adopted meant that they had experienced different identities that sometimes conflicted, sometimes switched from one to the other, sometimes blurred, and sometimes were experienced simultaneously. Some people felt that this experience allowed them to blend easily in new situations. But it also meant that they were not always certain who they were. The sense of a permanent, solid core self was sometimes missing. The result for many was a feeling that the self was dichotomised – genealogically, socially, racially, culturally, sexually.

Searcher SOPHIE
I feel like the whole of me is a dichotomy, you know there are many dichotomies and

many dualities running through my life. I'm mixed race, I'm nearly ambidextrous, I am bisexual. I'm married now but had bisexual relationships a lot when I was younger, and having spoken to other adoptees I understand that it is not an uncommon thing because our sense of boundaries is very different, we are less shockable to a degree ... so there's always been this duality in me and so I felt I fitted in, but stuck out like a sore thumb ... I will refer to myself as a Black woman but I'm fifty-fifty and I'm no more Black than I am White. So I try to see myself, well I do see myself as a world citizen with all sorts of cultural and racial rhythms running through my veins ... Sometimes when I'm in completely Black settings, I feel very, very White which is the weirdest experience because I've not ever been treated like a White person in my regular community ... there was no sense of being accepted anywhere.

Reasons for contacting The Children's Society and reaction of adoptive parents

The age at first contact with the Society was significantly younger for those placed transracially (25.8 years *v* 31.2 years).

Adopted people were asked to give one *main* reason for contacting the Society as well as *all* the reasons. Curiosity about one's origins stands out as the most frequently given reason by searchers. The distribution of the frequency of *main* and *all* reasons given for contacting the Society did not vary with the ethnicity of the adopted person.

Searcher GARY
One of the things that caused me unrest was that I went into the acting profession and I was going to lots of castings and it's about stereotyping and time after time people were asking me what my blood was ... and I was cast as playing a lot of Latin parts and Brazilians and occasionally Asian parts. I wanted to find out once and for all, what my roots were and to clarify the rejection thing that had been in my head for a long time – there was a big rejection thing I wanted to clarify, the circumstances around me being put up for adoption.

In those cases where the adoptive parent was still alive, the majority of adopted people had told them that they had contacted the Society for further background information about their adoption. Those who had been placed transracially were as likely to tell their adoptive parents of the approach to the Society as those who had been in same-race placements. Of those adopted parents who were told of the search for information, the majority were said to have been understanding and supportive. Adoptive parents of those placed transracially reacted in similar ways and in similar proportions to those in same-race placements.

Contact and reunion

People who had been placed transracially were as likely as those who had been in same-race placements to be still in touch with their birth relative after five years or more since their first contact.

Searcher   JANET
It is now five years on and the relationships I have with my adoptive and birth family just seems to come into its own really – there's no kind of antagonism – the only problem I do have is when it's time to visit them all – on holidays – that's the only difficulty! Because we are spread at three corners of the country – this half-term I'm going down on Saturday to stay with my adoptive mum and then I'm coming back on Tuesday and then on Thursday I'm up to Manchester to stay with my birth sister and that's how – to get both of them in at times … I don't like to leave it too long between … because it's difficult to get down for weekends and things. But there's no jostling or vying for who I'm going to visit or when or who I'm going to visit. My sister is a big gain in my life which grows every day. I don't know where I would be without her now and I don't know how we managed to live without each other.

Those who had been in White same-race placements were more likely than those who had experienced transracial placements to say 'my birth relatives are just like me' (52% v 28%, $p < 0.05$). This was reflected in answer to questions about where the adopted person felt most 'at home'. Feeling at home with birth relatives was less likely to be reported by those who had been placed transracially (see Table 15.2). For example, 23% of people who had been in transracial placements said they definitely felt at home with their birth relatives compared to 54% of people who had White same-race placements.

Table 15.2 Ethnicity and feeling at home with birth relatives

| | Feel at home with birth relatives | | |
	Agree (%)	Uncertain (%)	Disagree (%)
White adopted people	54	24	22
Black, Asian, mixed ethnicity	23	36	41

White n = 220; Black, Asian, mixed ethnicity n = 22; $p < 0.02$

Sixty-five per cent of those placed transracially said they felt more at home with their adoptive family, a statistically similar rate to that reported by those who had been in White same-race placements (56%).

Searcher   HEATHER
I just find her [birth mother] really demanding at times. I don't want her to be my

mum, if anything, I just want her to be a friend … I do want her to be in my life, don't get me wrong, I do, but not in any form of – just a friend – there's no room for another mum anyway. I don't feel attached to her at all … I just had to be honest with her: 'You are just the woman that gave birth to me' … I could be completely wrong, but I think it's affected her. I'm not saying she's mad but when I first met her she drank … I have not seen her for a long time, must be coming up for a couple of months at least and I know she is going to say to me, 'Oh we must meet up soon.' I just think, 'Oh God,' because every single time there's some type of scenario; something happens and I just think, 'Oh for God's sake! Can't you just be normal for once.'

As a result of the reunion, those who had been transracially placed were statistically less certain whether the contact had helped them feel more complete as a person (see Table 15.3). For example, although 44% of people who had been placed transracially did agree that they felt more complete since the contact, the proportion rose to 63% for people who had been in White same-race placements.

Table 15.3 Ethnicity and feeling 'more complete as a person' since contact

	Feel 'more complete as a person'		
	Agree (%)	Uncertain (%)	Disagree (%)
White adopted people	63	18	20
Black, Asian, mixed ethnicity	44	39	17

White n = 220; Black, Asian, mixed ethnicity n = 22; $p < 0.04$

However, overall both those placed transracially and those placed same-racially described a high level of satisfaction with the outcome of their contact and reunion (60% v 72%). Seventy-three per cent of adopted people who had been placed transracially said that the reunion had been positive compared to 86% of those who had been in same-race placements, a non-significant difference.

Searcher ISOBEL

It's just a bonus having them [birth mother and half-sisters] up there and I do feel very at home up there. We love the same sort of things. We are very alike … We ring each other up, we send cards … She'll be someone I go and see two or three or times a year, but it might develop more over the years, you never know … I feel I now know myself better … Seeing where a lot of me comes from. Genes really. Because I do think you get a personality as well. However much my parents brought me up, I've definitely got my natural mother in me … Now I don't worry … well, I still worry a bit but I don't worry so much about who I am because I can see me in them a little bit. I don't feel like I'm totally different or whatever. I feel there's people a bit like me – same sort of understanding – sense of humour. Whatever it is, I can't pinpoint it, but when I go up there I feel at home. I can just bung the kettle on, put my feet up, have a fag, whereas at home I get relegated to the garden!

Summary

In many respects, adopted people who had been placed transracially reported similar experiences and outcomes to those who had been in White same-race placements. They were as likely to be positive or negative about their overall adoption experience, have similar motives for searching, to be still in contact or to have ceased contact with their birth relatives, and to feel positive about the outcome of the reunion.

However, a number of significant differences were observed across a range of measures. People who had been placed transracially were much more likely to have felt different to their adoptive families when growing up. Transracially adopted people were also more likely than those who had been in same-race placements to be classified as Alienated (45% v 29%) or Differentiated (34% v 23%) and less likely to be categorised as Integrated (21% v 48%) in terms of their adoption experience.

Issues of identity ran through many of the qualitative interviews with both those who had been placed transracially and those who had not. However, the intensity of these issues was often more pronounced amongst those who had been in transracial placements and less likely to have been resolved by the contact. This was reflected in transracially placed people being much more likely to begin their search at a younger age. But having established contact, they were then less likely to say that they felt that their birth relative were 'just like' them (28% v 52%) or that they felt 'at home' with their birth relatives (23% v 54%). As a result, adopted people who had been in a transracial placement and who had had a reunion with their birth relatives were less likely to say that they felt 'more complete as a person' since the contact (44% v 63%). Interpretation of these findings is not straightforward, but matters of identity and belonging do seem more difficult for many of those who had been placed transracially. Although their reunion was described in most cases as a positive and satisfactory experience, it was less likely to resolve many of the issues concerning identity and belonging.

CONCLUSION

Part IV reviews the main findings of the study into the differences between adopted people who search for birth relatives and those who do not. Interpretation of the findings casts light on the similarities and differences between social (adoptive) and biological parenting. More particularly, the findings contribute to the debate about adopted people's search for identity. A complex but coherent picture emerges of relationships between people's experience of being adopted, the search for identity and the long-term outcome of reunions with birth relatives. The findings and their interpretation have implications for policy and practice, not just in the field of adoption but in allied areas where identity issues and family history are of primary importance.

CHAPTER 16

Identity and Relationships: Interpretation of the Findings

Introduction

The experience of being raised by parents to whom you are not biologically related and then meeting your biological parents in adult life has always been a subject of great human interest. Novelists have repeatedly explored the psychological and social dynamics of the encounter. Scientists have studied the experience from a number of viewpoints ranging from genetics to child welfare policy, from developmental psychology to the social construction of identity. It seems that key matters to do with who we are and how we become who we are, are thrown into sharp relief by adoption. Those who have studied the experiences of adopted people who search and compared them with those who do not, have found themselves trying to untangle complex issues to do with identity and relationships. What they have found and what they have to say seems to speak beyond adoption.

Adoption has held such interest because it separates what is normally undivided. Biological parents, or close relatives, normally raise their children. When adoption occurs, children and two sets of parents are involved. So, what is the adopted adult's relationship with and interest in these two sets of parents? Is there something special, primitive, fundamentally biological about the blood tie? If so, what? And why? Do the ties formed in childhood endure through life? Are they stronger than the ties of blood? Why do most people continue to keep in close contact with their parents? Is it habit? Is it some deeply established psychological bond formed during the years of being nurtured by our parents? Or is it just the product of various social expectations and cultural norms determining what we feel it is right and proper to do?

So far, the answers to such questions have not been clear cut. Given the relatively small number of studies to date, this should not surprise us. Some have been small in scale. Others have only looked at particular aspects of the search and reunion process. Only a few have examined large numbers or explored the broader picture (see Schechter and Bertocci, 1990). Issues around identity and the desire to establish a full personal history appear to crop up in most findings, but beyond that the picture remains blurred. There is still disagreement about whether there are biographical and psychological differences between those who search and those who do not.

Similar questions about what motivates people to search have not been fully settled, although matters are beginning to clarify around issues of identity, connectedness and rejection. The nature of the relationship adopted people form with their birth relative appears to vary across studies. And the long-term outcome of reunions has barely been explored. The present study and its findings engage with most of the above questions and answers, sometimes supporting the findings of one study, sometimes those of another. It also adds a number of new observations and insights of its own, particularly findings that compare searchers with non-searchers, and about the long-term outcomes of reunions. This chapter reviews the present study's main findings, and offers its own interpretation or lends support to those made in previous studies.

Who searches?

A perennial question in search and reunion studies concerns whether or not adopted people who search are different in some way from those who do not search. Adopted adults who have searched for information about or sought contact with their birth relatives have been examined in terms of their biographical characteristics, adoption experience and psychosocial wellbeing. A weakness of many previous studies has been the lack of a comparison between those who do search and those who do not. The things that have been said to distinguish searchers from non-searchers have been deduced from analysing the characteristics of searchers alone. The absence of a comparison group of non-searchers has meant that it was difficult to know whether what was found in a group of searchers was true for all adopted people or just for those in that group. For example, it is difficult to interpret the finding that most searchers think about their birth mother a lot during adolescence without knowing whether non-searchers have similar thoughts. On its own, the finding lends itself to two contrasting interpretations: thinking about your birth mother as an adolescent makes it more likely that you will want to search, or, thinking about your birth mother in adolescence is something that most adopted people do and therefore it does not predict who does and does not search. Although the findings of many previous studies alert us to many of the possible dynamics of the search and reunion process, without a comparison group of non-searchers, it is difficult to interpret the findings unambiguously.

The present study benefited from the inclusion of a comparison group of non-searchers. Many of the questions posed by previous investigations were asked of both the searchers and non-searchers. However, although the non-searchers themselves had not initiated contact with a birth relative, they were different from other non-searchers inasmuch as they had been approached by a birth relative with a view to contact. The majority of non-searchers, once contacted, chose to have some form of relationship with the birth relative. In other words, at the time of the study they differed from other non-searchers in that they had had contact with a birth relative. It remains possible that answers to questions about their 'non-searching' state and condition might have been affected in some way by the contact. Nevertheless, with this proviso in mind, the present study provided an opportunity to compare 78 non-searching adopted people with 394 adopted people who did decide to search for one or more of their birth relatives.

GENDER

The study confirms the established finding that women are much more likely to search than men. Twice as many women contacted the Society for information as men. However, when the birth relative initiates the contact, male adopted people are as likely to be sought as female adopted people. Nevertheless, the female gender bias is maintained in that most birth relatives who initiate contact are birth mothers (71%). The figure for searching female birth relatives is likely to be still higher when birth siblings are taken into account. Twenty-three per cent of birth relative initiated contacts were made by siblings. Unfortunately the sex of the sibling in these cases was not obtained, but it would seem reasonable to assume that at least half would be birth sisters. Searching, whether by adopted people or birth relatives, was therefore a predominantly female activity. Something in the order of 70% of searching initiatives, whether by adopted people or their birth relatives, were made by women.

The assumption that women are more interested in identity and relationship issues than men is supported by the finding that there were more female than male searchers. However, the reasons given for searching by the men who did search were broadly similar to those given by women. Curiosity about origins, the need to know more about oneself, and the need for background information topped the list of both sexes. Identity issues therefore seemed to lie behind most people's desire to search, whether male or female. Interestingly, women were slightly more likely to give more reasons for searching than men. They were also more likely to begin their search at a younger age than men, with two and a half years difference between their mean ages at first contact with the Society. A number of interpretations of these gender differences suggest themselves:

- Adopted women are more likely to think about matters of identity, biology and family relationships which means that more women feel motivated to search.

- Adopted women and adopted men are equally likely to think about matters of identity, biology and family relationships, but women are more likely to see searching as a way of helping them explore these matters.

- Adopted women and adopted men are equally likely to think about matters of identity, biology and family relationships, and women and men are equally likely to see searching as a way of helping them explore these matters, but men are less likely to feel confident/skilled/determined enough to pursue searching as a course of action.

The younger age at which women are more likely to make contact with the Society may reflect the general observation that women mature earlier than men physically and emotionally. Psychological developments in these areas continue to appear earlier in women than men, even in adulthood. Therefore, searching, as a way of tackling issues about identity, biology and relationships, is likely to be contemplated by women at an earlier age than men. It is still the case that demographically women enter long-term partnerships and have their first child at a younger age than men, experiences that are likely to heighten further thoughts about identity, biology and family relationships. The slightly higher number of reasons given by women for contacting the Society for information suggests that women are more likely than men to have more thoughts about matters of identity, biology and relationships, and that they are more likely to act on them.

FAMILY COMPOSITION

No differences were found between searchers and non-searchers in terms of their family composition. It has been speculated that the presence of siblings born to the adoptive parents, particularly after the placement of the adopted child, might be a factor that motivates adopted people to search. The present study found no evidence to support this conjecture.

DISCLOSURE, TELLING AND OPENNESS

No differences were found between searchers and non-searchers in terms of the age when they remember first being told that they were adopted. Around 70% of both groups said they had always known or certainly been told before the age of five that they were adopted. Delays in telling in themselves therefore did not appear to distinguish the two groups. Relatively high proportions of both searchers (70%) and non-searchers (74%) said that they definitely or sometimes felt uncomfortable asking their adoptive parents for information about their birth families and origins. There were no statistical differences between the two groups, but the finding does add weight to the idea that being adopted and being an adopter involves extra psychosocial tasks that affect the parent–child relationship (Brodzinsky, 1987; Howe, 1998).

Further evidence to support the idea that issues around identity formation and the lack of information affect the majority of adoptions is noted in the finding that 56% of searchers and 61% of non-searchers said that their parents gave them either no or very little background information. The discomfort experienced when discussing one's adoption or the paucity of background information available are therefore not matters peculiar to searchers. It cannot simply be argued that problems around telling and openness in themselves increase the likelihood of an adopted person wanting to search. The majority of adopted people, whether they searched or not, appeared to experience difficulties around telling and disclosure.

Where differences between the two groups did occur, they are seen in their reaction to these states of affairs. Non-searchers were more likely to believe that their adoptive parents had given them all the information they had, even if it was not very much. They were also more likely to feel satisfied with the level of information they did receive. These differences between the groups are not startling, but there is a hint that non-searchers are generally more inclined to be accepting and satisfied with the knowledge they do receive. If this is true, whether or not one becomes a searcher depends not so much on the quantity or quality of information available, or even how well the person's adoptive parents handled the telling, but rather on the adopted person's reaction to the perceived deficits. Even so, this can only be a partial mechanism explaining why some adopted people search and others do not.

As always with probabilities, not all people obey the increased likelihood of behaving one way or the other. For example, there were adopted people who felt they were told everything, felt comfortable discussing matters with their parents and were satisfied with the amount of background information they were given who, nevertheless, went on to search. In contrast, there were other adopted people who were told little, felt uncomfortable approaching their parents and expressed dissatisfaction but who did not go on to search.

THINKING ABOUT BIRTH RELATIVES WHILE GROWING UP

Most adopted people said they thought about their birth relatives while growing up, particularly during adolescence. It is during adolescence that many of the psychological tasks peculiar to adoption interact with the more general task of identity formation. The adopted adolescence has to think about their genealogy, what it means to have been adopted, loss of the original parents and the sense of rejection that it conveys, the difference between biological and psychological parenting, and the concept of having more than one family (Triseliotis *et al.*, 1997, p. 35). However, non-searchers were more likely than searchers to say that they had never thought about their birth relatives while growing up. For example, in adolescence only 2% of searchers but 22% of non-searchers said they had never thought about their birth relatives. This difference between the two groups continued into adulthood. Barely 1% of searchers (those who sought specific background information and said they were not interested in contact) said that they never thought about their birth relatives. In contrast, 22% of non-searchers said that as adults they had never thought about their birth relatives prior to contact.

Adopted people who did think about their birth relatives while growing up generally thought about similar things. In particular, people wondered what their birth relatives looked like, whether they looked like them, what their personality might be like, whether they were alive or dead, and whether they had any other children (who would therefore be the siblings of the adopted person). Wondering what birth relatives might look like and whether one looked like them stand out as the questions most likely to be asked by adopted people. There is the missing experience of encountering 'likeness-to-self' that is accentuated by feelings of difference. This is a strong reminder that identity and a sense of biological connectedness feature strongly in the minds of many adopted people. These thoughts do not necessarily imply the wish to have a relationship with the birth relative; rather they imply a desire to know where one has come from and where one fits in. In the case of searchers at least, the need to know why they were given up for adoption when added to the need to know who they looked like, partially explains why birth mothers are the birth relative most likely to be sought initially.

Subtle but significant differences in what was thought about did occur between searchers and non-searchers. Searchers (70%) were much more likely than non-searchers (48%) to wonder why their birth parents placed them for adoption. More searchers (77%) than non-searchers (52%) wondered whether their birth relative would want to be contacted.

Adding the above two elements together suggests that (i) more searchers than non-searchers thought about their birth relatives, and (ii) searchers were more likely than non-searchers to think about why they were placed for adoption and wonder if their birth relative wished to be contacted. Although wondering what birth relatives looked like was the most frequently mentioned thought by both groups, bearing in mind that 22% of non-searchers said they had never thought about their birth relatives, this means that in absolute terms, significantly fewer non-searchers appear to have been thinking about their birth relatives in terms of these basic identity issues. For example, an estimated 80% of *all* searchers thought about what their birth relatives looked like while growing up compared to 65% of *all* non-searchers. Nearly 70% of *all* searchers wondered why they were placed for adoption compared to only 37% of *all* non-searchers.

It seems, therefore, that issues of identity (Who am I?) and self-worth (Why was I given up? Was I wanted and loved before I was given up?) are more likely to have been actively thought about by those who eventually decided to search than those who did not. These differences are slightly reduced when gender is taken into account. Women are more likely than men to think 'a lot' about their birth relatives. There are also proportionately more female searchers than non-searchers. However, even when gender is controlled, the differences between the two groups in terms of thinking about birth relatives, issues of identity and issues of self-worth remain significant.

These differences between searchers and non-searchers need to be borne in mind when we come to examine people's experiences of reunion. Adopted people's thoughts, needs and motivations not only appear to affect whether or not they are likely to search, but, as we shall see, they also appear to have some influence on the outcome of the search and contact process.

ADOPTION EXPERIENCE

Half of all searchers said they felt different to their adoptive family when they were growing up, a rate twice that of non-searchers. In fact, over two-thirds of all non-searchers said that they did not feel different to their adoptive family as children. Although female searchers (55%) were much more likely than male searchers (40%) to say they felt different, rates for both sexes in the search group remained higher than for those in the non-search group.

The presence of siblings born to the adopters shows only a non-significant trend towards feeling different. However, the *total* number of siblings who are the biological children of the adopters does have a modest effect. The mean number of siblings born to adoptive parents was higher in the group who felt different than in the group who did not. There is a slight increased risk, therefore, of feeling different to the adoptive family for children who join families where there are (or will be) higher numbers of children born to the adoptive parents. This difference holds up even when age of placement is taken into account.

Feelings of differences were most likely to be reported by searchers who had been placed transracially, 71% of whom said that they had experienced such feelings while growing up. Many of the differences experienced by children placed transracially are more obvious and direct. Feelings of dissonance will therefore be greater, particular in areas of skin colour, race and culture. In turn, this is likely to generate greater and possibly earlier pressure on identity formation and the need to feel genealogically connected. To some extent, these hypotheses are borne out by the findings. Amongst searchers, people placed transracially were more likely to be classified as Alienated and Differentiated in terms of their experience of adoption (although those placed transracially were as likely to evaluate their adoption positively as those in same-race placements). People placed transracially were significantly more likely to begin their search at a much younger age than those in same-race placements (25.8 years v 31.2 years). As we have observed, feeling different is not necessarily connoted as a negative thing by adopted people (although for some it is). Nevertheless, it is a feeling more likely to be strongly felt by searchers than non-searchers, and people placed transracially than those in same-race placements.

Although not so pronounced, searchers were also more likely than non-searchers to say they felt treated differently by their extended adoptive family. The figure was highest for searchers who had been placed transracially, with 32% saying that they felt they were treated differently by the extended family. For all groups who said their extended family treated them differently, the experience was mainly negative, with relatives typically discriminating in favour of blood relatives.

When asked to describe the quality of childhood relationships with their adoptive parents and family, the majority of adopted people evaluated the experience positively. However, the proportions and degrees of positive assessment were at significantly higher levels for non-searchers than searchers. For example, although 65% of searchers said they were happy about being adopted, this proportion rose to 85% for non-searchers; 77% of searchers said that they felt loved by their adoptive mothers compared to 91% of non-searchers. When asked if they felt they belonged in their adoptive families whilst growing up, 68% of searchers compared to 85% of non-searchers said that they did.

Adoption theorists have often felt that handling feelings of difference and feelings of belonging are key tasks for both adopted children and their parents. Being adopted is a relevant difference that has to be acknowledged. This is most clearly seen in the advice parents are given about telling and being open. However, it is important for all children to feel that they belong in their new families, and for them to feel fully integrated. There is an inevitable tension between these two tasks of adoption (Kirk, 1964; Brodzinsky, 1987). Telling and openness deal with issues of difference. Integration requires that both children and parents feel that they belong and are part of the same family. Failure to carry out these tasks well increases the chances of the adoption being experienced negatively. The present findings offer some support to this line of thinking.

We looked at the answers given by adopted people to two particular questions: Did you feel different to your adoptive family when you were growing up? Did you feel that you belonged in your adoptive family? Although various combinations of the answers given to these questions are possible, we used three in particular (which accounted for 89% of searchers and 94% of non-searchers) to explore issues of difference and belonging. Adopted people who did not feel different to their adoptive families and felt they belonged were classified as having an Integrated adoption experience. Those who did feel different but also felt they belonged were classified as having a Differentiated adoption experience. The third group included people who said they did feel different to their adoptive families and who also felt that they did not belong or had mixed feelings about belonging. This group was classified as having an Alienated adoption experience.

Seventy-one per cent of the eligible non-searchers were classified as Integrated compared to only 46% of the eligible searchers. In contrast, 30% of searchers were classified as Alienated compared to only 15% of non-searchers. These group classifications were also associated with a number of other adoption experiences. For example, an Alienated adoption experience was associated with lower rates of adult contact with adoptive parents, higher rates of thinking about birth relatives whilst growing up, and higher numbers of reasons for wanting to contact the Society.

In the case of searchers, adopted people classified as Integrated (78%) were much more likely to evaluate their adoption positively than either those classified as Differentiated (54%) or Alienated (18%). Non-searchers (90%) classified as Integrated were the most likely to evaluate their adoption positively.

These categories suggest that having an Integrated adoption experience not only makes the adopted person more likely to evaluate their adoption positively, but it is more likely to decrease their desire to search. Having an Alienated adoption experience decreases the chances of the adopted person evaluating their adoption positively and increases the likelihood of them searching. Again, the counter-trends have to be noted. Just under a half of all searchers were classified as Integrated. And a small number of non-searchers were classified as Alienated. Therefore, although these three adoption experience states have some predictive power, on there own they fail to account for all cases. The fact that over 40% of all searchers said that they did not feel different to and that they did belong in their adoptive families (the Integrated adoption experience) means that other motivating forces to search must have been operating in these cases.

Evaluating the experience of being adopted as an overall experience, non-searchers were more likely than searchers to give positive responses. For example, while 74% of non-searchers evaluated their adoption positively, the proportion dropped to 53% for searchers. Turned around, 47% of searchers said they had either mixed feelings or felt negative about their adoption compared to 26% of non-searchers. Although there are only a small number of studies which have looked at non-searchers, their findings lend support to the idea that non-searchers do seem more satisfied with their adoption experience with a tendency to have higher self-esteem (Aumend and Barrett, 1984; Reynolds *et al.*, 1976; Sobol and Cardiff, 1983). In the present study, those placed after the age of two showed decreased rates of feeling positive. On the other hand, the presence of siblings who were also adopted appeared to offer a small amount of protection against feeling negative.

These findings about people's experiences of being adopted lend some support to the idea that searchers are more likely to be people who feel some degree of ambivalence, negativity or dissatisfaction with their adoption. It certainly seems to be the case that significantly more searchers than non-searchers describe relationships with their adoptive family and their overall experience of being adopted with mixed or negative feelings. This finding suggests that feeling ambivalent or negative about one's adoption might be one factor that motivates some people to search.

However, as we have seen, having mixed or negative feelings about one's adoption cannot be the only factor in the searching equation. Even though searchers are more likely than non-searchers to express negative views, it still leaves around half of the group describing their experience as a positive one. Dissatisfaction cannot be the motivating force to search in these cases. Other motivating factors must be present, which may or may not interact with the dissatisfactions felt by some people.

The identification of a number of factors affecting who searches and who does not suggests that *the decision to search is unlikely to be the result of a single or simple psychological process*. Individual needs and motivations appear both varied and complex. Although the desire to search by those with an Alienated adoption experience might seem self-explanatory, the mechanisms that explain the motivation of those with a positive, Integrated experience seem less obvious. There does appear to be a distinction to be made between those who search on the basis of dissatisfaction with their adoption experience who are looking for both a fuller sense of self *and* a relationship, and those who describe their adoption experience as positive whose interest in searching appears to centre on issues of self and identity and not the need to develop an alternative filial relationship with a birth parent.

Why search? Reasons for searching and not searching

It is now recognised by most adoption theorists that adoption is not a static condition, but a dynamic life-long process. Throughout childhood, adopted people are presented with a number of 'opposing, irreconcilable dilemmas' (Schechter and Bertocci, 1990, p. 63). They are told that they were born to different parents who cannot be contacted for reasons that are often difficult for young children to understand. Adoptive parents appear to have only the scantiest of knowledge about these mysterious but clearly significant people. And when information is given, it is often rendered in a rosy or sanitised way that does not quite square with being given up for adoption. Heredity and environment also impinge on the adopted person's experience in direct and regular ways. Physical and psychological differences between oneself and one's adoptive family might be just too stark to ignore. The search for likeness is very strong in many adopted people.

Dissonance is said to occur when there is not a clear, obvious or plausible fit between key elements in one's life. Dissonance is particularly likely to crop up repeatedly in the lives and experiences of people who have been adopted: parents who give birth to you and parents who choose you; the possibility (or impossibility) of drawing not one but two family trees; being told that your birth mother placed you for adoption because she loved you and knowing that people who love you do not reject and abandon you. The search is therefore seen, according to Schechter and Bertocci (1990, p. 81), as 'an attempt to reconcile cognitive dissonances, to bring order out of a sense of chaos, to gain active control over forces to which the adoptee has had to respond in the past.'

Schechter and Bertocci (1990, p. 63) wonder what it is in a certain percentage of adopted people that compels them to search for birth information or the birth parents themselves. Is it a reaction to a bad adoption experience? Is it an attempt to resolve feelings of loss and rejection? 'Or is there some yet-unexplained inner force compelling them to find someone who looks like them, feels like them, laughs like them, is artistic like them – a need to fill a void or give them a sense of completeness with a full familial history?' (p. 64). In short, is the need to search a response to external factors in their life experience (relationship with adoptive parents, feelings of social stigma etc.) or is it a response to internal forces (a desire for genealogical connectedness, a feeling of unresolved loss etc.)?

The three most frequently mentioned reasons for contacting the Society and conducting a search in the present study were:

- having a long-standing curiosity about origins (82%)
- needed to know more about myself (77%)
- need for background information (69%).

Although other triggers to search were mentioned, unlike the above three, none reached majority status. It seems that identity issues predominated in the desire to search, coupled with some need to know why one was placed for adoption (issues of self-worth). These quantitative observations are supported by the interviews. Most people talked about the need to have more information about themselves to help them feel more 'whole' or 'complete'. These findings agree with Bertocci and Schechter (1991, cited in Schechter and Bertocci, 1990, p. 70) who also observed that the desire to feel 'whole' and 'connected' was independent of the quality and evaluation of the adoption (also see Triseliotis, 1973; Pannor *et al.*, 1974; Depp, 1982). In the case of searchers, there appears to be a strong feeling that the self, prior to the search, is in some way incomplete. Information about whether looks and personality might have been inherited, and facts about birth families, the origin of mannerisms, weight at birth and a host of other self and identity matters were all keenly sought. What did not appear to be present in most cases was the desire to establish a relationship with a new set of parents or a new family.

These findings agree with the conclusions reached by Schechter and Bertocci (1990):

> The search therefore constitutes the adoptee's attempt to repair a sense of loss, relieve the sense of disadvantage, consolidate identity issues including body image and sexual identity, resolve cognitive dissonances, internalize locus of control, and satisfy the most fundamental need to experience human connectedness.
> (p. 89)

> On the basis of what we have learned about the strength of the desire to search and about its intrapsychic sources, we submit that the need to experience human connectedness through one's family of origin has innate (constitutional) origins in complex, interrelated sequences involving perception, cognition, emotion, and active response. In this sense the need for an internal sense of human connectedness meets the criteria of a drive state.
> (pp. 64–5)

The authors define a drive state as a genetically determined psychic system that when activated produces excitement and tension. Excitation of the system impels the individual to act, the goal of the action being to reduce the state of excitation. The absence of a sense of human connectedness in many adopted people becomes a psychologically consuming and energising force which ultimately can only be resolved by searching for birth information or meeting the birth parent. However, the presence of strong drive forces and powerful intrapsychic meanings must not be confused with psychopathology or clinical syndromes. They are normal and only receive strong expression in adopted people because there is an absence of human or genealogical connectedness.

As a result of gaining access to their adoption records, the majority of searchers (79%) said that they had received a lot of new information. Mirroring the reasons for searching in the first place, the most frequently mentioned benefits of receiving the new information were to do with increased knowledge about the self, the birth mother, early history and the reasons for being placed for adoption.

When non-searchers were asked why they had chosen not to approach the Society for background information, the main reasons involved feelings about the quality of relationship they had with their adoptive parents. In other words, although searchers appeared not to be looking for a new family relationship, non-searchers gave family relationship consequences as the main reasons for not searching. For example, 47% of non-searchers said that their adoptive parents were their 'real' parents, and 44% said they did not want to search fearing that it might upset their adoptive parents. Upsetting adoptive parents might well trigger old childhood feelings of anxiety that they might be rejected if they rock the boat. To search, though desired, might therefore lead to the loss of one's parents. A significant minority of non-searchers were worried they would not be emotionally strong enough to cope with the search process and its outcome. A significant minority (22%) said that they had no desire to learn more about their background.

These findings might be interpreted to mean that for most non-searchers, it is not a lack of any desire to search, it is more a fear that there might be adverse consequences for either the relationship with their adoptive parents or their own emotional stability. They have an *idea* of searching but decide against its *activation*. Partial support to this interpretation is given by the finding that 42% of non-searchers said they had actually thought about searching before the birth relative made their approach. Half of this group had gone so far as to take some very preliminary steps to see if and how they might locate their birth parents.

Upon closer examination, non-searchers, like searchers, appear not to be a homogeneous group in terms of their feelings and attitudes to the search process. Dividing them in a very rough and ready way suggests that around half of all non-searchers really did have no plans to search either because they had no curiosity, or they had a perfectly satisfactory relationship with their adoptive parents whom they had no wish to upset. The other half had contemplated searching, but had decided against it, possibly temporarily, mainly on the grounds that it might upset either their adoptive parents or themselves.

Although there is some evidence to support the suggestion that non-searchers are really just pre-searchers who will go on to search at some future date, the analysis offered here finds that this is only likely to be true for about half of all non-searchers. The other half show few signs that they had thought about searching. Indeed, around a fifth of this group refused to have any contact with the approaching birth relative.

The small number of non-searchers who refused contact raises issues to do with the right of birth relatives to initiate contact. Some members of this group, as well as other non-searchers who did agree to have contact, felt that birth relatives should not presume right of access to them or their adoptive parents. The request for contact, however delicately handled, was experienced as intrusive and unwelcome, an invasion of privacy that had no defence. In a few cases, the contact caused upset and anger. Some adopted people in this group wondered on what grounds the principle of privacy should, or indeed could be overridden by either birth relatives or agencies. Non-searchers who refused contact felt that the control of the contact process should lie entirely with the adopted person and that the Adoption Contact Register should be the vehicle that ensures that this is the case. The present study highlights the possible difficulties that can arise when the rights and needs of two parties conflict. The findings introduce some notes of caution into arguments for more relaxed and generalised levels of openness, access and contact.

Overall, searching appears to be mainly about identity issues and concerns about self-worth (Why was I given up? Was I wanted and loved before I was given up?). The main desire, therefore, was for autobiographical information, including wanting to know the reasons for being placed for adoption. It was thought that such information would 'complete the jigsaw'. About half of non-searchers experienced similar identity issues but anxieties about how the search process might affect their adoptive parents and their own emotional stability had inhibited plans to begin the process. Adopted people who felt no great need for further information were unlikely to have thought much about their birth relatives or had any desire to begin a search. Possibly around half of non-searchers fell into this definite no-search group. Nearly all of them said they did not feel different to their adoptive family, felt they belonged, and evaluated their adoption positively.

Conservatively, if about half of non-searchers and all searchers experience issues around identity and/or self-worth, then whatever proportion searchers are of the total population of adopted people, a majority of all adopted people must be experiencing these particular issues. For a majority of adopted people, questions of identity, genealogical connectedness, and the need to have the full-story appear to be endemic.

Contacting and being contacted by birth relatives

Of the searchers who managed to locate their birth relatives, 93% managed to have contact with at least one of them. Three-quarters of adopted people who decided to search found their birth mother. In practice, birth mothers often came with birth brothers and sisters, and sometimes maternal grandparents and extended family. Thus, if and when the birth mother was found, siblings and half-siblings would often be met in addition to the parent: 42% of all searchers said they had contact with both their birth mother and birth siblings. About a quarter of searchers found their birth fathers, and again this often entailed meeting brothers and sisters.

For most people, finding their birth relative was surprisingly easy and quick. For example, 41% of searchers found their birth mother within one month. By three months, 60% had been successful. Excluding those who had not managed to locate their birth relative and were still searching (the majority of whom were in the early stages of the search process at the time of the survey), only a small proportion of people who had located their birth relative failed to achieve a meaningful contact. Eight per cent of those who had successfully traced their birth mother attempted contact only to learn that she had already died. A similar story was told by 8% of those who had discovered the whereabouts of their birth fathers. Seven per cent of those who had located their birth relative were refused contact. The majority of these cases involved either the birth mother or birth father (who typically denied paternity).

Ninety per cent of non-searchers who were approached by a birth relative agreed to have some form of contact. The remaining 10% refused to have any form of communication with their birth relative. The birth relative most likely to make the approach was the birth mother (71%). However, it is worth noting that 23% of these birth relative initiated contacts were made by siblings.

Not surprisingly, once contact with the birth relative had been established, there was typically much activity – phone calls, meetings, visits to homes and other members of the family. Frequency of phone calls and visits was greatest in the first year. For example, 67% of searchers were having some form of contact with their birth mother at least once a month. However, in general, whatever the form of contact and with whichever birth relative, frequency of contact was more likely to be higher for searchers than non-searchers. This was particularly marked when it came to having face-to-face contact in the first year. In the case of birth mothers, searchers (96%) were more likely than non-searchers (61%) to be having face-to-face contact, whatever the frequency.

Adopted people reacted in a variety of ways when they first met their birth relative. People's descriptions of their feelings and the relationship they had on first contact were of four main types:

- felt like a friend
- there was an instant bond and connection
- felt like a stranger
- experienced emotional confusion.

Non-searchers (54%) were much more likely than searchers (37%) to say that during the initial contact they felt more like a friend. In contrast, searchers (29%) were more likely than non-searchers (11%) to say that they felt an instant bond and connection with the birth relative. Although only just under a third of searchers said they felt an instant bond, feeling socially and emotionally attracted to a person to whom one is genetically related was a powerful experience for many people. *Indeed, across all categories there was a high proportion of people who said they were transfixed by the looks, behaviour and mannerisms of the birth relative.* Meeting someone who looked like you and just staring at them, not remembering what was said, was for many people the overriding memory of the first contact.

The frequency of contact and the quality of the relationship with the birth relative over the years following the first reunion varied a great deal. The broad trends were for:

- a slight majority of both searchers and non-searchers still to be in contact with their birth relative after five years;
- a steady number of people to cease contact with their birth relative year on year;
- non-searchers to be more likely to cease contact with their birth relative than searchers;
- searchers who were still in contact to be more likely than non-searchers who were still in contact still to be having *face-to-face* contact with their birth relative;
- adopted people, whether or not they were still in contact with a birth relative, still to be in contact with their adoptive parents (if they were still alive);
- adopted people who were in contact with both their adoptive and birth parents to be more likely to have more frequent contact with their adoptive parents than their birth parents.

For example, 63% of searchers compared to 55% of non-searchers were still in contact with their birth mothers five years after the initial reunion. Seventy-five per cent of searchers compared to 50% of non-searchers were still in contact with a birth sibling five years after the initial reunion. Of those adopted people who were still in contact with both their adoptive mothers and birth mothers five years on, 67% were having at least weekly contact with their adoptive mother and 24% were having at least weekly contact with their birth mother.

These findings suggest that for most adopted people, reunion with a birth relative did not affect the strength of the relationship with their adoptive parents. In fact, 21% of searchers and 15% of non-searchers said that relationships with their adoptive parents had actually improved as a result of the contact. Only one in ten people said that the contact had put their relationship with their adoptive parents under some strain. The bonds formed in childhood therefore appear to be strong and durable. Measured crudely in terms of how long the relationship was sustained and the frequency of contact in adult life, *the adoptive parent–child relationship in most cases was more robust than the birth parent–child relationship*. Although the blood tie seems to have great importance in terms of identity, self-worth and self-understanding, its strengths are not necessarily greater than the socio-emotional ties established with parents during childhood.

However, to complicate this picture a little further, seeing more of one's adoptive parents did not necessarily mean that one did not feel 'at home' with one's birth family, or in some cases feel even more 'at home' with them. Complex feelings to do with duty, shared history, loyalty, love, class, culture, familiarity, attraction, genetic compatibility, and physical and psychological similarity influenced people's emotional relationships with both their adoptive and birth families. So, for example, although a half of searchers said they felt 'at home' with their birth family, only a third of non-searchers felt the same. When pushed to opt for feeling more comfortable in one setting than the other, 60% of both searchers and non-searchers said they felt more 'at home' with their adoptive family. This bias was even stronger in the case of people who had evaluated their adoption positively and those whose adoption experience was classified as Integrated. In contrast, those who had evaluated their adoption negatively (25%) or whose adoption experience was classified as Alienated (31%) did not agree that they felt more 'at home' with their adoptive family.

It is possible, therefore, that whereas identity/autobiographical needs might be the major or only motivating force to search in the case of adopted people who had a positive adoption experience, identity/autobiographical *and* relationship needs might be the forces at work in the case of those whose adoption experience was more negative. We shall hold on to this line of thought when we try to model the different search and reunion pathways taken by adopted people.

There is clearly a nature–nurture dynamic at work in the reunion process that must inform any interpretation of the findings. The results, again, suggest that rather than look for a single mechanism to explain contact patterns over the long-term, we might be alert to the possibilities of a complex interaction between people's adoption experiences and the psychosocial tasks associated with being adopted. Let us remind ourselves that non-searchers are people (i) who had chosen not to search, but (ii) when given the opportunity to meet a birth relative mostly decided to go ahead with the reunion, although (iii) in the event, they were more likely than searchers to be in less frequent contact or cease contact with their birth relative altogether. The different pre-reunion and post-reunion experiences of searchers and non-searchers provide some possible clues about how to prise open and reveal the dynamic relationship between issues of identity and understanding on the one hand, and parent–child relationships based on either nature (biology) or nurture (social experience) on the other.

The impact of the reunion experience

Whether or not the contact with the birth relative was short-lived and abrupt, or comfortable and long-lasting, most searchers and non-searchers said the reunion had been a positive experience. Rates of satisfaction tended to be marginally higher for searchers at 85% than non-searchers at 72%.

These high rates of satisfaction and positive evaluation, even in cases of rejection or where the relationship with the birth relative had ceased, are explained by examining which aspects of the contact and reunion experience were rated most highly. Over 80% of both searchers and non-searchers said that the contact had answered important questions about their backgrounds. Half of all searchers and a third of non-searchers said that they had an improved sense of identity and wellbeing as a result of the contact. People talked about feeling more complete; the 'missing bits' of their story had been found.

Men, non-searchers and those whose adoption experience was classified as Integrated were the most likely to say the experience had not changed them.

Although the broad picture is a positive one, it has to be noted that a significant minority of searchers (11%) and non-searchers (24%) felt the reunion experience had been upsetting and for some it was evaluated negatively.

Summary

A number of significant biographical and adoption experience differences were found between searchers and non-searchers. Searchers were more likely than non-searchers to have actively thought about issues of identity (Who am I?) and self-worth (Why was I given up? Was I wanted and loved before I was given up?), particularly during their adolescence. Women, who show a greater interest in matters of biology, identity and close relationships, are more likely than men to think 'a lot' about their birth relatives.

The findings lend some support to the idea that searchers are more likely to be people who have felt some ambivalence or dissatisfaction about being adopted. Significantly more searchers than non-searchers describe relationships with their adoptive family and their overall experience of being adopted with mixed or negative feelings. This suggests that feeling ambivalent or negative about one's adoption might be one factor that motivates some people to search. However, the decision to search appears to involve a complex interaction between a number of factors. A distinction might be made between those who search on the basis of dissatisfaction with their adoption experience who appear to be looking for both a fuller sense of self *and* a relationship, and those who describe their adoption experience as positive whose interest in searching appears more to do with issues of self and identity and not the need to develop an alternative filial relationship with a birth parent.

Adopted people who search are looking for answers to questions about who they might look like and why were given up for adoption. In contrast, half of non-searchers felt very satisfied with their adoption and said they had no curiosity about their origins or background. The other half of non-searchers did express some interest and curiosity but they worried that searching might seriously upset either their adoptive parents or themselves. Searchers and non-searchers who did have a reunion were typically intrigued by the looks and mannerisms of their birth relative. About five years after their initial reunion, around 50 to 60% of adopted people were still in contact with their birth relative, although searchers were slightly more likely than non-searchers still to be in touch. At all stages of the contact and reunion process, most adopted people maintained a higher rate of contact with their adoptive parents. The findings suggest that the social ties formed with parents during childhood tend to be more robust and durable than the ties with parents based solely on biology. However, whatever the outcome of adopted people's contact and reunions with their birth family, most people viewed the experience as worthwhile and not to be regretted. Contact and reunion experiences were good at helping people answer questions of identity. They did not necessarily imply the desire for, or achievement of a second or alternative family relationship.

CHAPTER 17

Roots, Reasons and Relationships: A Model of the Searching Process

Introduction

The two strongest themes in the search and reunion experience were the wish to develop a more complete sense of identity and the need to understand why one was placed for adoption. These two themes of 'roots' and 'reason' tap into (i) issues of self and the formation of identity; and (ii) feelings around loss, rejection and grief. Contact with a birth relative is for most people initially a means to an end. However, meeting someone who possesses (biologically, physically, historically, socially, emotionally) so much information about who you are inevitably entails the development of some kind of relationship, one which may be charged with powerful feelings. The search for identity is primary. The emergence of a relationship with the birth relative is a secondary achievement. The relationship may or may not last once the primary goal of the search process has been reached.

Identity refers to a stable sense of knowing who one is and what one values. Abend (1974, quoted in Schechter and Bertocci, 1990, p. 80) defines identity as 'a loosely organized set of conscious and preconscious self-representations that serve to define the individual in a variety of social contexts.' Personal identity, writes Grotevant (1997, p. 4), concerns 'interconnected issues of uniqueness and similarity.' The individual wonders in what ways they are different and unique, and in what elements they are like and connected to others. Identity continues to evolve over the lifespan. Identity forms and re-forms within the dynamic between self and context, difference and sameness, uniqueness and connectedness. Changes in the cognitive state of the self or the information found in the environment produce tension in the identity dynamic that needs to be resolved. For the adopted person, identity development:

> becomes increasingly complex as additional dimensions of 'differentness' from other family members are added, such as differences in physical appearance, ethnic or cultural origin, disabilities, or talents. The identity process also involves integrating other aspects of one's pre-adoption history, including experiences such as multiple foster placements or abuse.
>
> (Grotevant, 1997, p. 8)

Adopted people who search are seeking to consolidate their identity by filling in a whole range of missing elements to do with looks, origins, accounts and explanations. 'Depending on how well this [self-] structure is developed, individuals can feel whole and unique or confused and different' (Triseliotis *et al.*, 1997, p. 41). There is evidence from the present study and others that many of the dissonances experienced in adoption between nature and nurture, born and chosen, love and rejection, Black and White, belonging and difference do lead to a self which is experienced as divided, uncertain, incomplete, ambiguous, fluid, unanchored, or shifting. As Sophie (p. 150) said, 'I feel like the whole of me is a dichotomy, you know, there are many dichotomies and many dualities running through my life – I'm mixed race, I'm nearly ambidextrous, I am bi-sexual.' The search for self is part of the attempt to unite the fragmented pieces of experience, to ground what was previously drifting and loose.

Brodzinsky *et al.* (1992) prefer the term 'self' rather than identity. They recognise three types of self (Triseliotis *et al.*, 1997 p. 42):

- the *physical self* which includes awareness and feelings about one's own body: how it looks, feels, smells;
- the *psychological self* which includes personality, temperament, intelligence, emotional make-up;
- the *social self* which includes our awareness of ourselves in relation to others and our view of how others see us.

In terms of the present study, this is a very useful division. Differences experienced by adopted people, often strongly felt, can be easily categorised as physical, psychological and social. Not at all three differences need be experienced. An adopted individual can have a range of identities in the realms of the personal, genealogical, social, cultural and racial. The psychological need is to make these different aspects of the self fit and cohere into a connected whole. However, the experience of being adopted is inclined to split, confuse, deny and obfuscate many of these selves so that a sense of the self as whole and complete is more difficult to achieve. The more these different elements of the self remain in a state of dissonance, the more compelling the drive to search and the greater the need to experience human and genealogical connectedness. Different individuals either experience or are exposed to different quantities and qualities of these dissonant physical, psychological and social selves. Being transracially placed in a family where there are birth siblings is likely to amplify dissonance and increase the need to search for self, connectedness and identity. Children who have been physically matched with their adoptive parents, who are raised in families where there are other adopted children ('It's not just me') and where there is a good deal of background information available and delivered in a comfortable manner might feel the pressure to search is less immediate and might delay it until later.

A model of the search process

The present study has provided a range of findings that give further insights into the search and reunion experience, particularly in relation to the search for self.

The three most basic clusters of input variables for the search and reunion experience are that:

- significant differences exist between searchers and non-searchers in terms of their biographies and experiences of being adopted;
- these differences are not absolute: a significant minority of searchers are indistinguishable from the majority of non-searchers in terms of their biographies and experiences of being adopted;
- there are wide ranges of difference amongst searchers and to a lesser extent non-searchers in terms of their biographies and experiences of being adopted.

The two most basic clusters of outcome variables for the search and reunion experience are:

- most searchers and non-searchers expressed satisfaction and positive feelings about the search and reunion experience;
- over the medium to long term, the numbers of adopted people remaining in contact with their birth relative fell year on year so that after five years just over a half of searchers were still in contact and just under a half of non-searchers were still in contact.

Is it possible to develop a model that links inputs with outcomes? Such a model would need to represent why searchers search and non-searchers do not in terms of their observed differences. It would also need to explore the similarities and subtle differences between searchers and non-searchers, and between the various sub-groups within the searcher group in terms of reunion outcomes and length of contact with the birth relative.

The intensity of the wish to search, or the *motivation* to search, is taken to be a consequence of the intensity of feelings associated with the search for a wholeness and coherence of self, identity, understanding and improved wellbeing. However, in the light of the study's main findings, the intensity of these wishes and feelings is moderated by how the individual adopted person *evaluates* and *experiences their adoption*. In turn, a third level of *biographical and placement characteristics* influences the evaluation and adoption experience. Turned around, an individual's biographical and placement characteristics influence his or her evaluation and experience of being adopted. This moderates the universal task facing all adopted people of the search for self and identity completion, which may or may not include self-understanding, self-esteem and psychological adjustment to experiences of loss and rejection (see Figure 17.1)

The model holds that biographical and placement characteristics, and some of experiences of being adopted, independently affect whether or not an adopted person is likely to search. These same characteristics also affect whether an adopted person is likely to evaluate their adoption positively, with mixed feelings or negatively. Not surprisingly, therefore, adoption evaluation as a factor also affects a person's likelihood of searching. However, it should be noted that although certain biographical characteristics are statistically associated with certain types of adoption experience, in any one case it is not inevitable that the presence of a characteristic leads to a certain kind of adoption experience. Not all factors have been incorporated in Fig. 17.1; some of those with more modest effects have been omitted simply to avoid too much clutter in the diagram whose main purpose is to illustrate the principles of the model.

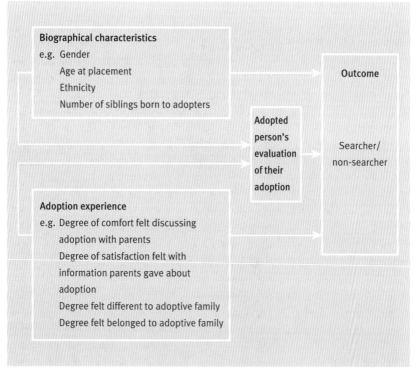

Fig. 17.1 Model of the search process.

The model accommodates the findings of previous studies, but gives them only partial power to explain whether or not an adopted person is likely to search. Each factor (e.g. number of siblings born to the adopters, gender etc.) weights how an adopted person is likely to evaluate their adoption, and whether they are likely to search. The weighting power of each factor varies. For example, we have observed that gender and feelings of difference have a strong influence on who is likely to search. The presence of other adopted siblings and age at placement also influence who is likely to search, but their effect is weaker.

In an individual case, the values of some factors might pull in different directions in terms of whether or not a person might decide to search. For example, men are less likely to search than women, but a particular man might have been placed transracially at an older age. Given these facts, predicting whether or not he searches is less clear-cut and more finely balanced.

In other cases, the values of particular factors might all be weighted in the same direction. For example, consider an adopted person who is female, felt unloved by her adoptive mother as a child, was placed at the age of four, and has three siblings who are the biological children of the adopters but no adopted brothers or sisters. The model would predict that such a person would be highly likely to search.

It will be apparent from the findings of this study that there is an association between an adopted person's biographical and placement characteristics and (i) their evaluation of being adopted, and (ii) whether or not they are likely to search. Perhaps not surprisingly, there is also an association between a person's evaluation of their adoption and whether or not they are likely to search. We have seen, for example, that people who evaluate their adoption with mixed feelings or negatively are more likely to search. Although it might be sufficient just to know a person's biographical and placement characteristics in order to predict whether or not they are likely to search, his or her evaluation does appear to have some independent effect on this decision. This means two things might be predicted from people's biographical and placement characteristics: how they might evaluate their adoption, and whether or not they are likely to search. Knowing how they evaluate their adoption allows us to predict one thing: whether or not they are likely to search. Because people's evaluation of their adoption has a degree of independence in predicting whether or not they are likely to search, combining biographical/placement characteristics with people's evaluation of their adoption generates the more powerful formula for predicting who might search and who might not.

For example, men in White same-race placements who had an Integrated adoption experience which they evaluated positively are less likely to search than women placed after the age of two who had a Differentiated adoption experience which they evaluated with mixed feelings.

The premise is that most, if not all, adopted people think about their identity – Who am I and where do I come from? Many also think about their value: Why was I placed for adoption? Was I wanted and loved before I was given up? The prime purpose of the search is to seek answers to these questions in order to resolve issues of identity and worth. But if the premise holds good, why are there non-searchers? The study identified a number of possible explanations, not necessarily mutually exclusive:

- non-searchers do think about issues of identity and worth but do not experience any great pressure or need to address them; their experience is one of feeling highly integrated into the life of their adoptive family about which they feel very positive;

- non-searchers' anxieties about upsetting their adoptive parents is sufficiently strong to suppress the desire to search;
- non-searchers have stronger fears about what a search may unearth.

These different explanations also suggest that non-searchers appear to be a heterogeneous group in terms of what inhibits or suppresses their decision to search. Although some have no great wish to search, others would like to search but feel that the emotional consequences for their parents or their own stability are too great. We have already recognised that searchers are a differentiated group in terms of why they choose to search. Some searchers are curious and seek genealogical connectedness, some want to know why they were placed for adoption, and some feel unhappy and dissatisfied with their adoption and the adopters.

Grotevant's (1997, p. 11) ideas lend support to this line of interpretation. He suggests that adopted people who construct a narrative that helps make sense of their adoptive status are more likely to feel that things are going well. Their narratives cohere and give meaning to the adoption experience. 'Such outcomes,' continues Grotevant (1997, p. 11), 'are presumably associated with psychological wellbeing and resilience. Conversely, the inability to construct a coherent narrative that confers meaning to the individual's life circumstances can be related to various forms of psychological distress.' Grotevant then describes a process that affects the identity development of adopted people. Initially there is little awareness and a lack of conflict about some of the tasks and tensions involved in being adopted. This is followed by 'sensitising experiences' in which the adopted person becomes aware of differences and what is implied in being adopted. This might lead to feelings of incongruence, confusion or disequilibration. The final stage sees the individual acknowledging, exploring, understanding and incorporating the new information into who they are and what it means to be adopted. The end result produces 'a more fully integrated sense of identity that incorporates adoptive status' (Grotevant, 1997, p. 16). The process can be repeated throughout the life-cycle as different issues and realisations appear. Each cycle of the identity quest deepens the sense of personal integration.

So, let us recap on what has been said so far. Thinking about origins and identity issues is likely to be a universal experience for most adopted people, although it comes in various strengths. The strength of the experience is likely to vary naturally in people, independently of the family circumstances in which they happen to find themselves. However, biographical and circumstantial characteristics interact with both the strong and weak versions of adopted people thinking about their origins and identity.

For example, strong curiosity and a drive for genealogical connectedness felt by a person in an adoptive family which historically has been open, relaxed and supportive is very likely to lead to a search. However, strong curiosity in a family which historically has not been comfortable talking about and reflecting on adoption might result in a decision not to search. Unhappy adoptive experiences, whether curiosity is naturally weak or strong, are likely to lead to a search for reasons more complex than simply to find out more about origins and background.

All of this rather tortuous reasoning is necessary if we are to make sense of the second element of the study, the outcomes of contact and reunion, particularly over the long term.

Modelling reunion outcome experiences and patterns of contact over the long term

The main reunion outcome findings are:

- the large majority of adopted people, whether searchers or non-searchers, felt that receiving new information and having a reunion with a birth relative was a positive and worthwhile experience, and had answered important questions about their backgrounds;
- searchers were more likely than non-searchers to review the overall experience as positive, and to say they felt more complete as a person;
- people whose adoption experience was classified as Alienated reported the greatest change and felt the biggest improvements in self-esteem, the quality of their personal relationships, and feeling more complete as a person;
- although there was a steady fall in the numbers of people remaining in contact with their birth relative, searchers were more likely to remain in contact than non-searchers over the long term, particularly face-to-face contact;
- (i) non-searchers were more likely than searchers, (ii) those who had evaluated their adoption positively were more likely than those who had not, and (iii) those whose adoption experience was classified as Integrated were more likely than those whose experiences were either Differentiated or Alienated, to say they felt more 'at home' with their adoptive family than their birth family.

Can these outcomes and their broad patterns be explained? Are there connections between initial motivations to search and outcomes? Can exceptions to the rule be explained? What are the differences between those who cease and those who maintain contact with their birth relatives?

We have found that both searchers and non-searchers felt that receiving new information about their origins and background was a positive experience that helped answer important questions. This helps confirm the thesis that the search for identity and self-completion is a fundamentally important task for most adopted people. Information received might include details about the birth family, who looks like who, medical history, and reasons for being placed for adoption. For many people, receipt of this information is sufficient and helps them complete their prime task – the search for self and identity. This is most likely in the case of those who evaluated their adoptions positively and had an Integrated adoption experience. This might also explain why people in this group are more likely to say that they continue to feel more 'at home' with their adoptive family.

The findings also show that non-searchers are more likely to evaluate their adoptions positively and to have had an Integrated experience, hence they are most likely to say they feel more 'at home' with their adoptive families and least likely to say they felt 'at home' with their birth family, even though they might have rated the contact experience positively. This line of reasoning also explains why, once having received background information, non-searchers are more likely than searchers to cease contact with their birth relative. They are not particularly looking for another parent–child or family–child relationship.

Adopted people who felt unhappy in their adoption, and who felt that they were different and did not belong, might be looking for some kind of more meaningful relationship with their birth family. They might find that their need for background information is heightened by their unhappiness. Thus, they approach contact and reunion not only looking for information but also with the possibility of forming a birth parent–child or birth family–child relationship as an alternative one to the relationship they had with their adoptive parents and family. Some measure of support for this conjecture is provided by the findings. Adopted people who evaluated their adoptions negatively or whose adoption experience was classified as Alienated reported the greatest change and felt the biggest improvements in self-esteem, the quality of their personal relationships, and feeling more complete as a person. They were also less likely to say that they felt more 'at home' with their adoptive families after their reunion experience.

However, to complicate an already complicated picture even further, one final twist needs to be added to the findings and their interpretation. Over the long term, no differences were found between searchers who continued contact and those who ceased contact with their birth relatives in terms of their biographical and placement characteristics, how they evaluated their adoption, or how their adoption experience was classified. In other words, of those still in contact five years or more after their initial reunion, those who positively evaluated their adoption or who were classified as Integrated were as likely to be still in contact with their birth relative as those who negatively evaluated their adoption or who were classified as Alienated. The only group who were less likely to still be in contact after five years or more were those who had not set out to search in the first place – the non-searchers. However, even amongst non-searchers, 55% were still having some form of contact with their birth mothers after five years or more.

The establishment of a long-term relationship with a birth relative appears to be based on forces that operate with a degree of independence of the need to search for identity. The search for identity, worth and understanding catapults the adopted person into a relationship with the birth relative, but new forces seem to operate once the parties meet. These forces are only a little modified by the adopted person's earlier biographical and placement characteristics. To some extent, these new forces are the jokers in the reunion pack and their appearance, or not, cannot easily be predicted.

Some people, whether or not they evaluated their adoption positively or negatively, whether or not they started out as searchers or non-searchers, felt an instant bond with their birth relative. They could not explain the feeling, but the interest and attraction were experienced as powerful. There is no agreed explanation for this experience – other than to call it a drive for socio-genealogical connectedness – but promising evidence is emerging from behavioural genetics. People who are physically similar or who have similar personalities are more likely to be attracted to one another or to get on than those who have very different physical and psychological characteristics. If physical appearance, personality characteristics and temperamental traits have a high heritability (e.g. Plomin, 1994; Kagan, 1994; Loehlin, 1992; Wachs, 1992), when an adopted person meets a birth relative, they will be meeting someone who is more likely than a stranger to look like them, behave like them and react like them. This will increase feelings of attraction and compatibility, irrespective of the adopted person's biographical and placement history. This is a strong basis for a long-term relationship. This is also an argument for bringing a genetic perspective to the interpretation of reunion outcomes.

These feelings and relationships operate independently of the relationship adopted people have with their adoptive parents and family. It is perfectly possible, and not at all unusual, for many adopted people to be having good long-term relationships with both their adoptive and biological parents. In the most rewarding outcomes, adoptive and birth parents also meet, and they too establish a friendly relationship, much to the delight and pleasure of the adopted person. On the other hand, if adopted people feel 'at home' with their birth relatives and their relationship with their adoptive parents has been poor, then they are likely not only to continue seeing their birth relatives but also to cease or decrease their relationship with their adoptive parents. Although the study did find examples of this outcome, they were relatively few in number. Adopted people whose adoptive parents had died found no difficulty keeping in contact with birth relatives with whom they got on. In contrast, the absence of any strong feelings of attraction to or similarity with birth relatives was likely to mean that once the search for identity had been satisfied, the relationship petered out and often ceased altogether.

However, more generally, adopted people's relationships with their adoptive parents were not only much more likely than relationships with their birth relatives to continue over the long term, they were also more likely to be conducted with greater intensity (measured in terms of frequency of contact, and frequency of face-to-face contact). Explanations for these findings rest on the embeddedness and durability of attachment relationships formed in childhood with primary caregivers. A rich and dense matrix of emotional and social bonds form between children and their parents throughout childhood. Families also share histories, class, culture, expectations and a vast range of experiences that not only play a large part in shaping the psychological make-up of individual family members, but also connect and embed them in the same, shared narrative and psychosocial universe. This is a very strong basis for a long-term relationship. This is also an argument for retaining an environmental/ experiential perspective when interpreting reunion outcomes.

Given a positive adoption experience and given feelings of attraction to and compatibility with the birth relative, and all else being equal, adopted people are likely to maintain a relationship with both their adoptive and birth families. However, the relationship with the adoptive family is more likely to be conducted on a more frequent and familiar basis. This balance suggests that early environmental experience (nurture) has the edge on genetic ties (nature) in terms of filial relationships, their frequency and sustainability. Nevertheless, there is no getting away from the fact that the pull of the biological tie remains present and strong in many cases. That so many people choose to meet up with 'relative strangers' in adult life and then get on with them so well for so long does suggest that something is going on above and beyond chance or social convention.

The explanation of who forms a long-lasting relationship with birth relatives and who does not is unlikely to be either one of either nature or nurture, but rather one of nature and nurture in some elaborate interplay.

The adult adopted person therefore brings to the reunion (i) physical and psychological characteristics derived from their genes, (ii) psychological and social characteristics derived from their environment and upbringing, and (iii) a range of psychosocial needs and tasks to do with being adopted. The interaction between these three elements influences both the approach to and outcome of the reunion. However, birth relatives also bring their own histories and personalities to the reunion. They, too, will have their own views, needs and feelings about the adoption, depending on whether they are a birth mother, father or sibling. In other words, just as the adopted person brings to the reunion a complex psychosocial agenda, so does the birth relative, particularly the birth mother.

It is not possible to map all the permutations that might exist when these two agendas meet. Personalities, class, culture, race, unresolved feelings of loss, and issues of identity and understanding all come into play. Genetic compatibility and attraction is a powerful force in many cases, but may be dampened by lack of a shared history or a difference in class and culture. 'We had nothing in common,' is a typical closing statement in these cases.

One of the more common reasons given by adopted people for ending the relationship was that the psychological needs and demands of the birth relative were too great. In cases where the main need of the adopted person was to search for and complete their identity, and the main need of the birth parent was to re-establish a filial relationship or sort out personal problems, tensions often occurred. Having satisfied their identity needs, and finding no basis for a relationship, adopted people in these cases would end the contact. Typical comments by adopted people included: 'Emotionally draining; for her benefit not mine'; and 'She needed a family and I didn't need another mother.'

However, in cases where there was compatibility, and where the pressures on both sides were not too great or oppressive, where the relationship was not too forced, and where understanding developed, a long-term relationship was likely to develop. For most adopted people, the relationship was a secondary gain. It was not what they were looking for initially, but if it happened it was valued. It rarely affected people's relationship with their adoptive parents. Indeed, just over half of all adopted people who had achieved a reunion said that it had made them appreciate their adoptive families more.

Conclusion

The study found that most adopted people thought about their birth relatives. Issues around identity and a search for self were common. There was in the mind of the majority of adopted people the *idea* of searching for background information and the possibility of meeting birth relatives. However, whether or not the idea of a search and reunion turned into action depended on a range of factors. Some were internal or intrapsychic (gender, temperament, feeling different or not, feeling that one did or did not belong, feeling positive or negative about being adopted). Others were external and circumstantial (age at placement, same-race or transracial placement, adoptive parents' openness and comfort with adoption, presence or not of birth and adoptive siblings). The interaction between these many internal and external factors affected whether or not a person was likely to search. There were broad, but discernible differences between those who decided to search and those who did not.

But whether people searched or were searched for, most felt the new information and the achievement of reunion had been a positive and satisfying experience. The self was said to feel more complete, more connected and less fractured. Nevertheless, the differences that marked searchers from non-searchers still echoed throughout these evaluations. Although most people did feel positive, searchers were slightly more likely than non-searchers to view the experience as self-enhancing. More non-searchers than searchers said that they felt the experience had left them unchanged.

Most people who had achieved a reunion with a birth relative did not regret the contact. Five years or more later, just over a half were likely to be still in some kind of contact, with slightly higher and more intense rates to be found amongst searchers than non-searchers. In cases where the adoptive parents were still alive, most adopted people were still having fairly regular and frequent contact. The study casts some light over the nature of filial relationships over the long term. Filial relationships established in childhood tend to endure into and throughout adulthood. Filial relationships based solely on biological ties in which children were not raised by their birth parents are less likely than those with adoptive parents to endure post-reunion. Although there is a powerful psychological interest in the birth relative that makes the idea of reunion compelling and the experience of contact highly emotional, the search for self does not necessarily translate into a long-term filial relationship. The dynamics of the nature–nurture interplay that reverberate through childhood continue to sound across the years into adulthood.

CHAPTER 18

Implications for Practice and Policy

Investigating people's experiences of being adopted and searching for their birth relatives has identified a number of important messages for current child care practice, not just in adoption, but also in areas where identity and information about family history are of primary importance. We conclude by discussing these messages and their implications for both adoption policy and practice. The findings suggest ways in which service provisions designed to meet the needs of adopted people and their relatives might be improved and delivered with greater awareness and sensitivity.

Information about origins and family history

The study has confirmed that having knowledge about one's origins and understanding the reasons for being placed for adoption are important stages of the adopted person's search for identity. To help achieve a fuller sense of identity and connectedness between the past and present, adopted people should be given information about their origins and family history. Information helps adopted people develop a greater understanding of themselves, who they are, and what makes them tick. For example, the provision of photographs of birth parents can help answer many adopted people's strong need to know who they look like. However, the study indicates that factual information, although important, may not be sufficient for everyone. People often need an actual physical meeting with their birth relative to satisfy their curiosity and need to complete their sense of identity and connectedness.

Current child care practice in the UK does recognise the importance of background information. Children who are adopted typically have a life-story book containing background information of their history with photographs of family members. Adopted children today are likely to receive more detailed information (including photographs) of their original family background and the reasons why they were placed for adoption.

Complete severance with the birth family is not taken lightly in contemporary adoptions. More often than not the possibility of contact, either through an annual letter-box system or personal meetings, is considered as part of the adoption plan. For adopted children who do have face-to-face contact, the need to search becomes unnecessary. For those who have indirect contact, the search process will inevitably be more straightforward.

Counselling adopted people

PROCESS OF SEARCHING

Most adopted people in the study valued the opportunity to receive counselling about their adoption records, plans to search, and desired reunion with a birth relative. Each stage of the search process can throw up practical and psychological difficulties. The support, knowledge and advice of counsellors can be invaluable at such times. Thoughts and feelings around origins and identity invariably arise. Many people want to know why they were given up for adoption, wondering whether it might say something about them or their parents. These can be emotionally demanding questions that require skilled, sensitive and supportive responses. Counsellors need to have a thorough understanding of what motivates people to search, what it feels like to begin a search, and how the search and reunion experience affects people. For many adopted people, the search provides an opportunity to connect the past with the present; to heal, in Verrier's (1995) evocative words, the 'primal wound' that opens when mother and baby are separated.

Counsellors need to explore with adopted people the reasons for setting out on a search, both in terms of how far their search is one for identity, and how much one of resolving feelings of loss and rejection. In practice, although both these basic reasons for searching are described by most people, the balance and effect of each is unique for each individual. Perhaps the majority of adopted people come to a birth record counselling interview having given a great deal of thought to the searching process. In contrast, a few people approach the task with very little emotional forethought or preparation. But whatever stage of reflection and anticipation the adopted person has reached, the counsellor has to help them explore and think about the issues that a search might raise, and the different outcomes that might follow a contact and reunion. Discussion and recognition of such things as motivation, feelings, hopes and fears allows people to reflect on, consider and even anticipate the nature of their journey. As a result they are less likely to be taken unawares or feel confused during the search and reunion process. With support and reflection, breakdowns of either the self or the new relationship are less likely. And when the search is for information only, it may help people avoid having expectations about themselves or their birth relative that are unrealistic.

Many non-searching adopted adults also achieved an improved sense of identity as a result of being searched for rather than doing the searching. In the majority of these cases, the unplanned contact brought new knowledge and understandings that were said to be helpful. Although birth relative initiated contacts remain a practically and ethically complex area, the benefits reported by large numbers of non-searchers offer new insights and add to the debate about whether or not birth relatives should have the right to search and seek contact.

OUTCOME OF THE SEARCH

It is not unusual for adopted people who are setting out on their search for a birth relative to imagine that the process will be long and difficult. In practice, nearly two-thirds of people found and had contact with their birth relative within three months of beginning their search. Adopted people in this study had access to information from agency records as well as agency advice and support about how to conduct a search for birth relatives. This may well have affected both the speed with which the adopted person located a birth relative and the actual outcome of the contact. Access to such support systems may help speed up the search process.

The Adoption Contact Register allows adopted people to record their wish for contact with a birth relative. However, what the Register does not do is automatically recommend that people receive counselling to help them consider the possible implications of searching for and having contact with a birth relative. The value placed by adopted people on the support and advice provided by post-adoption services does suggest that those seeking contact and reunion, whether facilitated by the Contact Register or adoption agency, do benefit from expert and informed counselling and that such services should be built into all routes that lead to contact on a routine basis.

Adopted people often imagine that even if they find their birth relative, they might be rejected by them. In practice, only 7% of those who approached a birth relative suffered an outright rejection. However, for this group of people, this often felt like a second rejection. It triggered difficult and upsetting feelings. Most rejected people described feeling disappointment, frustration and hurt. It is therefore important for post adoption workers to help searchers anticipate that being rejected is one possible outcome of the search process and discuss how best to handle it. There are a variety of reasons why birth relatives might refuse to see the adopted person. Few of them are to do with the searcher themselves. Rather, they concern the birth relative's own feelings and current circumstances. The re-appearance of the adopted child can provoke painful memories or threaten long-held secrets.

IMPACT OF THE CONTACT AND REUNION

Just over half of adopted people were still in touch with their birth relative five years after their initial reunion. It is important for successful searchers to think about how contact might affect not just themselves but also their birth relative, their birth family, their adoptive parents and their adoptive family. A few people decided to keep the contact secret but keeping such an emotionally powerful experience a secret can increase feelings of stress and may distort and damage close relationships. For other adopted people, meeting their birth relative was not the experience they had hoped for. They either began to withdraw from the relationship or decided to end it. A number of adopted people felt that the reunion failed to answer some of their questions or meet their emotional needs. This often led to feelings of anger and rejection. Contact can stir up deep, unresolved feelings about being adopted. Old issues of loss and abandonment can be reawakened. Experience has taught counsellors that it is often helpful, for both the adopted person and their birth relative, to be clear about their wishes and feelings. Communicating what is being thought and felt can prevent misunderstanding and unnecessary hurt.

Over the long term, maintaining relationships with birth relatives can be complex and demanding, joyful and rewarding, frustrating and annoying. For some, having invested so much in the search and reunion, it can be difficult to acknowledge disappointment, dissatisfaction and disinterest. Rather than renegotiate, some adopted people bring the relationship to an end. Access to skilled counselling and post-adoption services may help identify what is happening in the context of the reunion relationship. Rather than end the relationship abruptly or on a note of anger, people can be helped to form a more considered view so that whether the relationship ends or not, the adopted person is left feeling comfortable and positive about their decision. However, for many people, their reunion is experienced as happy and exhilarating. Relationships are said to be good, long-lasting and very satisfying. It is impossible to predict the kind of relationship any one adopted person might develop with their birth relative. People are encouraged to set off on their search with an open mind; a positive outlook, whatever the outcome; and the recognition that they have a lot of emotional and practical support on which to draw.

Intermediary services for birth relatives and work with non-searching adopted people

In the past decade a growing number of adoption agencies have acknowledged the need for consistency in the provision of intermediary services for birth relatives. This need has recently been endorsed by the Department of Health (forthcoming) in their guidance to local authorities and adoption agencies.

The Adoption Contact Register was set up to assist adopted people and birth relatives to register their interest in one another and their willingness for contact. The present study confirmed the long-held suspicion that many adopted people are unaware of the existence of the register: 75% of non-searchers said they had not heard of it. Research conducted by Mullender and Kearn (1997) also found that there was a lack of publicity for the register. If the Adoption Contact Register is to work as intended, much more thought must be given to publicising its existence and improving access to it so that it can be of value to both adopted people and their birth relatives.

Many birth relatives want to know what has happened to the adopted person. In many cases, birth relatives also want the adopted person to know that they would be willing and pleased to have contact if it was desired. Some agencies have created intermediary services somewhat tentatively, proceeding cautiously, waiting for more knowledge about how birth relative initiated contact affects non-searching adopted adults. Without presuming to resolve the ethical issues surrounding this, 76% of non-searchers approached on behalf of a birth relative in the present study said they felt that the agency had been right to inform them of the birth relative's enquiry, even though some of these people declined to have any form of contact with the enquiring birth relative. Nevertheless, this form of contact remains emotionally, morally and politically complex. Its impact on all three parties – the adopted person, the adoptive parents, and the birth relatives – is often difficult to predict. Although it can upset adoptive parents, this is no more likely than the adoptive parents of searchers feeling upset. While some adopted people may be prepared for an approach and have given the prospect some thought, others may be psychologically unprepared or have made very definite decisions about not wanting contact. The birth relative initiated approach can threaten adopted people's feelings of security and emotional equilibrium. Practitioners need to address these issues when they counsel birth relatives. Even though an adopted person may be pleased to hear of their birth relative's interest, they may not be ready for or feel the need to develop an ongoing relationship. Some adopted people stop all contact once they have received information that relates to their sense of self, identity and medical history.

Some agencies, practitioners and policy makers remain reluctant or unsure about providing intermediary services for birth relatives because of fears that it places the adopted person in a difficult emotional position, and that it invades the right to privacy presumed by some adopted people. A small minority (6%) of non-searching adopted people in the present study did feel strongly that birth relatives had no right to contact them. They said that their birth relative's enquiry had been an extremely unsettling, intrusive and unwelcome experience. These strongly held, albeit minority, views of non-searching adopted adults raise concerns about utilitarian arguments based on the idea that the views, wishes and outcome experiences of the majority should prevail over the rights and wishes of the minority. The difficult moral issues that surround practice in this area require clear and careful thought by practitioners and their agencies. The findings of the present study certainly provide some new facts and insights into the experiences of non-searchers, but as ever, what *is* the case cannot tell us what *ought* to be done. Certainly, questions of what is to be done are better answered when there are clear facts on which to draw. Nevertheless, the posing of such questions remains firmly in the realm of politics and moral judgement.

Possible ways forward include lobbying for new legislation which will not only acknowledge birth relatives' right to an intermediary but also inform adopted people and adoptive families about the service. Legislation will need to consider including a provision for those definitely not wanting an approach to make their wishes known. The findings of the study also suggest that the profile of the Adoption Contact Register needs to be much higher if the majority of adopted people are to become aware of its existence.

In practice, non-searchers appear almost as likely as searchers to stay in touch with their birth relative over the long term. For example, five years after their initial reunion, 55% of non-searchers, compared to 63% of searchers, were still in some form of contact with their birth mother. Even over the medium to long term, both searchers and non-searchers report that the relationship with the birth relative can still throw up problems and emotional surprises around the issues of loss and identity, rejection and belonging. It seems important that all those involved or affected by the reunion experience, at whatever stage, continue to have access to post-adoption counselling services. The life-long nature of the adoption process suggests that people ought to have access to supports and services that facilitate that process as and when needed. Searching, contact and the long-term effects of reunions can last right through adulthood.

The adoptive parents

One of the reassuring messages from the study, for both adoptive parents and adoption practitioners, is the continuing significance and durability for most adopted people of their relationship with their adoptive parents. It is not uncommon for adoption workers to hear adoptive parents express anxiety about what might happen if their son or daughter decided to embark on a search for birth relatives. As well as being concerned about the effects on the adopted person, they worry that it might destroy the relationship they have had with their son or daughter, that they might lose him or her to the birth mother. In the vast majority of cases, this fear is totally unfounded. In terms of frequency and intensity of contact, durability and affectivity, in most cases the adoptive parent–child relationship appears more robust than the biological parent–child relationship. These reassurances may enable adoptive parents to be supportive and understanding of their adopted son or daughter's need to search for identity and reunion.

For many adopted people, the search for their birth parent is more a search for identity and less a search for a relationship, although a relationship with a birth relative might be a secondary gain. In most cases, the contact poses little or no threat to the adoptive parent–child relationship. However, although this might be reassuring for adoptive parents, it presents birth parents with a more difficult emotional picture. If the prime needs of most adopted people are ones of identity (and not ones of relationship), this may not sit well with the prime needs of birth parents, which are much more likely to be ones of wanting to re-establish the filial relationship.

The study provides some evidence suggesting the more fragile nature of the birth parent–adopted child relationship. Five years after their initial reunion, 40 to 50% of adopted people were no longer in contact with their birth mother or birth father. Birth relatives who approach adopted people who are still relatively young (typically under 25 years), are more likely to be rejected or find the adopted person ceases contact after only a short time. Although the majority of adopted people who cease contact say they still got a lot out of the reunion in terms of new information and an improved sense of completeness, there are clearly hazards for birth relatives as well as adopted people. Counsellors will need to help birth relatives see where the adopted person is coming from in terms of how they approach contact and reunion. If the adopted person's prime needs are ones of identity, and those of the birth parent are ones primarily of renewed family relationships, there is potential for misunderstanding, conflict and disappointment. These are difficult matters on which to reflect in counselling, for both the adopted person and the birth parent, but the findings clearly point to a need for both parties to ponder their own as well as the other's emotional needs, psychological perspective and personal motivations.

Communication and openness

It appears that most adopted people – searchers and non-searchers – thought about their birth parents as they grew up, particularly during adolescence. However, it also seems that many adopted people felt uncomfortable asking questions about their origins and birth family. They were acutely aware of their adoptive parents' feelings. There was a concern not to cause them unnecessary hurt or upset by raising the subject of birth parents and the circumstances of their adoption. Strong feelings of loyalty to adoptive parents who had raised them were expressed. All of these elements appeared to inhibit asking questions about people and matters that were clearly of growing importance to adopted people as they progressed through childhood. Talking openly about their adoption therefore seemed less than easy for a surprising majority of adopted people, whether they were searchers or not.

Parents may feel that discussions about adoption are a reminder of their own and their child's adoptive status, and the fact that there are other significant people in the adopted child's life. The adopted person may feel inhibited about raising the subject and sharing the natural curiosity they may have about their birth parents and birth family, in case it is interpreted by the adoptive parents to mean that the adoptive family and experience has not been good enough. The situation that can often arise is one where the adopted person is keen to know, the adoptive parents are willing to tell, but communication breaks down or fails to begin because each believes the other is either reluctant to discuss or anxious about all matters to do with the adoption. What adoptive parents perhaps should not do is interpret a lack of questions about origins and background as necessarily meaning that there is no curiosity about birth family, background and beginnings.

The study mainly investigated the experience of adopted people who were adopted before the Children Act 1975. It therefore has to be recognised that a significant number of people in the study were probably brought up by adoptive parents who were encouraged by adoption agencies to raise their child as if s/he was their own 'birth' child and only answer questions if and when they were raised. Preparation of adoptive parents today accepts that parents should be encouraged to talk more openly with their children, to help them feel comfortable about asking questions and talking about their origins. A Department of Health funded initiative, Project 16–18 (Hundleby and Slade, 1999), consulted 58 adopted young people aged 14–21. The study showed that this climate of unease persists: many adopted children said they found it difficult to talk to their parents about their adoption and birth family. Similarly, Tizard (1977) and Craig (1991) showed that, even with the best of preparation, when it comes to the crunch a tiny proportion of adoptive parents will still find it difficult to go beyond the telling to the sharing of genealogical and other information. The indication is that even for contemporary adoptions more attention needs to be given to helping adoptive parents and adopted people feel more comfortable talking to one another about their adoption and their early history. Ideally, adopted people need to be given a clear and reassuring message from adoptive parents that talking about the past and birth relatives is something they can manage and with which they feel comfortable.

Adolescence is the time when most adopted people really begin to think very actively about their adoption – Why was I given up? Who do I look like? What does my birth mother look like? Do I have any birth brothers or sisters? This is a powerful reminder that the tasks of adoption are not only life long, but their nature and complexion change over time. 'Telling' and talking about being adopted can never be a one-off event, dealt with and tucked away during the safe years of early childhood. Of course, adolescence is a time when communication between parents and children is often difficult, whether or not adoption is a factor. All of this conspires to make the time when the fact of being adopted is perhaps most important to the adopted child also the most difficult to address, discuss and consider in an open, relaxed and supportive way. Post-adoption services should be available to provide information, guidance and advice to those parents and adopted adolescents who feel they might need it. Workshops might be held, local support groups run, personal counselling offered. Even though many parents and children may choose not to avail themselves of such services, the knowledge that they are there and that those who place children for adoption recognise that needs continue to exist and express themselves in different ways at different times, can be experienced as a source of support and reassurance.

Transracial adoption

The experience reported by adopted adults who were placed transracially reveals that this group faced additional challenges in their search for a fuller sense of identity. Again, it should be noted that the findings of the present study apply only to people placed transracially who decided to search. It is not possible to say how representative they are of all adopted people placed transracially.

Even when contact with a birth relative was achieved, transracially adopted people were less likely than people raised in same-race placements to feel a sense of wholeness. The reasons behind this are complex but in some cases it may be that the lack of racial and cultural input during childhood alienates them from their communities of origin. The act of complete separation from the family and culture of origin appears to create a tension that few found easy to resolve. This can compound feelings of not belonging. However, although this cultural split may partly explain the psychological difficulties experienced by some transracially placed people who met their birth relatives, it does not explain all cases. A significant proportion of those who were placed transracially were of mixed ethnicity. In many of these cases, the birth mother was white and the birth father was black. Thus, a meeting with a birth mother would not always be with someone whose cultural background was either Black or Asian. The dynamics of reunion and identity appear more complex in these cases.

Most transracially adopted people felt loved by their adoptive family. They reported good family experiences. They were as likely as same-race adopted people to evaluate their adoption positively. However, people placed transracially were significantly more likely than those placed in the same race to say that they felt different to their adoptive family. Again, although the findings send complex messages to policy makers and practitioners alike, issues around identity and connectedness, difference and wholeness point to the potential psychological benefits of same-race placements wherever and whenever possible.

Perhaps some of the starkest findings emerged when people of Black, Asian and mixed ethnicity talked about the racism and racial abuse they suffered throughout their childhood. However, although most people felt that their parents supported them as much as they could, practically as well as emotionally, it was often felt they lacked that deep knowledge of what it was like to be on the receiving end of regular and persistent racism, and therefore their help unavoidably lacked an element of understanding and effectiveness. Such reports raise issues about the ability of White adoptive parents to help their Black children cope with these very difficult and often painful social and psychological experiences. Many adopted people said they felt ill equipped to deal with such abuse. They did not tell their parents whom they felt could never fully understand or appreciate their position. This meant that many transracially adopted children often felt they had to struggle alone with the hurt and abuse.

All of this lends weight to those who argue that being transracially placed for adoption presents extra challenges for adopted children. Indeed, since the mid-

1980s it has been policy within the UK to only place children with families whose ethnic origin is similar to their own. However, recent Department of Health guidance issued to social service departments (Local Authority circular LAC (98) 20) recommends that children should not be kept waiting for placements because of their race. There is a delicate balance between meeting children's cultural, racial and identity needs on the one hand, and the developmental risks posed by delaying their permanent placement. If, for whatever reason, it is decided to place a child transracially, then the preparation of prospective adopters of children of a different race needs to be very clear about helping parents develop a much greater understanding of what it feels like to look very different from other family members. Family placement workers and adoptive parents will also need to explore how they can help the child to deal with the racism and hostility that they will inevitably encounter outside the home. Adoptive parents should also recognise the importance of giving their child the knowledge and experience of the culture from which they originated, and to this end all those in adoption must feel collectively responsible for generating resources and supportive services to help both parents and children to meet these fundamental needs.

Inter-country adoption

It was not until the early 1990s that inter-country adoption services and procedures started to develop. This was largely in response to concern about the numbers of children entering the UK from Romania where there had been no proper assessment or preparation of adoptive parents. In 1992, the Overseas Adoption Helpline was first established by the Department of Health and subsequently it became an independent charity. Its function is to provide information and advice to prospective adopters, adoptive families, adopted people from foreign countries and professionals working in inter-country adoption. It aims to promote good practice and to ensure that the interests of the child remain paramount.

The Hague Convention on the Protection of Children and Co-operation in Respect of Intercountry Adoption (1993) based in the 1989 UN Convention on the Rights of the Child, sets a framework of measures designed to protect children involved in inter-country adoption. It provides the basis for international cooperation between states of origin (of the children) and receiving states. The Adoption (Intercountry Aspects) Act 1999, once implemented, will provide the legal framework necessary for the UK to ratify the Hague Convention.

There continues to be some professional objection to inter-country adoption on both political and ethical grounds. Many of the concerns expressed about transracial adoptions apply with at least equal force to inter-country adoptions. However, whatever the objections, inter-country adoption is likely to remain an option available to those wishing to build or extend their family. Whilst there has been a general improvement in recent years in the procedures and practice of inter-country adoption, there is still much to be learned from people who have experienced a transracial placement. As reported in the present study, a significant proportion of people adopted transracially expressed strong feelings of difference, not belonging and alienation, a finding that has serious implications for people who seek to adopt a child from overseas. The experience of loss is endemic to being adopted. However, for children transposed from one country, culture and race to another, experiences of loss are both multiplied and amplified. Furthermore, many children adopted from abroad also lose, or never learn, the language of their country of origin. Clearly, many of the tasks involved in inter-country adoption are more complex and challenging than domestic adoption. We need to be sure that the interests of children adopted inter-country are as well guarded as those of a child adopted domestically.

The repeated message given by most adopted people is that rich, detailed and accurate background information about their origins is crucially important if they are to negotiate issues of identity successfully. However, the provision of such information is often said to be extremely difficult where inter-country adoptions are concerned. Some children were literally abandoned or no information was obtained from the mother when her child was received into care. In some countries, it is normal practice automatically to destroy the original records of children once they have been adopted. Although it is extremely difficult to ensure that such background information is routinely obtained, there are strong psychological and moral arguments for demanding that all those involved in the practice of inter-country adoptions are as active and assertive as possible in acquiring and recording as much detail as they can about birth parents, birth families, the reasons for the adoption, background material, and so on.

We need to remember that even when people have full information, they might still want to go on and search for their birth family. For inter-country adopted people who no longer speak the language of their country of origin, this can be an enormous challenge. Developing relationships with birth family members or their community of origin is a complex experience often made even more difficult by the barriers of language.

Our findings reveal some of the very strong needs and feelings around issues of race and identity expressed by many of those placed transracially. Ideally, prospective inter-country adopters might try to provide their adopted children with opportunities to learn what would have been their mother tongue. As parents, they would be recognising the importance for the child of being able to communicate should they decide to return to their country of birth, either to search for birth relatives or simply to visit. Adopters should be willing to maintain links with the child's country of birth and to be involved in parent support groups so that the child can be in touch with other children in a similar position to themselves. Taking such positive steps can help children adopted inter-country begin the complex journey of self-discovery.

Donor-assisted conception

Approximately 7500 children are now born each year as a result of all forms of licensed fertility treatment in the UK. Of these about 2500 are born as a result of treatment involving donated gametes and embryos, but unlike adopted or surrogate children they do not have any legal rights to identifying information about their origins. In other countries such as Sweden, Austria and New South Wales, Australia, access to identifying information is not denied.

It is perhaps difficult to understand why the rights of donor children differ so greatly from adopted children when it is likely that both share the same fundamental needs relating to identity and the desire for important background and medical information.

Article 8 (1) of the UN Convention on the Rights of the Child states, 'Respect the right of the child to preserve their identity including nationality, name and family relations as recognised by law without unlawful interference.' Article 7 of the UN Convention provides the child with the right ' as far as possible … to know … his parents'. But as Blyth (1998) points out, exercising this right hinges on the definition of 'parent':

> When the U.K. government ratified the Convention it stated its intention to restrict definition of the term 'parents' to persons who are treated as such in law. Since the Human Fertilisation and Embryology Act 1990 provides that a donor whose consent to donation has been properly obtained is not regarded in law as a parent of the child, it may be argued that Article 7 has no relevance to the issue of donor anonymity in the UK.

Whilst the UK practices in adoption reflect the importance of children having the right to know who their genetic parents are, this clearly is not the case for children born as a result of donated gametes. Many donor offspring children are unaware that one or both of their parents are not genetically related to them. People who need to use donated sperm or eggs to start a family have no obligation to tell the child (McWhinnie, 1996; also Cook *et al.*, 1995). The fact can remain secret as even legal documents, such as the birth certificate, are not required to show who the genetic parents are.

Donor-assisted conception is currently an adult-centred service provided by the medical profession. It does not appear to have addressed or incorporated the long-term needs of children into its practices (for examples of these needs, see Donor Conception Support Group of Australia Inc. 1997; also see Cook *et al.*, 1995).

The lessons learnt from the needs and experiences of adopted people appear to have had minimal influence on the attitudes and practices of donor-assisted conceptions and the legislation that allows it. The Human Fertilisation and Embryology Act 1990 (SS 27–29) gives children born as a result of donated gametes the right to apply at the age of 18 years to the Human Fertilisation and

Embryology Authority to ask whether a person they are proposing to marry is genetically related to them. However, this right is only given to children born from 1991 onwards. No identifying information is permitted. It is difficult to understand why in one situation the government recognises the importance of people having information about their origins, as reflected in adoption legislation and subsequently in the 1998 government's Health Select Committee enquiry into the welfare of former child migrants, while in another situation children's identity needs are largely ignored.

If adopted people and donor offspring have various shared needs around matters of identity and connectedness, as seems likely to be the case, the manner of meeting those needs is likely to require similar legislation and professional practices. For example, on a very practical level, it could be argued that couples who choose to have a child using donated gametes should be prepared in a similar way to prospective adopters about the tasks of parenting a child to whom one or both of them is genetically unrelated. More generally, the debate surrounding donor-assisted conceptions is now at a stage where the debate about openness and contact in adoption was at some twenty or thirty years ago. The relevance of the research findings in adoption identity and reunion studies to donor-assisted conceptions seems strong and compelling. It is hoped that some of the results of the present study might contribute to the discussions currently taking place about donor-assisted conception and the children it produces.

Conclusion

Adoption is a way of providing a family for children who are not able to remain in their family of origin. However, being adopted remains a life-long process. The issues inherent in adoption around difference and belonging repeatedly surface in the lives of adopted children, adoptive parents and birth parents. The overwhelming message for practitioners, policy makers and legislators is that appropriate high quality advice, support, information, mediation and counselling needs to be available for people as and when they need it, whatever stage of life they have reached. Such services need to be planned and delivered with skill, knowledge and sensitivity by appropriately trained people. Statutory services, voluntary agencies and self-help groups need to work together in partnership to provide a comprehensive service for all people affected by adoption.

Although adoption continues to evolve, with generally fewer babies and more older children (typically with complex histories of abuse and neglect) being placed, the underlying psychological needs peculiar to all adopted children, including those to do with identity and connectedness, remain the same. Many of the findings, interpretations and issues presented here are as relevant to the adoption practices of today as they are to those who are the living testimony of the adoption practices of yesterday.

References

Access to Birth Records (1976). Notes for Counsellors. London: HMSO.

Adamec, C. and Pierce, W.L. (1991) *The Encyclopedia of Adoption*. London: Facts on File Limited.

Anderson, R. S. (1988) 'Why adoptees search: motives and more.' *Child Welfare* **67** (1), Jan–Feb, pp. 15–19.

Aumend, S.A. and Barrett, M.C. (1984) 'Self concepts and attitudes towards adoption: a comparison of searching and nonsearching adult adoptees.' *Child Welfare* **63** (3) May–June, pp. 251–9.

Bertocci, D. and Schecter, M.D (1991) 'Adopted adults perception of their need to search: implications for clinical practice.' *Smith Collection of Studies in Social Work* **61** (2), pp. 179–96.

Blyth, E. (1998) 'Donor assisted conception and donor offspring rights to genetic origins information.' *International Journal of Children's Rights* **6** (3), pp. 237–53.

Bouchier, P., Lambert, L. and Triseliotis, J. (1991) *Parting with a Child for Adoption: The Mother's Perspective*. London: BAAF.

Boult, B. (1992) 'The complexity of adult adoptees' needs to search for their origins: a research finding.' *Social Work* **28** (1), pp. 13–18.

Brodzinsky, D. (1987). 'Adjustment to adoption: a psychosocial perspective.' *Clinical Psychological Review* 7, pp. 25–47.

Brodzinsky, D. and Schechter, M. (Eds) (1990) *The Psychology of Adoption*. New York: Oxford University Press.

Brodzinsky, D.M., Schechter, M.D. and Marantz Henig, R. (1992) *Being Adopted: The Lifelong Search for Self*. New York: Anchor Books.

Campbell, L., Silverman, P. and Patti, P. (1991) 'Reunions between adoptees and birth parents: the adoptees' experience.' *Social Work* **3**, pp. 329–35.

Carstens, C. and Jullia, M. (1995) 'Legal, policy and practice issues for intercountry adoption in the United States.' *Adoption and Fostering* **19** (4), pp. 26–33.

Cook, R., Golombok, S., Bish, A. and Murray, C. (1995) 'Disclosure of donor insemination: parental attitudes.' *American Journal of Orthopsychiatry* **65** (4), pp. 549–59.

Cowell, J., Crow, K. and Wilson, A. (1996) *Understanding Reunion: Connection and Complexity*. New South Wales: Post Adoption Resource Centre.

Craig, M. (1991) 'Adoption: not a big deal.' Unpublished report. Edinburgh: Scottish Adoption Society.

Day, C. and Leeding, A. (1980) *Access to Birth Records*. London: BAAF.

Department of Health (1990) *Inter-Departmental Review of Adoption Law*. London: HMSO.

Department of Health (1996) *Adoption – A Service for Children*, Adoption Bill. London: HMSO.

Department of Health (forthcoming) *Intermediary Services for Birth Relatives*. London: HMSO.

Department of Health Government White Paper (1993). *Adoption – the Future*. London: HMSO.

Depp, C.H. (1982) 'After reunion: perceptions of adult adoptees, adoptive parents, and birth parents.' *Child Welfare* **61**, pp. 115–119.

Donor Conception Support Group of Australia Inc. (1997) *Let the Offspring Speak: Discussions on Donor Conception*. Donor Conception Support Group of Australia Inc. Georges Hall: New South Wales.

Feast, J. (1992) 'Working in the adoption circle: outcomes of section 51 counselling.' *Adoption and Fostering* **16** (4), pp. 46–52.

Feast, J. and Howe, D. (1997) 'Adopted adults who search for background information and contact with birth relatives.' *Adoption and Fostering* **21** (2), pp. 8–15.

Feast, J. and Smith, J. (1993) 'Working on behalf of birth families – The Children's Society experience.' *Adoption and Fostering* **17** (2), pp. 33–40.

Feast, J. and Smith, J. (1995) 'Openness and opportunities – review of an intermediary service for birth relatives.' *Adoption and Fostering* **19** (3), pp. 17–23.

Feast, J., Marwood, M., Seabrook, S. and Webb, E. (1998). *Preparing for Reunion: Experiences from the Adoption Circle*. London: The Children's Society.

Feigelman, W. and Silverman, A. (1983) *Chosen Children: New Patterns of Adoptive Relationships*. New York: Praeger.

Freud, A. (1973) *Annual Report, January 1942. The Writings of Anna Freud*, Vol. 3. New York: International Universities Press.

Gediman, J.S. and Brown, L.P. (1991) *Birth Bond – Reunions between Birthparents and Adoptees*. Far Hills, NJ : New Horizon Press.

Gonyo, B. and Watson, K.W. (1988) 'Searching in adoption.' *Public Welfare* Winter, pp. 14–22.

Goffman, E. (1963) *Stigma: Notes on the Management of Spoiled Identity*. Englewood Cliffs, NJ : Prentice-Hall.

Greenberg, M. (1993) 'Post adoption reunion – are we entering uncharted territory?' *Adoption and Fostering* **17** (4), pp. 5–15.

Grotevant, H. (1997). 'Coming to terms with adoption: the construction of identity from adolescence into adulthood.' *Adoption Quarterly* **1** (1), pp. 3–27.

Haimes, E. and Timms, N. (1985) *Adoption, Identity, and Social Policy: The Search for Distant Relatives*. Aldershot: Gower.

Hill, M. (1991) 'Concepts of parenthood and their application to adoption.' *Adoption and Fostering* **15** (4), pp. 16–23.

Hollingsworth, L. (1998) 'Adoptee dissimilarity from the adoptive family: clinical practice and research implications.' *Child and Adolescent Social Work Journal* **15** (4), pp. 303–319.

Hoopes, J. (1990) 'Adoptions and identity formation.' In D. Brodzinsky and M. Schecter (eds) *The Psychology of Adoption*. New York: Oxford University Press.

Houghton Report (1972) *Report of the Departmental Committee on the Adoption of Children*. London: HMSO.

Howe, D. (1997) 'Parent reported problems in 211 adopted children: some risk and protective factors.' *Journal of Child Psychology and Psychiatry* 37, pp. 401–412.

Howe, D. (1998) *Patterns of Adoption: Nature, Nurture and Psychosocial Development*. Oxford: Blackwell Science.

Howe, D., Sawbridge, P. and Hinings, D. (1992) *Half a Million Women: Mothers who Lose their Children by Adoption*. London: Penguin Books (now available from and published by the Post Adoption Centre, Torriano Mews, London).

Hughes, B. and Logan, J. (1973) *The Hidden Dimension*. London: Mental Health Foundation.

Humphrey, M. and Humphrey, H. (1989) 'Damaged identity and the search for kinship in adult adoptees.' *British Journal of Medical Psychology* 62, pp. 301–309.

Hundleby, M. and Slade, J. (1999) *Project 16–18*. Nottingham: Catholic Children's Society.

Hurst Report (1954) *Report of the Departmental Committee on the Adoption of Children*. London: HMSO.

Iredale, S. (1997) *Reunions: True Stories of Adoptees' Meetings with their Birth Parents*. London: The Stationery Office.

Kagan, J. (1994) *Galen's Prophecy: Temperament in Human Nature*. London: Free Association Books.

Kirk, H. (1964) *Shared Fate: A Theory of Adoption and Mental Health*. New York: Free Press.

Kirton, D. (1995) *Race, Identity and the Politics of Adoption*. Working Paper 2, Centre for Adoption and Identity Studies. London: University of East London.

Kowal, K.A. and Schilling, K.M. (1985) 'Adoption through the eyes of adult adoptees.' *American Journal of Orthopsychiatry* 55, July, pp. 354–62.

Lichtenstein, T. (1996) *Child Welfare* 75 (1), Jan–Feb, pp. 61–72.

Lifton, B.J. (1979) *Lost and Found: The Adoption Experience*. New York: Dial Press.

Lifton, B.J. (1983) *Journey of the Adopted Self*. Oxford: Basic Books.

Loehlin, J. (1992) *Genes and Environment in Personality Development*. Newbury Park, CA: Sage.

March, K. (1995) 'Perception of adoption as a social stigma: Motivation for search and reunion.' *Journal of Marriage and the Family* 57, pp. 653–60.

McMillan, R. and Irving, G. (1994) *Heart of Reunion. Some Experiences of Reunion in Scotland*. Essex: Barnardo's.

McWhinnie, A.M. (1996) *Families – Following Assisted Conception: What Do We Want to Tell Our Children?* Dundee: Department of Social Work, University of Dundee.

Miall, C.E. (1996) 'The social construction of adoption; clinical and community perspectives.' *Family Relations* 45, Part. 3, pp. 309–317.

Moran, R.A. (1994) *Stages of Emotion: An Adult Adoptee's Postreunion Perspective*, pp. 249–260. Child Welfare League of America.

Mullender, A. and Kearn, S. (1997) *I'm Here Waiting*. London: BAAF.

Ngabonziza, D. (1988) 'Inter-country adoption: in whose interests?' *Adoption and Fostering* **12** (1), pp. 35–40.

Pacheco, F. and Eme, R. (1993) 'An outcome study of the reunion between adoptees and biological parents.' *Child Welfare* **72**, pp. 53–64.

Pannor, R., Baran, A. and Sorosky, A. (1974) 'Birth parents who relinquished babies for adoption revisited.' *Family Process* **17** (3), pp. 329–37.

Parish, A. and Cotton, P. (1989) *Original Thoughts: The View of Adult Adoptees and Birth Families Following Renewed Contact.* Essex: Barnardo's.

Plomin, R. (1994) *Genetics and Experience: The Interplay between Nature and Nurture.* Newbury Park, CA: Sage.

Post Adoption Centre (1990) *Feeding the Hungry Ghost.* London: Post Adoption Centre.

Pugh, G. (1999) *Unlocking the Past: The Impact of Access to Barnardo's Childcare Records.* Aldershot: Gower.

Raynor, L. (1980) *The Adopted Child Comes of Age.* London: Allen and Unwin.

Reynolds, W., Eisnitz, M., Chiappise, D. and Walsh, M. (1976). 'Personality factors differentiating searching and non-searching adoptees.' Paper presented at the 84th Annual Convention of the American Psychological Association, Washington, DC.

Rozenberg, K.F. and Groze, V. (1997) 'The impact of secrecy and denial in adoption: practice and treatment issues.' *Families in Society* **78** (5), pp. 522–30.

Rushton, A. and Minnis, H. (1997) 'Annotation: transracial family placements.' *Journal of Child Psychology and Psychiatry* **48**, pp. 1–13.

Ryburn, M. (1995) 'Adopted children's identity and information needs.' *Children and Society* **9** (3), pp. 41–6.

Ryburn, M. and Rockel, J. (1988) *Adoption Today: Change and Choice in New Zealand.* Auckland: Heinemann Reed.

Sachdev, P. (1988) *Reunions and Aftermath.* Prepared for Parent Finders of Ontario, Canada.

Sachdev, P. (1989) *Unlocking the Adoption Files.* Toronto: Lexington Books.

Sachdev, P. (1992) 'Adoption reunion and after: a study of the search process and experience of adoptees.' *Child Welfare* **71**, pp. 53–68.

Sanders, P. and Sitterly, N. (1981) *Search Aftermath and Adjustments.* Costa Mesa, CA: Independent Search Consultant Publications.

Sants, H. J. (1964) 'Genealogical bewilderment in children with substitute parents.' *British Journal of Medical Psychology* **37**, pp. 133–41.

Schechter, M.D. and Bertocci, D. (1990) 'The meaning of the search.' In D. Brodzinsky and M. Schechter (eds) *The Psychology of Adoption*, pp. 62–90. New York: Oxford University Press.

Silverman, P., Campbell, L., Patti, P. and Style, C. (1988) 'Reunions between adoptees and birth parents: the birth parents' experience.' *Social Work* **33**, (6), Nov–Dec, pp. 523–8.

Silverman, P.R, Campbell, L. and Patti, P. (1994) 'Reunions between adoptees and birth parents: the adoptive parents' view.' *Social Work* **39** (4), Sept, pp. 542–9.

Simon, R., Alstein, H. and Bertocci, D. (1994) *The Case for Transracial Adoption.* Washington DC: American University Press.

Simpson, M., Timm, H. and McCubbin, H. I. (1981) 'Adoptees in search of their past.' *Family Relations*, Oct, pp. 477–83.

Slaytor, P. (1986) 'Reunion and resolution: the adoption triangle.' *Australian Social Work* **39** (2), pp. 15–20.

Sobol, M. and Cardiff, J. (1983) 'A sociopsychological investigation of adult adoptees search for their birth parents.' *Family Relations* **32**, pp. 477–83.

Sorosky, A. Baran, A. and Pannor, R. (1974) 'The reunion of adoptees and birth relatives.' *Journal of Youth and Adolescence* **3** (3), pp. 195–206.

Sorosky, A., Baran, A. and Pannor, R. (1978) *The Adoption Triangle*. New York: Anchor Press/Doubleday.

Stevenson, P.S. (1976) 'The evaluation of adoption reunions in British Columbia.' *Social Work* **4**, pp. 9–12.

Thoburn, J., Norford, L. and Rashid, S. (2000) *Permanent Placement for Children of Minority Ethnic Origin*. Jessica Kingsley: London.

Thompson, J. et al. (1978) *The Adoption Rectangle*. Toronto: Children's Aid Society of Metropolitan Toronto.

Tizard, B. (1977) *Adoption: A Second Chance*. London: Open Books.

Triseliotis, J. (1973) *In Search of Origins: The Experiences of Adopted People*. London: Routledge and Kegan Paul.

Triseliotis, J. (2000) 'Identity formation and the adopted person revisited.' In I. Katz and A. Treacher (eds) *The Dynamics of Adoption*. London: Jessica Kingsley.

Triseliotis, J., Shireman, J. and Hundleby, M. (1997) *Adoption: Theory, Policy and Practice*. London: Cassell.

United Nations (1989) *United Nations Convention on the Rights of the Child*. London: HMSO.

Verrier, N. (1995) *The Primal Wound*. Baltimore: Gateway Press.

Wachs, T. (1992) *The Nature of Nurture*. Newbury Park, CA: Sage.

Wadia-Ells, S. (1996) *The Adoption Reader. Birth mothers, Adoptive Mothers and Adopted Daughters tell their Stories*. London: The Women's Press.

Wadsworth, M.E.J. (1986) 'Grounds for divorce in England and Wales: a social and demographic analysis.' *Journal of Biosocial Science* **18**, pp. 127–53.

Wells, S. (1993). 'Post-traumatic stress disorder in birth mothers.' *Adoption and Fostering* **17** (2), pp. 30–32.

Winkler, R.C. and van Keppel, M. (1984) *Relinquishing Mothers in Adoption: Their Long-term Adjustment*, Monograph no. 3. Melbourne: Institute of Family Studies.

Winkler, R.C., Brown, D.W., Van Keppel, M. and Blanchard, A. (1988) *Clinical Practice in Adoption*. Elmsford, NY: Pergamon Press.

Index

THE CHILDREN'S SOCIETY
A POSITIVE FORCE FOR CHANGE

The Children's Society is one of Britain's leading charities for children and young people. Founded in 1881 as a Christian organisation, The Children's Society reaches out unconditionally to children and young people regardless of race, culture or creed.

Over 90 projects throughout England and Wales

We work with over 30,000 children of all ages, focusing on those whose circumstances have made them particularly vulnerable. We aim to help stop the spiral into isolation, anger and lost hope faced by so many young people.

We constantly look for effective, new ways of making a real difference

We measure local impact and demonstrate through successful practice that major issues can be tackled and better resolved. The Children's Society has an established track record of taking effective action: both in changing public perceptions about difficult issues such as child prostitution, and in influencing national policy and practice to give young people a better chance at life.

The Children's Society is committed to overcoming injustice wherever we find it

We are currently working towards national solutions to social isolation, lack of education and the long-term problems they cause, through focused work in several areas:

- helping parents whose babies and toddlers have inexplicably stopped eating, endangering their development;
- involving children in the regeneration of poorer communities;
- preventing exclusions from primary and secondary schools;
- providing a safety net for young people who run away from home and care;
- seeking viable alternatives to the damaging effects of prison for young offenders.

The Children's Society will continue to raise public awareness of difficult issues to promote a fairer society for the most vulnerable children in England and Wales. For further information about the work of The Children's Society or to obtain a publications catalogue, please contact:

The Children's Society, Publishing Department, Edward Rudolf House, Margery Street, London WC1X 0JL. Tel. 020 7841 4400. Fax 020 7841 4500. Website: www.the-childrens-society.org.uk

The Children's Society is a registered charity: Charity Registration No. 221124.